Border Queen Caldwell

TOUGHEST TOWN ON THE CHISHOLM TRAIL

Bill O'Neal

EAKIN PRESS Fort Worth, Texas
www.EakinPress.com

For Jim and Theresa Earle

Who for three decades have provided publication to

authors of the Early West

Copyright © 2008
By Bill O'Neal
Published in the United States of America
By Eakin Press
An Imprint of Wild Horse Media Group
P.O. Box 331779
Fort Worth, Texas 76163
1-888-982-8270
www.EakinPress.com
ALL RIGHTS RESERVED
1 2 3 4 5 6 7 8 9
ISBN 978-1-934645-66-6
Library of Congress Control Number 2008931277

Contents

Acknowledgments v

CHAPTER ONE
First Chance on the Chisholm Trail.............................. 1

CHAPTER TWO
Shootouts and Vigilantes... 18

CHAPTER THREE
Trail Town on the Grow 32

CHAPTER FOUR
Caldwell Becomes a Community................................. 45

CHAPTER FIVE
Boss Town of the Southwest...................................... 61

CHAPTER SIX
Last Railhead on the Chisholm Trail............................. 77

CHAPTER SEVEN
The Town Tamers... 101

CHAPTER EIGHT
Caldwell's Outlaw Marshal 109

CHAPTER NINE
Tragedy at Medicine Lodge 124

CHAPTER TEN
The End of Caldwell's Gunfighter Era............................ 140

CHAPTER ELEVEN
The Cherokee Strip Live Stock Association 148

CHAPTER TWELVE
Life in the Border Queen... 172

CHAPTER THIRTEEN
Boomers and Land Rushes 196

CHAPTER FOURTEEN
Celebration of the Border Queen 214

Endnotes. 221

Bibliography 235

Index 239

Acknowledgments

My first expression of gratitude is to Karen Sturm, a Caldwell native who is president of the local historical society and a major force in community activities. While on a trip during the summer of 2006, I wanted to show my wife a diorama of 1880s Caldwell that I had placed in the Border Queen Museum more than a quarter of a century ago. Karen graciously opened the Border Queen and a downtown museum for us. When I asked Karen if the rich photo collections of these museums might be available to me for a book about early Caldwell, she enthusiastically agreed. Karen suggested other ways to facilitate my research, and throughout the ensuing two years she has connected me with numerous local experts while making a variety of arrangements on my behalf. Karen Sturm, along with her husband Harold, whose family dates back to Caldwell's pioneer days, provided me with invaluable assistance throughout the development of this book.

Author Rod Cook, a highly knowledgeable historian of his hometown, took two days off from work to tour me throughout Caldwell and vicinity. Rod shared his incomparable knowledge of frontier Caldwell with me, as well as photographs and other materials he has accumulated. My debt to Rod runs deep—and so does my appreciation.

A delightful Caldwell couple, Don and Gloria White, welcomed me into their home and allowed me to inspect their vast collection of historic photographs and other artifacts. They generously permitted me to copy a great many photos for use in this book. At the venerable Stock Exchange Bank, President Gage Overall and Vice President Kim Miller cordially made available to me an impressive array of financial records and historical materials. Then I was allowed to inspect and photograph the second floor of the bank building, where the offices of the famous Cherokee Strip Live Stock Association once were located.

David Mardis, a funeral director with numerous business interests in Caldwell, took time during a busy workday to escort me into the basement of a venerable commercial building he owns on Main Street. David permitted me to inspect and photograph a unique water well from the 1880s. At the historic LX Ranch, two miles east of Caldwell, owner-manager Carson Ward conducted me on a highly informative tour of the original ranch headquarters, a two-story stone structure which I was allowed to photograph.

At the Caldwell Public Library I met with the library board to explain the project and my need to examine carefully microfilm of the weekly newspapers of the Border Queen. The board voted to loan me the newspaper microfilm for an extended period of time. Head Librarian Lisa Moreland presented me with eleven reels of microfilm, which I was allowed to bring back to Texas. This newspaper microfilm proved to be my single most important research tool, and I am indebted to Librarian Moreland and the board members for generously permitting me lengthy access to this crucial resource.

Another genial librarian, Sherri Baker, is the inter-library loan specialist at the M. P. Baker Library in Carthage, Texas. Sherri facilitated the loan of the microfilm reels from Caldwell, and with her customary resourcefulness she procured a number of other useful items for me. In Caldwell I met Bob Klemme of Enid, Oklahoma. Bob has placed markers for the Chisholm Trail from Texas to Kansas, and he commands a broad and detailed knowledge of the Chisholm Trail. Bob brought his impressive collection of government maps and reports to Caldwell for my instruction, and he patiently answered a battery of my questions.

I first studied and wrote about Caldwell in my second book, *Henry Brown, The Outlaw Marshal*, published in 1980 by Creative Publishing Company of College Station, Texas. Publishers Jim and Theresa Earle graciously granted me permission to use excerpts from *Henry Brown* in this book. For many years, through their Early West Series, Jim and Theresa have provided encouragement to a great many western authors, publishing numerous books of frontier history. I am only one of a host of western historians who is deeply indebted to the Earles.

While researching Henry Brown during the early 1970s, I was helped in Caldwell by Leo Oerke, Harry Jenista, Doyle Stiles, Emma Wiedower, Jane and Peggy Glover, and Grace and Mashlon Reck. In Medicine Lodge I was assisted by Gus Palmer, Luke Chapin, Gary Parker, and Mrs. H. J. Czirr. At the Kansas State Historical Society in Topeka, I was extended great cooperation by Nyle H. Miller and Joseph W. Snell.

My wife, Karon, chair of the Math and Science Division of Panola College, found the time to provide her customary assistance with this project. Karon twice traveled with me to Caldwell, shot photographs, served as a sounding board, and converted my handwritten manuscript to hard copy and disk. I cannot imagine putting together a book without her cheerful and invaluable help.

BILL O'NEAL
Carthage, Texas

CHAPTER ONE

First Chance on the Chisholm Trail

"It was said by many that Caldwell was started with a population of two, and both of them were non-residents."
—G. D. Freeman, blacksmith

Caldwell was born amid a dusty parade of longhorn cattle and trail-weary cowboys. Each summer for two decades herd after herd came up from Texas along the most famous of all cattle routes, the Chisholm Trail. "The Trail—and Trail deserves to be capitalized—pointed to the North Star," stated Texas historian Joe B. Frantz.[1] From 1867 through 1871 the North Star brought Texas herds as far as Abilene, Kansas. And each herd ambled and bawled its way through the future site of Caldwell.

"As I write my memory takes me back to the scene," recalled noted cattleman and ranch manager John Clay, writing forty years after he first witnessed herds coming up from Texas. "You saw a steer's head and horns silhouetted against the sky line.... Then comes another and another, til you realize that it is the herd. On each flank is a horseman. Along came the leaders with a swinging gait, quickening as they smell the water of the muddy river. More cattle, more men, a small bunch of horses, a mess wagon, with a tattered tarpaulin over it, drawn by four mules. The thirsty cattle walked straight into the river, horses also."[2]

Clay saw longhorn herds coming up the Western Trail into Dodge City in 1884, the last great year of the long drives from Texas, and "the muddy river" he referred to was the Arkansas, just south of Dodge. But that same year, 130 miles to the southeast, Texas herds entered Kansas along the Chisholm Trail and were driven into the stockyards south of Caldwell.

Caldwell came to life in 1871, just before the busiest season of the fabled Chisholm Trail. That year more than 600,000 head of cattle emerged from Indian Territory to cross Bluff Creek and, a mile beyond, Fall Creek, before angling up a gradual rise past a tiny collection of crude structures. And anyone in the hamlet of Caldwell who watched an approaching herd top the rise would have experienced the same impression as John Clay:

2 Border Queen Caldwell

"You saw a steer's head and horns silhouetted against the sky line.... Then comes another and another...."

This scene was repeated hundreds of times before the season of 1871. Hundreds of herds crossed Bluff Creek and Fall Creek that summer. Since 1867, when the Chisholm Trail opened, many herds had bedded down for the evening on the flat grassland between the two streams. John Clay described how "thirsty cattle" and horses would stand for a time in the water as the outfit established camp. "The driver swung his wagon downstream, unhitched his team and began preparations for dinner. The mules rolled two or three times in the sandy banks of the stream and then drank their fill." The next day, after watering and grazing, the herd would begin to be moved up the rise at mid-morning.

But when herds began arriving in 1871, the fifth season of the Chisholm Trail, a few log buildings and dugouts were scattered around an official townsite named after Kansas Senator Alexander Caldwell. With so much traffic each summer it was inevitable that frontier entrepreneurs would recognize opportunity where the Chisholm Trail left Indian Territory.

"You saw a steer's head and horses silhouetted against the sky line," remembered John Clay. "Then comes another and another.... On each flank is a horseman." Volunteers erected these silhouettes just south of Caldwell in 1995. —Courtesy Caldwell Historical Society

The first trail driver to shove a herd of cattle into Kansas was Francisco Vasquez de Coronado in 1541. *Conquistadores* Hernán Córtes and Francisco Pizarro recently had made spectacular discoveries of gold and silver in, respectively, Mexico and Peru. When rumors of gold-encrusted cities in the north reached Mexico in 1536, Viceroy Antonio Mendoza began planning an expedition of conquest to be led by Coronado, the governor of a province in northwestern Mexico. The expedition marched northward in 1540, with more than 300 Spaniards, at least 800 Mexican natives, and large herds of horses, mules, cattle, and sheep. The horses and mules provided transportation, while the cattle and sheep were meat on the hoof in an unknown land.

The far-ranging expedition discovered Grand Canyon and Palo Duro Canyon and claimed the North American Southwest for Spain. Angling toward the northeast into modern Kansas in 1541, the expedition halted near the future site of Dodge City on June 29 to celebrate the first Catholic mass held in the North American interior. Coronado led his men deep into Kansas before realizing that there were no cities of gold.

Although bankrupted by the financial failure of his expedition, Coronado brought back a wealth of information about Spain's new territory, including the existence of buffalo. "The prairies were as full of 'crooked-back oxen' as the mountains of Spain were sheep," he reported. And he had trailed a herd of cattle into Kansas more than three centuries before any crew of Texas cowboys. Indeed, it long was believed in Caldwell that "on June 1, 1542, Coronado and his army, according to their historic records, camped on the bluffs south of Caldwell. The next day they passed through the county...."[3]

Spanish colonizers introduced cattle to the Western Hemisphere in the early 1500s. On the ranges of northern Mexico *vaqueros* handled these animals from horseback, developing special techniques, tools, and attire. Roping, branding, heavy-duty saddles, jingling spurs, leather *chaparejos*, high-heeled boots, wide-brimmed *sombreros*—everything had utilitarian purposes, but came to seem colorful and even romantic.

Through the years countless expeditions marched into Texas along *El Camino Real* (The Royal Highway), some going as far as Spanish Florida. Every expedition drove cattle, often to stock the Catholic missions in Texas (one mission had a herd of 15,000, another of 10,000). Cattle inevitably strayed into the brush country above the Rio Grande, multiplying freely in this unpopulated region. It was a harsh land where cattle had to become hardy survivors, good at finding water and any kind of forage, and aggressive in battling predators—with horns that evolved into long, dangerous weapons.

In the 1800s Anglo-American frontiersmen adapted the techniques and equipment of the *vaqueros*. Texas "cowboys" drove a few herds of longhorns to distant markets such as New Orleans and California during the 1840s and 1850s. But before the long drives could become a regular activity the Civil War blocked Texas from almost all cattle markets. Unattended and ignored, the longhorns continued to multiply.

At the end of the Civil War Texas, like the other ten states of the defeated and occupied Confederacy, faced an uncertain future with a devastated economy. Throughout the South trade and commerce had been disrupted by years of blockade, banks had failed, transportation facilities were destroyed, capital vanished with Confederate currency, and a labor system based on slavery no longer existed. To make matters worse, much of the South was plagued by severe droughts in 1865 and 1867.

Alone among the ex-Confederate states Texas held a major economic asset. Between four and five million longhorn cattle now ranged across the grasslands of Texas, most of them in the southern part of the state and along the western frontier. A hungry market existed in the Northeast, which throbbed with industrial growth. Longhorns costing no more than three or four dollars in Texas would bring thirty to fifty dollars in the Northeast.

The major obstacle to such profits was transportation. The nation's first transcontinental railroad began construction during the Civil War. Although other lines were laying track toward the West, there remained a gap of several hundred miles between the Texas cattle and a rail connection to the Northeast.

But longhorns were lean and agile and tough. These half-wild beasts could walk to market, and in the spring of 1866 Texas cattlemen launched 260,000 head of longhorns along the Shawnee Trail (or Sedalia Trail) toward Sedalia, Missouri, railhead of the Missouri Pacific. But the timbered, mountainous terrain of southeastern Indian Territory, northwestern Arkansas, and southwestern Missouri proved difficult for trailing cattle herds. Furthermore, Missouri farmers resisted the presence of Texas longhorns which spread "Texas fever" or "tick fever" (Texans preferred the label "Spanish fever"). Tough longhorns were immune to the disease, which was carried by ticks. When longhorn herds passed through farm country, ticks dropped into pastures and fatally infected domestic cattle.

Few herds managed to reach the Sedalia market in 1866, but

the cattle that found buyers produced impressive profits. Texas cattlemen stubbornly led herds up the Shawnee Trail again in 1867.

But an enterprising cattle buyer, twenty-six-year-old Joseph McCoy, was working to establish a railhead to the west, which would create a trail through more favorable terrain—land where few farmers had yet settled. McCoy secured a shipping contract from the Eastern Division of the Union Pacific Railroad, then building westward across northern Kansas. (This U.P. line soon would be called the Kansas Pacific.) Although farm communities along the line resisted his overtures to become a shipping point for longhorn cattle, McCoy finally found his railhead at a hamlet which had nothing to lose.

Cattle buyer and promoter Joseph G. McCoy developed Abilene into the first railhead on the Chisholm Trail, and later he was a familiar sight around Caldwell, the last railhead. (From the frontispiece of McCoy's 1874 Historic Sketches of the Cattle Trade)

"Abilene was a very small, dead place," observed McCoy, "consisting of about one dozen rude huts," including "the inevitable saloon." McCoy erected a stockyard, bank, livery stable, hotel, and other facilities. He sent riders south to intercept herds already bound for Sedalia.[4] Although it was late in the season, several herds changed course, using a trader's trail that had been blazed into Indian Territory by half-blood Jesse Chisholm, whose trading post was near the future townsite of Wichita. In mid-August 1867 the first herds arrived in Abilene, and 35,000 longhorns were shipped from McCoy's stockyard. The next year 75,000 head were shipped from Abilene, and in 1869 the total exploded to 350,000.

"About this time selling Texas mares in the North proved profitable," stated rancher and trail boss H. H. Halsell.[5] Through the years as many as one million horses were driven up the Chisholm Trail, along with a total of five million cattle. Another four or five million head of Texas cattle were driven up the Goodnight-Loving Trail, the Western Trail, and other thoroughfares during the 1860s, 1870s, and 1880s.

During this period America became captivated by the western range cattle industry. This frontier enterprise "burned its image like a smoking cattle brand into the consciousness not

---

A Rose by Any Other Name...

"Chisholm Trail" identifies the most famous of all cattle trails. But before this famous name became iconic, other labels were provided by cowboys, cattlemen, and Kansans:

McCoy's Trail

Abilene Trail

Kansas Trail

The Great Cattle Trail

The Texas Cattle Trail

Wichita Trail

THE Trail

★★★

only of North America but the entire world," in the powerful words of Texas historian T. R. Fehrenbach. Texas cattlemen and cowboys conducted their picturesque venture "with a barbaric magnificence equaled nowhere. They exploded not a business, but a new way of life, across the entire North American West."[6]

The West long had attracted adventurous youngsters, and now adolescents and young men eagerly went to Texas to become a cowboy on a trail drive—just as farm boys once had sought adventure before the mast. Booted and spurred, clad in

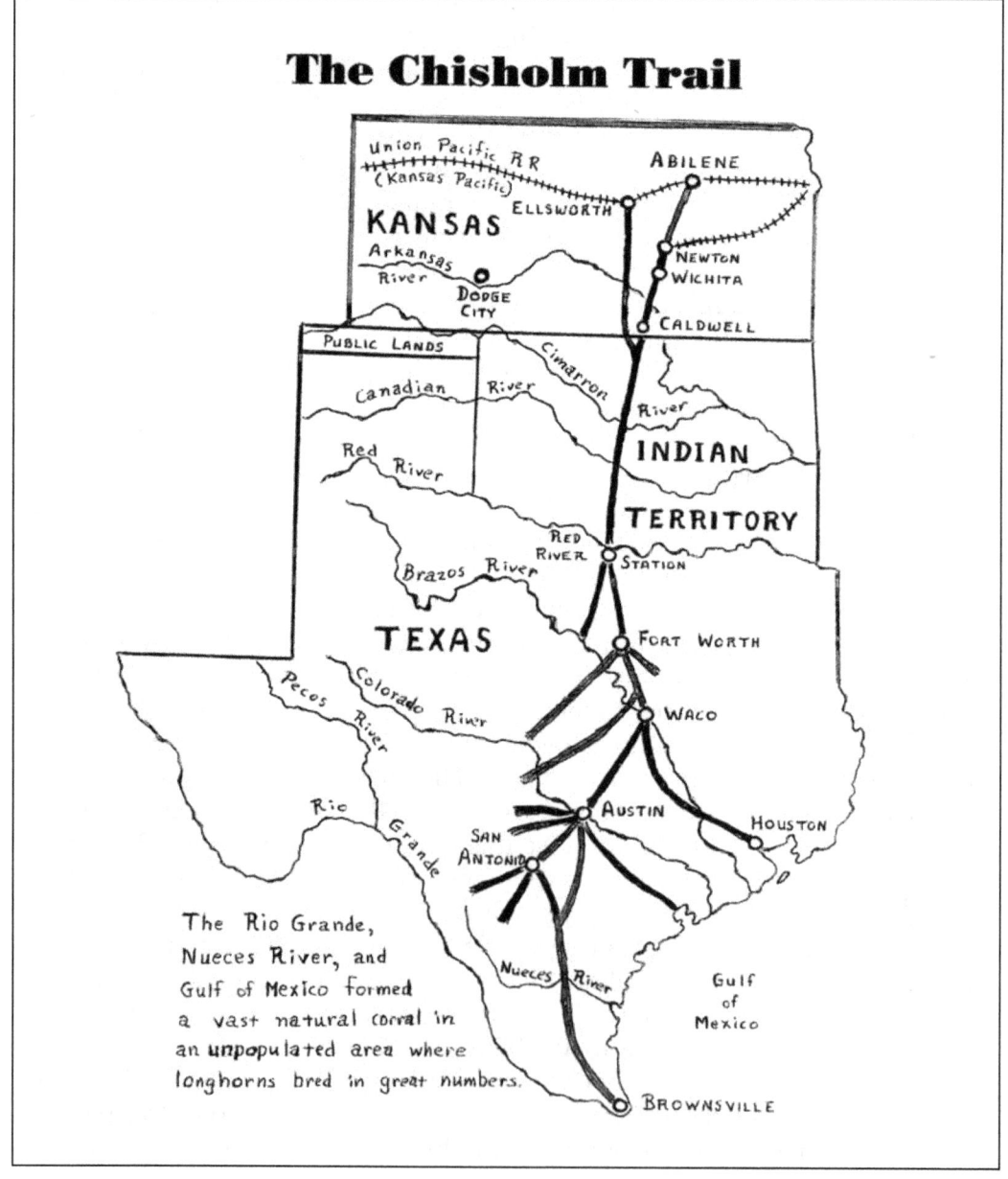

big hats and chaps and bandannas, cowboys were high-spirited, proud, tough. "Timid men were not among them," admired legendary cattleman Charles Goodnight.[7] Cowboys possessed the majestic feeling of power and height and superiority of mounted men throughout history, but their work proved hard and dangerous. Longhorns were big, ornery beasts, capable of inflicting harm upon men and horses. Cowboys had to ride, rope, and master other athletic skills to handle those cantankerous creatures.

Long cattle drives bristled with hazards, particularly treacherous river crossings and stampedes—or "stompedes"—which usually erupted at night. "Chain lightning caused more stampedes than anything else, and next came lobo wolves—the smell of them," related veteran trail driver Alonzo Mitchell. "After we got them up into Indian Territory, we could depend upon nearly all the storms coming from the northwest. We and the cattle both generally got warnings out of the sky, but the storm nearly always broke with great suddenness and fury."[8]

Alonzo Mitchell, quoted above, stands at the far right. Pink Higgins, trail boss of this crew of Texas drovers from Lampasas County, is seated at far right. Jess Standard, great-grandfather of the author, is seated second from left.
— Author's collection

The flamboyant combination of dangerous frontier journeys and brave, colorful cowboys immediately created a romantic adventure that would prove unforgettable to the American public. The exciting climax to that adventure was the arrival of the herds and crews in Abilene or Dodge City or other railhead cattle towns—including Caldwell. These towns became part of the cowboy legend.

In 1869, during the third year of the Chisholm Trail, hundreds of thousands of longhorns emerged from Indian Territory, crossed Bluff Creek and Fall Creek, and headed north into Kansas toward Abilene. Longtime trail boss H. H. Halsell observed that "at the time we are describing there was nothing in the Indian Territory from Red River to Caldwell but cattle, Indians, and wild game."[9] There were no towns, and federal law prohibited the sale of liquor in the Territory. A few frontier entrepreneurs began to realize that opportunity existed where the Chisholm Trail crossed into Kansas.

Just north of the Bluff Creek crossing, former army scout John E. "Curly" Marshall erected "a double log house." He sold liquor, feed, and provisions to the scores of crews that emerged from weeks in Indian Territory. Marshall put up the famous "First Chance–Last Chance" sign. It was the "First Chance" cowboys had at liquor since Texas, and when they returned from Abilene Marshall provided the "Last Chance" before the long ride south into Indian Territory. Because of its proximity to Indian Territory, the First Chance–Last Chance became "the favorite resort of the desperado and horse thief," according to early settler G. D. Freeman. But Curly Marshall was a strong, heavy-set man and a noted pistol shot who could hold his own in tough company.[10]

Caldwell historian Rod Cook standing on the site of the First Chance–Last Chance (looking east). — Author's photo

Marshall doubtless had a busy summer in 1869, selling everything he could stock into his double log cabin. The following summer saw almost as much traffic at the First Chance–Last Chance, as 300,000 longhorns came up the Chisholm Trail to Abilene.

By that time Wichita was in its formative stage, nearly fifty miles northeast of the First Chance–Last Chance along the Chisholm Trail. In Wichita Capt. Charles H. Stone, a cattle buyer and promoter, noted the potential of the First Chance–Last Chance site. By late in 1870 Stone formed a town company with other local businessmen, including wholesale liquor dealer James H. Dagner, G. W. Smith, George Vantilberg, C. F. Gilbert, and Chris Pierce. Gilbert was named president of the company, Smith was the secretary, and Stone was treasurer. This founding company hoped to attract a railroad and turn Caldwell into a railhead boomtown.

On a scouting expedition Stone and Dagner determined the location of their townsite, about a mile above the First Chance–Last Chance. The town would be centered on a rise just west of the Chisholm Trail and adjacent, on the west and south, to Fall Creek. In January 1871 Stone returned with Smith, along with a third member of the company and a surveying crew. Setting up camp, these men surveyed a townsite of 116 acres and laid out lots. The party went back to Wichita and filed their township claim, officially naming the site after U.S. Senator Caldwell. On February 7, 1871, Sumner County was organized, encompassing the planned townsite.[11]

The last week in February Captain Stone returned with teams and a work party. The workmen began felling cottonwood and hackberry trees along the banks of Bluff Creek. The logs were hauled up to the townsite, then hewn and fitted into a stout structure eighteen by thirty-six feet. Caldwell's first building was completed on March 15 at the northwest corner of Main and Fifth. The workmen also erected a ten by fourteen dwelling. On May 29 Stone received an appointment as postmaster—at one dollar per year—and Caldwell was rated a post office of the fifth rate. Handling mail, of course, was merely a service to be provided to the community. By May Stone and James Dagner had stocked the log store with provisions. G. D. Freeman remarked that the establishment was "a grocery store, with liquid groceries predominating."[12]

The first large sale was not to a crew of cowboys but to a regiment of cavalry. The Sixth Cavalry, divided between Fort Sill in southwestern Indian Territory and Forts Griffin and Richardson

The first building on the Caldwell townsite was on the northwest corner of Main and Fifth. Built of cottonwood logs early in 1871 by Col. C. H. Stone, the structure served as a store, post office, and residence.
—Courtesy Border Queen Museum, Caldwell

in Texas, was ordered to congregate and march to Fort Riley, Kansas. On Thursday, May 4, 1871, a column of several hundred cavalrymen and a baggage train came off the Chisholm Trail. Col. James Oakes ordered the regiment to camp at the grassy, well-watered area where cattle herds soon would follow. In need of resupply, commissary officers purchased $711 worth of provisions. The cavalry continued their march northward after twenty-four hours, and Charles Stone sent to Wichita for more supplies.[13]

At the townsite James M. Thomas soon erected a log building, renting it to Cox & Epperson of Kansas City for a saloon. Thomas worked for Cox & Epperson, sometimes as a clerk and sometimes herding cattle they acquired. A frame saloon also was built, fourteen by sixteen feet, and operated by Milam Fitzgerald.[14] Counting the First Chance–Last Chance outside the city limits, most of their trail town's first buildings dispensed liquor. During the summer and fall of 1871 more than 600,000 cattle trudged past the fledgling community, and many of the three or four thousand drovers must have been elated to find this collection of new whiskey mills.

The crews coming out of Indian Territory needed reprovisioning, and Captain Stone and Caldwell's other pioneer merchants hustled to bring in supplies. William B. Slaughter, "foreman" of his third drive up the Chisholm Trail, led 1,800 longhorn steers in 1871 "to Bluff Creek where Capt. Stone had a store." A herd of 1,200 steers took the trail late in March 1871, and cowboy Nate Rachal remembered emerging from Indian Territory. "When we reached Bluff Creek at the Kansas line the first house of Caldwell was being put up. It was a log house." He found that an old acquaintance, merchant Milam Fitzgerald, was at the new townsite "with a tent full of trail supplies, so we stocked up." A charter citizen of Caldwell observed that as soon as trail drivers reached town "they would visit the supply stores, lay in a supply of coffee, flour, bacon, and gather in the entire stock of liquids."[15]

The town company touted Caldwell's prospects in Kansas newspapers, emphasizing the heavy traffic in cattle herds and the availability of prime homesteads. Promotional stories attracted such men as G. D. Freeman, a young farmer and blacksmith from Augusta, twenty miles east of Wichita. Freeman "read flattering reports of the country around Caldwell, and of the probability of that town being the new metropolis of the Southwest."[16]

With a wife and three children, "we all stood greatly in need of a home to call our own," and Freeman became excited about the prospects of Caldwell. "I thought that the transient trade, afforded by the travel over the trail by Texas men with herds from Texas, could not fail to make a red hot town. Yes indeed a red hot town was what it did become; for many a time did the wild and wooly cow-boy 'paint the town red.'"[17]

Deciding to inspect Caldwell, Freeman enlisted a neighbor, 300-pound W. B. "Buffalo" King, then set out in his wagon "for the famous border town" in May 1871. Freeman and King spent the first night in Wichita, then camped along the Chisholm Trail the next two nights. En route they met A. M. Colson and J. A. Ryland, who would become noted pioneer settlers of Caldwell. Colson and Ryland accompanied Freeman and King into Caldwell, arriving during the afternoon of May 25. These men set up a camp along Fall Creek, which flowed along the west and south sides of the townsite.[18]

All four emigrants decided to settle in Caldwell. While George Freeman and Buffalo King traveled to Augusta to pack up their families, A. M. Colson and J. A. Ryland entered a partnership. Filing a claim six miles northeast of Caldwell on the Chikaskia River, the two young bachelors built a log dwelling and began buying sore-footed cattle from passing herds. These animals cost little and most of them healed while grazing on the Colson-Ryland place.[19]

George Freeman, Buffalo King, and their wives and children arrived in Caldwell on June 6, 1871. They took adjoining claims about a mile and a half west of town, although King soon moved to better land along Bluff Creek six miles farther west.[20]

On the day of their arrival the two families camped beneath a cottonwood tree with a spring nearby. The weather was "delightful," and they began planning to build dugouts. But about ten o'clock the next morning James Thomas rode up to spread the news that two Osage warriors had attacked and wounded Fred Crats, a homesteader whose claim was on Bluff Creek only five or six miles away. Freeman's wife was badly shaken, even though C. H. Stone soon arrived to offer reassurances. Stone was a Union veteran of the Civil War, and so were Freeman and King and many other early settlers of Caldwell. These frontiersmen were not easily spooked. They would not be frightened away from their homesteads or businesses by Indian scares or roistering cowboys or much of anything else.

Freeman mentioned to James Thomas that he was about to begin constructing a dugout for his family. Thomas, as eager as Stone to secure permanent settlers, said that he would send help from town. "Soon after several men came," recalled Freeman, "bringing spades, shovels, and axes with them. We were soon at work plowing, digging, and shoveling dirt." From log rollings to quilting bees to cattle drives, American pioneers had a genius for teamwork. By nine o'clock a dugout—fourteen by twenty-eight feet and six feet deep—was completed and roofed. While the wagons were unloaded the women prepared a late meal. "Our friends and co-laborers ate supper with us and several remained over night at our dugout."[21]

Despite the misgivings of Mrs. Freeman, the family stayed. George soon opened a blacksmith shop in Caldwell, and later was elected constable and appointed a deputy marshal—a representative of the law in a lawless, unincorporated trail town. Big Buffalo King stayed and put down family roots on his homestead. A crack shot, King spent a season buffalo hunting, then returned to his home, where he could work and raise his youngsters for the next decade and a half.

A. M. Colson prospered as a cattleman and banker, married and had children, and served Caldwell as mayor during the 1880s and again two decades later. J. A. Ryland also married and worked successfully as a farmer and stockraiser.

C. H. Stone, James Thomas, A. M. Colson, George Freeman and other charter citizens of Caldwell were urban pioneers. Mountain men, gold prospectors, cowboys riding on frontier cattle trails, and homesteaders in covered wagons were not the only pioneers in the West. Indeed, the settlement of each successive frontier was concluded by urban pioneers who created towns in a wilderness. Like fur trappers, prospectors, and land-hungry farmers and ranchers, urban pioneers sought opportunity in an undeveloped West while relishing the adventure of a new land.

"The attitudes of urban pioneers differed from those of eastern city dwellers," stated frontier historian Ray Allen Billington. "Most were restless seekers after wealth who ... deliberately selected a promising frontier community as the site of their next experiment in fortune making. There they built a mill, opened a general store, set up a portable printing press, or hung out a shingle as a lawyer or ... teacher, confident that the town's rapid growth would bring them affluence and social prominence. When they guessed right and the village did evolve into a city they usually stayed on as prosperous businessmen or community leaders.... Their mobility and restlessness distinguished them from the more stable souls who filled the eastern cities."[22]

The first risk-taking frontier entrepreneurs to try their luck in Caldwell established saloons, supply stores, blacksmith shops, and other businesses. Caldwell soon attracted other urban pioneers: lawyers, doctors, editors, teachers, preachers, and their wives, who would shape the culture of the Border Queen.

Among the frontiersmen who were in and out of Caldwell during the first year of the Border Queen were buffalo hunters. Beginning in the 1860s contract hunters were employed to supply railroad construction crews with buffalo meat, and passengers shot the lumbering beasts from trains. The northern and southern herds were vast, totaling perhaps 13,000,000 head. But by the late 1870s railroads offered easy transportation from western hunting grounds to eastern tanneries, which paid three dollars or more per hide. Hide hunters swarmed onto the plains in the early 1870s with powerful, long-range rifles. In 1871, with provisions and liquor available in Caldwell, buffalo hunters and their skinners began gathering in the little community. Caldwell would be a jumping-off place for buffalo ranges in southwestern Kansas below the Arkansas River.

Wyatt Earp, a twenty-three-year-old frontier adventurer, determined to try his hand as a buffalo hunter in 1871. "I had definitely decided to hunt buffalo, and late in August I left Kansas City for Stone's Store, a trading-post that was to be Caldwell,

Kansas, to purchase an outfit of wagons, animals, and supplies. I wanted to get to the range early in September."[23]

Earp and his skinner headed west and, after crossing the Medicine Lodge River, encountered an enormous herd. "I shall never forget a herd we sighted in the fall of '71," he reminisced. In April 1872 Earp returned to Caldwell to deal with hide buyers, clearing $2,500 for the 1871-72 hunting season. "In my first season as a buffalo-hunter, many buyers made headquarters at Caldwell, which had not yet been reached by a railroad. In Caldwell, the hides were collected to fill the bull-wains [wagons] which took them by the thousands to the railhead."[24]

Buffalo hunters and hide and bull-wain drivers were transients, like cowboys, but during Caldwell's first year the buffalo trade added much-needed business for local merchants. The slaughter of the bison herds was so great, however, that by the 1872-73 season many hunters roamed much farther west.

As a young frontiersman Wyatt Earp outfitted himself in 1871 at "Stone's Store" for a season of buffalo hunting. —Courtesy Arizona State Historical Society

Rough and heavily-armed, the buffalo hunters of 1871 added to the rugged makeup of Caldwell's early population. Saloonkeepers in raw frontier communities were tough men, capable of doing business with a rowdy, inebriated clientele. The first professional gamblers to drift into a lawless trail town like Caldwell dealt cards to hard-drinking, volatile cowboys and buffalo hunters. Prostitutes who were willing to work in a pioneer village without amenities were at the bottom of their profession, hard women, no longer young or pretty or shapely. G. D. Freeman observed that more settled Kansas communities "gave up their most reckless citizens to make up a band of rustlers, horse thieves, and bad characters to populate Caldwell."[25]

Such a society often exploded in violent personal altercations, making gunplay inevitable. The first fatal shooting erupted on Monday, July 3, 1871—less than five months after Captain Stone erected the first building on the Caldwell townsite.

George Peay was a recent settler who lived on a claim near Bluff Creek about five or six miles east of the new town. A formidable man, Peay was six feet tall and weighed 200 pounds. "He was a very quarrelsome man when under the influence of whiskey," described G. D. Freeman, "always boasting of his physical strength." It was suspected that Peay was a "claim taker" and a stock thief.[26]

Five or six friends lived on claims near Peay, and on July 3 these men rode into Caldwell and began drinking. Peay drank heavily and became surly, and as a precaution his friends took his pistol.

Peay soon encountered a man named O'Bannon, a native of Canada who held a claim about five miles west of Caldwell. O'Bannon lived in a dugout with two friends who helped him tend a small cattle herd. Small of stature, O'Bannon was bullied by the drunken Peay on July 3. O'Bannon tried to avoid trouble and went into one of Caldwell's stores. Peay followed the smaller man inside, hurling insults and challenging O'Bannon to fight.

O'Bannon instead left the store, but Peay stalked him outside. Suddenly O'Bannon pulled a cap and ball revolver and pulled the trigger. The gun would not fire, but Peay backed off for the moment. O'Bannon borrowed a pistol from a friend and jammed it into his belt.

A short time later Peay lurched toward O'Bannon with more insults. O'Bannon pulled his borrowed gun and triggered a round into the drunken aggressor.

"God, boys, I'm shot," gasped Peay, who staggered backward and collapsed.

O'Bannon, with his blood up and smoke curling from the pistol in his fist, turned toward Peay's friends. "Gentlemen, I have killed Peay, now is there is any one here that wants to take it up, they have the privilege of doing so, for I am in good shooting order."

No one wanted to take it up, so O'Bannon mounted his horse and rode west. Peay's friends carried his body into a building, then resumed their drinking. They drank most of the night, periodically climbing aboard their horses and riding "up and down the street yelling like demons and firing off their revolvers," according to G. D. Freeman. Then they would dismount, "talk to their dead friend, and beg him to get up and take a drink."

Within a short time Deputy Sheriff T.H.B. Ross arrived in Caldwell to arrest Peay's killer. Although Ross was a deputy in Cowley County, to the northwest, he probably held a deputy U.S. marshal's commission. Deputy U.S. marshals were not salaried, collecting only modest travel expenses, arrest fees, and perhaps rewards. But a deputy U.S. marshal's badge permitted county and local officers to act outside their primary jurisdictions.

After reaching Caldwell Deputy Ross learned that "O'Bannon had said no live man could arrest him," since he had shot Peay in self-defense. Although O'Bannon lived only a few miles away, Deputy Ross prudently stayed in Caldwell for several days "thinking O'Bannon would come to town." O'Bannon received word that a lawman was in Caldwell, and he departed the area. Caldwell's first shooting went unpunished, receiving scant attention from the law.

Less than two weeks after Peay was killed, citizens called a meeting to establish authority in Sumner County. Shortly after the formation of Sumner County, temporary commissioners were appointed to set up an election for county officers. The temporary commissioners had done nothing and ignored the Caldwell meeting of July 15, 1871. An election finally was held on September 26 to select "permanent" county officers, but the regular November election was little more than a month away. Most of the winners in September did not even post the bond required for county officials. In the November 7 election 805 votes were cast. Caldwell was in the Fourth Precinct of Sumner County. Elected Fourth Precinct Trustee was Charles Sullivan, who had recently arrived and built a combination "hash house" and residence of logs. One of the precinct's two justices of the peace was George Mack, a partner of O'Bannon, and one of two constables was George Epps, who would kill a man within a few months.[27]

Election day was a festive occasion in Caldwell. The area polling place for the September election was the ranch of A. M. Colson and J. A. Ryland. But on November 7 Caldwell was a voting precinct. In anticipation of the usual celebratory mood of election day in frontier America, Caldwell's saloons and grocery stores were restocked with whiskey.

G. D. Freeman observed "that all voted who were inclined to do so. I did not hear any questions asked relative to the residing place of the voter.... I know there were votes cast by men whose homes were in New York City, and other voters who lived as far South as Mexico."[28]

A number of cowboys were present and there were impromptu horse races. An occasional pistol shot was triggered toward the sky, and empty cans were tossed up as moving targets. The principal sport, however, was drinking, and after the votes were counted the winners were expected to donate ten or fifteen dollars to "a whiskey fund." Then everyone adjourned to the saloons where drinking and gambling and general revelry rocked Caldwell until late in the night.

This raucous celebration was a fitting climax to the inaugural year of the wild, ramshackle trail town. A new wolf howl community had been born in the West.

CHAPTER TWO

Shootouts and Vigilantes

"By means of rope logic, [the vigilantes] persuaded him to pilot them to McCarty's hiding place."
—*Sumner County Press*, April 26, 1872

The second killing in the Caldwell area occurred in February 1872. George Epps, elected constable the previous November, lived in a dugout on a homestead claim a few miles west of town along Bluff Creek.[1]

Jim, John, Frank, and William Manning had driven a herd from Texas and were wintering the cattle near Bluff Creek. The large Manning clan was from Alabama, but migrated to Texas after the Civil War. Four brothers had fought for the Confederacy, although William was too young to serve, and the Mannings would create a legacy as troublemakers.[2]

During the winter of 1871-72 the Mannings contracted George Epps to cut and stack hay for their cattle. But Epps and William disagreed over the arrangements. Following a heated quarrel the two antagonists vowed to shoot on sight.

On the day of the shooting G. D. Freeman rode to the Epps dugout in search of a missing horse. Epps had not seen the animal, so Freeman decided to look around the creek. After proceeding only a couple of hundred yards Freeman encountered William Manning: "I spoke to him and I noticed his greeting was not cordial."

Apparently looking for trouble, William Manning rode to the dugout. But Epps intended to "shoot on sight," and Freeman "heard the report of a gun in the direction of Epps' dug-out." Wheeling his mount, Freeman hurried back to the dugout, where he found Manning sprawled in front of the door. The fallen man was dead, shot in the chest.

Epps promptly surrendered himself and a frontier jury acquitted him on grounds of self-defense, "for had he not defended himself, in all probability Manning would have killed him."

William Manning was buried by his brothers on a little peak a couple of miles south of Caldwell. Unhappy with the acquittal

18

Shootouts and Vigilantes

The Manning Brothers

The oldest of the fighting Manning boys, George Felix, was born in 1837 on a plantation near Huntsville, Alabama. Felix would have several younger sisters and four brothers: Frank, Jim, John, and William. Felix studied medicine at the University of Alabama and in Paris. A dedicated physician, he would be called "Doc." During the Civil War he served as a staff officer under Gen. Joe Wheeler. Jim, John, and Frank also were Confederate soldiers, but William was too young to go to war.

After the war the brothers migrated to Texas. Doc practiced medicine in

(cont. next page)

of Epps, the brothers threatened his life. But Epps rode to the newly-designated county seat, Wellington, and swore out a warrant for the arrest of Jim, John, and Frank Manning. A deputy sheriff was dispatched to Caldwell, where he organized a posse of about twenty men, including G. D. Freeman.

The posse rode out of town and about two o'clock in the morning located the Manning brothers, holed up in the dugout of H. H. Davidson and his family. The deputy sheriff hailed the dugout, but the Manning brothers refused to surrender. Realizing they were cornered but wanting reassurance from influential citizens, the Manning brothers asked for the presence of C. H. Stone and another Caldwell merchant, N. J. Dixon. A rider set out for town and returned after dawn with Stone and Dixon.

The brothers surrendered about eight o'clock. The deputy sheriff selected two men to help him take the Mannings to Wellington. The little posse and their trio of prisoners stopped for the night at a two-room ranch house eight miles north of Caldwell. After supper a card game was started, and soon players began drinking. As the evening progressed the Manning brothers were left unguarded in the back room. A window was opened and the Mannings left the house. While the guards drank and gambled, the brothers saddled their horses and rode south.

The Mannings reached Caldwell about two hours after midnight, rustled up a meal from someone, then headed for Texas. The possemen slept off their liquor at the ranch before riding into Caldwell. By then the Mannings had vanished.

The arrival of the fugitives in the middle of the night and their consumption of a late supper could not have gone unnoticed around the little town. But there were no officers in Caldwell, and citizens gave the brothers free rein.

It seemed clear that civic officials were needed in Caldwell. A township election was held in April, but Caldwell would remain unincorporated for several more years, with little civic or taxing organization. Elected justice of the peace was Caldwell's first physician, Dr. B. W. Fox, who operated out of a drugstore he had established.[3]

G. D. Freeman was elected constable in April 1872. In addition to his homestead claim a few miles west of Caldwell, Freeman had opened a blacksmith shop just off Main Street. But he already had ridden as a posseman, and he obtained a commission as a deputy U.S. marshal. Being the only peace officer in "Caldwell and vicinity" soon overwhelmed his other occupations.

"The office I held placed me under obligations to be with the rougher element the greater part of my time...," reminisced Freeman. "Many times I have sat in the saddle, day and night, in search of the fugitive fleeing from justice, and have returned to my home, utterly worn out from exposure and fatigue, after a long, weary fruitless chase."[4]

By the time Constable Freeman assumed office a local man-killer was yielding to the dark side of his nature in and around Caldwell. Michael McCarty, handsome and boasting a strong physique, had claimed a homestead a short distance south of Caldwell. "He was well educated and in manner resembled a cultured gentleman," said G. D. Freeman, who knew him. An expert pistol shot, McCarty often practiced in public before on-

George Freeman was one of Caldwell's first settlers—homesteader, blacksmith, constable, photographer. (From the frontierpiece of his 1892 account of Caldwell, Moonlight and Noonday)

Giddings and engaged in a bloody knife fight with a medical competitor. His four brothers began driving cattle to Texas. After the death of William the brothers drifted west, settling in El Paso. Jim, John, and Frank engaged in rustling activities, then turned toward to running saloons.

The Manning brothers began feuding with El Paso City Marshal Dallas Stoudenmire. In 1882 Jim Manning fatally wounded Stoudenmire's brother-in-law, Doc Cummings, during a saloon fight. Soon afterward Doc and Jim Manning shot Stoudenmire to death during a brawl. Soldiers. Knife fighters.

(cont. next page)

Gunmen. When William Manning sought trouble with George Epps in 1871 he exhibited the combative nature of his family.

★★★

lookers. Rumors abounded that he had killed a man, or several men, in Texas or Colorado or Kansas.[5]

Just over a month after William Manning was shot to death, Michael McCarty became inebriated with drinking companions during a spree in Caldwell. That night McCarty rode to his dugout a couple of miles south of Caldwell on Bluff Creek. He shared the dugout with another homesteader, Eugene Fielder. Fielder already had gone to sleep, but McCarty wanted him to get up, and drunkenly pulled him out of bed by his hair. Fielder shook off McCarty's intoxicated behavior and went back to bed. When McCarty again grabbed a handful of hair, Fielder administered a beating, then both men went to bed.

McCarty brooded over being whipped. A few days later McCarty again became drunk in Caldwell and rode to the dugout looking for trouble. Informed by someone that McCarty was drinking again, Fielder took the precaution of arming himself and riding to the nearby dugout of early settler John Reid.

Finding their mutual dugout empty, McCarty rode back to town, where he was told that Fielder was spending the night at Reid's. Was this information dispensed innocently, or did someone knowingly incite trouble, much like boys egging on a schoolyard fight?

McCarty rolled a blanket around his torso, hoping its folds could absorb or deflect a pistol ball. Arriving at Reid's McCarty dismounted and called for Fielder. Fielder appeared in the doorway, a revolver in his fist. "Here I am," he announced, "come in here if you want anything."

McCarty reached for his revolver. Fielder fired, but the bullet burrowed into the blanket and glanced off McCarty. McCarty whipped out his gun and triggered round after round. One bullet found Fielder's lung. "Don't shoot any more," gasped Fielder. "I am killed." McCarty remounted and spurred toward Indian Territory. Fielder, "in great agony and covered with perspiration," died within an hour. His sorrowful friends provided a respectful burial at the little boothill a mile south of town.

A week later McCarty boldly rode back into town, accompanied by a man named Webb. McCarty and Webb drank heavily, then idly went into the store of J. M. Thomas (who had built the structure and now had bought out Cox & Epperson). Thomas was examining the goods of a merchant named Doc Anderson, who had closed out his store in Butler County and was trying to sell the last of his merchandise in Caldwell.

Anderson wore a plug hat, which was bait to a drunken

Westerner like McCarty. Perhaps contemplating another public demonstration of his prowess with a pistol, McCarty told his drinking companion that he would like to shoot a hole in the plug hat. "No," said Webb, "you won't shoot through a man's hat."[6]

"Oh no," replied McCarty sarcastically as he drew a revolver, "of course I wouldn't unless the man wanted me to."

McCarty fired just as Anderson turned to pick up more goods. The ball ripped through the top of Anderson's head and he dropped dead at the feet of McCarty. McCarty's aim was spoiled by drunkenness or Anderson's movement or both. McCarty said something about "he is out of luck, that's all."

Having killed two men within a week, McCarty mounted up and again rode toward Indian Territory. Constable Freeman was not in town when Anderson was slain, but the next morning an arrest warrant was delivered to his dugout.

By then a group of Caldwell men already had taken drastic action to apprehend the killer. McCarty shot Anderson about four o'clock in the afternoon and by evening as many as a score of men had decided to resort to vigilantism to thwart the violent direction of their new community.

Vigilantism and lynching were extralegal activities that had been commonplace since the 1760s, when violence was directed against British authority in the years leading up to the American Revolution. While the Revolution still raged in 1780, a prominent Virginian, Col. Charles Lynch, presided over a court designed to combat outlawry in Bedford County. Illegal trials were held regularly, with flogging as the common punishment. The court thus dispensed "Lynch Law," and in time the term came to mean a far more lethal form of justice than flogging.[7]

During the eighteenth, nineteenth, and early twentieth centuries, more than 6,000 men—and a few women—were executed by vigilante activities. Vigilantism flourished on the frontiers of the nineteenth century, when the westward movement repeatedly outraced the establishment of courts, law officers, and even jails. Indeed, vigilante action was quicker and cheaper than any system of courts, judges, juries, attorneys, trials, appeals, and institutional punishment. When the westward movement leaped across half a continent to the California gold fields, vigilante committees were organized in one community after another. San Francisco's Committee of Vigilance was formed in 1851 to control a soaring crime rate, and was revived on a large scale, with 6,000 members, in 1856. In Montana in 1864, a vicious outlaw gang led by Sheriff Henry Plummer committed more than one hundred murders in gold fields around Bannack and Virginia City. Citizens finally banded together as vigilantes and hanged Plummer, along with more than a score of his gang members.

By 1872 vigilantism was a century-old tradition in America, and across the frontier many westerners embraced extralegal violence as a necessary means to impose order. Throughout its Wild West period Caldwell was the site of a classic struggle between rowdyism and order, between frontier violence and legal authority that could provide a safe environment for commerce. At the same time that Caldwell's first saloonkeepers were ladling out whiskey to cowboys and buffalo hunters, merchants were selling provisions and homesteaders were beginning to develop their property and bring in their families. Caldwell was a raw trail town, but from its earliest months businessmen, wives, and children exerted civilizing pressures.

The embodiment of this conflict was J. M. Thomas, who sold whiskey in his store, but who was trying to buy goods when his fellow tradesman was murdered by a drunken gunman. Such unrestrained violence clearly was an impediment to serious commerce. Caldwell would face the same problem in the 1880s when the Border Queen at last became a railhead, while the continued threat of gunplay might frighten away eastern cattle buyers.

At the same time that Michael McCarty gunned down his second victim, Curly Marshall was in Wichita looking for prostitutes to bring to the First Chance–Last Chance. Marshall had built a frame "dance hall" beside his double log cabin. "He had made arrangements with some women of ill repute to come from Wichita and aid him in running the hall," complained Constable G. D. Freeman. Freeman added that "public sentiment was against the starting of such a house...."[8]

The same element that disapproved of Michael McCarty's two killings also would object to a new bawdy house masquerading as a dance hall. If Curly Marshall was in Wichita rounding up "women of ill repute," then he was absent from the First Chance–Last Chance—and unable to defend his property with the shooting skills for which he was noted.

As soon as darkness fell fifteen or twenty citizens from Caldwell proceeded with the same angry resolve as vigilantes in other lawless areas of the West. Rationalizing that McCarty might have ridden no farther than the convivial confines of the First Chance–Last Chance, the vigilantes approached the dive and demanded to search the premises. When they were rebuffed, most of the vigilantes rode to a ravine about 200 yards away, while two or three men returned to town for siege materials. Soon rejoining the posse, they brought two pails of coal oil and two bed quilts.[9]

The First Chance–Last Chance had grown quiet by the time the vigilantes crept up to the new frame building. The quilts were soaked in coal oil and "fastened to the sides of the house with two pins." The remaining oil was thrown onto the structure, than a match ignited Curly Marshall's new dance hall. A sudden burst of flames illuminated the building. There was a commotion inside as men who apparently were slumbering leaped up and began rolling whiskey barrels and carrying a bar to safety.

As they emerged outside, the inmates of the burning building spotted the surrounding posse. There was a quick exchange of gunfire. None of the vigilantes was hit, but two of the inmates were slightly wounded with buckshot. Vigilantes could see by the bright flames that McCarty was not present. Leaving two men in the ravine to watch for McCarty, the posse retreated to town.

Early the next morning a warrant for McCarty was delivered to Constable Freeman. He sent a rider to Butler County to relate the news of Anderson's murder, then organized a sweeping manhunt. "We scoured the country in every direction, rode over hill and plain, up and down the banks of the streams, through ravine and hollow, but all in vain," stated Freeman. "Our chase was a long weary one to both horse and man, and we were utterly worn out from want of sleep and rest."

On the third day of the search the weary posse members returned to Caldwell. But while they were scouring the countryside, a few vigilantes stayed behind to watch the First Chance–Last Chance. Suspicious of a hardcase named Nicholson, they confronted him inside the dive and became convinced that he knew where McCarty was hiding. Nicholson denied any knowledge of the murderer, but the vigilantes produced a rope and threatened to hang him from a rafter. Unwilling to die for McCarty, Nicholson revealed that his hideout was in Indian Territory on Deer Creek, about twelve miles south of Caldwell.

Constable Freeman arranged to meet a posse at four o'clock in the morning, then rode to his dugout for a few hours of sleep. But the vigilantes did not intend to give McCarty any extra time to escape. A grim band of justice seekers rode south after dark.

The vigilantes spotted McCarty at dawn. The fugitive was sleeping with his head on his saddle. His horse was tethered by a thirty-foot rope tied to the saddle horn. The posse surrounded McCarty, then called for his surrender. He sprang up and opened fire with a Sharps carbine, at the same time trying to gather his horse for an escape ride. But a daring young man named Newt Williams sprinted in and, while McCarty fired twice at him, cut the rope. Williams darted away unhurt—and so did McCarty's horse.

McCarty continued to work his carbine until a spent shell jammed in the breach. As he tried to clear the shell a ball disabled his right hand. McCarty pulled a revolver but was clumsy with his left hand. He raised his hands in surrender and, according to Mrs. J. B. Rideout, "begged for his life in a most distressing manner, his lips quivering and tears flowing freely."

The posse discussed their next step. Although some men wanted to turn McCarty over the authorities for trial, others wanted to hang him, while still others favored shooting. Dan Fielder, the brother of McCarty's first victim, had ridden with the posse. "Now is your chance," urged a fellow posse member, "give it to him." Admitting that he had come for vengeance, Fielder decided that "now his conscience would not let him become a murderer."

A less squeamish vigilante—apparently a friend of Dan Fielder—asked which of McCarty's revolvers had killed Fielder. He pulled the indicated weapon from its holster, pressed the barrel against McCarty's head, and pulled the trigger. No one tried to stop him, and McCarty died instantly. His body was left where it fell for several days until his mother and brother came to Caldwell. Someone guided them to the site of the fight, and McCarty's remains were interred nearby in a lonely grave.

Like many other vigilante bands, the Caldwell men felt empowered to take further steps. Eighteen men, regarded as "sympathizers with murderers, outlaws, and desperadoes," were notified to leave the area. Sixteen complied. But ignoring the vigilante threat was a desperado named, ironically, John D. Lynch. Details are sketchy, but on April 28, 1872, Caldwell vigilantes summarily hanged Lynch at Wellington.[10]

"Some guilty one had to suffer at the hands of the Vigilant's Committee," commented Constable Freeman, "or in other words be used as an example for the good of others. While I did not uphold the methods of Vigilant's, yet it is the only way lawlessness can be subdued in a new country."[11] Lynching was a pragmatic means of dealing with frontier outlaws, and Constable Freeman seemed quietly to appreciate the extralegal assistance of the vigilantes.

In Wichita Curly Marshall learned that his new dance hall had been burned, and he quickly returned to the First Chance–Last Chance without the prostitutes he was trying to engage. After learning details of the attacks against his establishment and upon Michael McCarty, Marshall announced his intention to kill Newt Williams, and he issued other threats. Defiantly Marshall set off to Wichita to buy lumber to replace his dance hall, but the vigilantes were just as determined to thwart him.

Marshall came back to Caldwell driving a wagon loaded with lumber, a pistol strapped around his waist. Constable Freeman was seated in front of a store with Newt Williams. Williams promptly drew his revolver and hailed Marshall, then hurried over to the wagon. "I understand, Mr. Marshall, you intend to kill me on sight."

Freeman alertly followed Williams, and now wrestled the pistol from his hand. At the same instant another citizen snatched Marshall's revolver. During the next few moments it was communicated to Marshall that he would not be allowed to rebuild his dance hall or to import prostitutes from Wichita. Freeman watched Marshall's "characteristic bravado" desert him, saw "the tears of the conquered, unbidden," flow down his cheeks. Now understanding the lethal resolve of Caldwell's vigilantes, Marshall pledged that if permitted to leave town he would never return.[12]

Marshall wheeled his team around and headed back toward the north. On the outskirts of town he stopped and unhitched his team. While the animals grazed, Marshall conferred with Dave Terrill. Within minutes Marshall arranged to sell the First Chance–Last Chance to Terrill. Curly Marshall took the lumber back to Wichita, where he died the following November.

Within a six-week period early in 1872, four men had been shot to death in and around Caldwell and another hanged by vigilantes—and the first cattle herds had not yet arrived. But when the herds began passing through, two Texas cowboys became the next victims of gunplay.

In June 1872 a Texas herd plodded past Caldwell and was bedded down about a mile north of town. There were twelve men in the crew, and that afternoon about half the cowboys rode expectantly back to Caldwell. They purchased provisions and small articles for the remainder of the journey, then sat down to drink and play cards.

At nightfall the cowboys left these pleasures to return to camp. But two of the boys, Frank Moore and James Harris,[13] were having such a good time that they decided to stay. G. D. Freeman remembered that "occasionally the cowboys' yell could be heard to ring out in the clear night air. They kept on drinking and reveling until near the midnight hour," when they finally stumbled out to their horses to head toward camp.[14]

A short time later two revolver shots rang out, but everyone who heard the gunfire assumed that the cowboys were shooting the sky as part of their drunken hilarity. The next morning the cook spotted them lying across the grass near camp, presumably sleeping off their spree. When one of the cowboys went to rouse them for breakfast, he was horrified to discover that both were dead. Each man was shot in the chest, and it was surmised that a drunken quarrel had led to one shot apiece, resulting in immediate death. A man in Caldwell was paid twenty-five dollars to handle the burial. As the trail drive, now short-handed, moved north, the impromptu undertaker fashioned a crude pine box large enough for two. The dead cowboys were enclosed in the box, then buried without ceremony only a foot and a half beneath the prairie.

Another cowboy killing occurred in June 1872, after a herd led by "one Oliver, a cattleman from Texas," passed through Caldwell. ("Oliver" may have been Print Olive, oldest son of a pioneer Texas cattleman. Print Olive had brought a herd

Caldwell's Boot Hill was north of the trail town and one mile east of the later City Cemetery. Prairie fires, trampling herds, and plowing destroyed almost all of the flimsy markers. But a few gravestones have been salvaged and clustered inside a fence near the City Cemetery. — Author's photo

through Caldwell in 1871, and trailed another herd from Texas to Kansas in 1872. The hot-tempered Olive was involved in numerous shootings, including an 1886 affray in which Print himself was killed.) Oliver—or Olive—had contracted to pay off one of his men in Caldwell. The amount was to be paid in coin, but the trail boss carried only currency and there was no bank in Caldwell.[15]

The herd departed Caldwell and was driven twelve miles north before being bedded down beside the Chisholm Trail. But in town the employee who had been paid in currency obtained legal papers against "Oliver," and Constable Freeman had to ride out to the herd to serve the trail boss. The constable anticipated a touchy situation, but "Oliver" politely invited both Freeman and his former employee to supper, then agreed to return to town that night.

Arriving in Caldwell too late to attend court, "Oliver" spent the night with Freeman in the blacksmith shop. While they were breakfasting the next morning, a cowboy rode into town with news that there had been a killing in the cow camp. Following a quarrel between the two drovers, one was fatally wounded and the killer fled for his life. "Oliver" quickly settled up with his former employee, then headed for the camp. He led several men in pursuit of the killer, but the man escaped.

Just as the trail boss and his drover headed back to camp, another rider galloped into Caldwell. It was Freeman's brother, who blurted out that G. D.'s prized horses, harness and wagon had been stolen. Freeman had paid $550 for the matched sorrels, a team of "large Illinois horses," and his younger brother was working the claim when two armed men took the outfit at gunpoint. Later it was learned that the thieves had lurked about waiting for the younger brother—who worked unarmed—to appear with the team, instead of the constable.

Stock thieves were rampant throughout the region, and in the Caldwell area rustlers often congregated at the First Chance–Last Chance, which stood just a short distance from the outlaw haven of Indian Territory. Stock theft was a common threat, and three dozen men volunteered to ride in pursuit with Constable Freeman. The entire community rallied behind Caldwell's sole peace officer, while the spirit of vigilantism throbbed just below the surface.

"The ladies of the town began preparing eatables for us to take with us," related Freeman, "and the proprietors of the stores kindly offered us any thing they had in the line of provisions."[16]

C.H. Stone asked Freeman if he needed money. After Freeman counted his cash, Stone gave him an additional twenty dollars in case funds were needed on the trip. Asa Overall, a young man who had just settled in Caldwell, wanted to ride with the posse but had no horse. Captain Stone went to the livery stable and procured a horse and saddle for the eager posseman. Destined to become a prominent citizen of Caldwell, Overall proved to be Freeman's right hand man and personally arrested one of the thieves.

The large posse rode west to the site of the theft and soon picked up the tracks of wagon tires and the hoofprints of the big horses. In the meantime, an anonymous note was delivered to Freeman stating that the thieves were "Tom Smith and — Dalton," who were headed for Boyd's Ranch. The Boyd place was a rustler hangout east of Fort Larned, which was more than 120 miles to the northwest through virtually uninhabited land.

Within a few days both the provisions and the trail became exhausted. The posse fanned out into groups, but after a few more days all but one contingent drifted back to Caldwell. Freeman, of course, doggedly continued pursuit, accompanied by Asa Overall, bachelor homesteader Ballard Dixon, and four other men. Freeman and his companions killed a buffalo, found the trail again, and finally located the wagon and team parked near the Arkansas River. Closing in, the posse found Dalton in the wagon. Dalton, in his early twenties, surrendered and revealed that the other thief was Tom Smith. ("Tom Smith" was the alias of Civil War veteran Thomas G. Moore, who was born Thomas G. Ford. His natural father was Thomas Ford, former governor of Illinois, but after Ford's death the boy was adopted by Thomas Moore of Peoria. Tom's older brother, "One-armed Charley Smith," also was a stock thief in the Caldwell area.)

After a time Tom Smith approached the camp, but he spotted the posse and wheeled his horse. Freeman loosed both barrels of a shotgun but inflicted only slight wounds. Using a knife to cut his horse, Smith surged ahead of any pursuit.

Freeman led the party to Fort Larned, where they bought food with the cash Stone had provided. Showing his deputy U.S. marshal's commission to the post commander, Freeman secured a squad of soldiers to accompany him to Boyd's Ranch, where they found and arrested Smith. With their two prisoners shackled and placed in the wagon, the posse started back to Caldwell. At night Dalton, whose shackles were a little large, pulled off his boots and removed the shackles. Putting his boots back on, he slipped away from camp and escaped on his horse.

When the posse finally reached Caldwell, after an arduous trek of a week and a half, they were met by cheering townspeople. Freeman placed Tom Smith in the top floor of J. M. Thomas' log building, shackled and guarded by several men. A large crowd of excited men gathered, and Constable Freeman and Justice Fox both feared a lynch mob. Freeman sent for his brother, and as soon as he arrived Fox hastily convened a trial. Young Freeman identified Smith, who admitted his guilt.

Justice Fox directed the constable to take the prisoner to Wellington without delay. Freeman borrowed a wagon and team from I. N. Cooper, whose homestead was just west of town. The wagon had three seats, and Cooper drove the team. Three other men, as well as Freeman, accompanied the prisoner.[17]

The party started for Wellington at sunset. It was dark when the wagon reached the Chikaskia River, six miles north of Caldwell. From the timber and brush along the riverbank as many as one hundred men suddenly emerged and halted the wagon. Tom Smith gamely stood up and announced, "I am the one you are after."

Freeman told his prisoner to sit down and be quiet. A revolver was leveled at Freeman's face, but the constable shoved it aside. A couple of vigilantes seized Smith. Freeman protested, but a double-barreled shotgun was thrust at him, "and I was told if I said one word I would be shot." The constable realized that he was hopelessly outnumbered by the vigilantes, "and the shining barrels of the shotgun looked as large as stovepipes."

Smith was pulled off the wagon, and the team was led across the river. The men in the wagon were told that anyone who came back across would be shot. Freeman decided that his only sensible option was to proceed to Wellington and report to the sheriff. Arriving about dawn, Freeman and his men ate breakfast at the hotel. Word about the vigilante mob spread quickly, and the hotel filled with men wanting to know more.

About two o'clock, after the horses had fed and rested, the wagon headed back toward Caldwell. Freeman and his party spotted their former prisoner hanging from the branch of an elm tree. A justice of the peace and ten or twelve citizens were gathered around the victim holding an inquest. Freeman related that the verdict "was to this effect: that Smith was taken from the constable by a gang of desperadoes and horse-thieves and hanged for fear he would divulge the secrets of the order to which he belonged."

This verdict probably was believed by no one. While there may have been a number of stock thieves in and out of the region, there never was a congregation in the West of one hundred "desperadoes and horse-thieves." And if such a force of outlaws had ridden together, they would have freed Smith instead of hanging him, and they also would have stolen Cooper's team of horses.

Undoubtedly the one hundred men who seized and hanged Tom Smith were vigilantes. Lynch mobs of one hundred or even more vigilantes were not uncommon. Inquests usually were conducted after lynchings, and members of the coroner's juries often were men who had participated in the execution. Little wonder that such juries almost always ruled that a criminal suspect was executed by "unknown parties," which closed any legal proceedings. But the verdict that Tom Smith was hanged by an enormous gang of fellow horse thieves was an especially imaginative — and unbelievable — fiction.

During five months of 1872, February through June, six men were killed by gunplay in and around Caldwell, and three more were executed by Caldwell vigilantes. Nine fatalities in a five-month period indicated an unruly and dangerous environment. But repeated and large-scale vigilante actions revealed a stern resolve within the community to curb violent anarchy. The struggle between the forces of outlawry and order was a classic frontier conflict that would agitate Caldwell for an especially long period. For years to come gunplay would erupt in Caldwell — saloon fights, street shootouts, and murders. But with sufficient provocation vigilantes would regroup, and tough, lethal lawmen were employed — although a dismaying number of Caldwell officers would be killed. The battle for law and order that would be romanticized in countless Western movies was embodied, year after year, in Caldwell.

CHAPTER THREE

Trail Town on the Grow

*"In my vision I saw the locusts eat up
every green thing in the land."*
— The Prophet Amos

Although 600,000 cattle were driven up the Chisholm Trail in 1871, this banner season was Abilene's last as a railhead. The Atchison, Topeka & Santa Fe was building west across central Kansas, roughly parallel to but considerably south of the Kansas Pacific. With the distance to a Kansas railroad thus reduced for Texas herds, rowdy Abilene suddenly became a sleepy farm town.

Before the end of the 1871 season, herds were being shipped from Joseph McCoy's new stockyard at Newton, located at the juncture of the Chisholm Trail and the AT&SF. By the next summer the AT&SF built a branch line, the Wichita and Southwestern, southward to Wichita, where McCoy built another stockyard. Wichita was twenty-six miles south of Newton, which ended its brief tenure as a railhead. The new terminus of the Chisholm Trail stood less than fifty miles northeast of Caldwell.

Whether the Texas herds were shipped out of Abilene or Newton or Wichita, the cattle and cowboys passed through Caldwell. During the summer of 1872, Caldwell's second season as a trail town, 350,000 cattle were driven to Newton and Wichita. Between May 1 and November 1, 1872, Captain Stone of Caldwell tallied 272 herds with a total of 349,275 head—an average of 1,195 cattle per herd.[1] The next year was Wichita's busiest, with more than 400,000 cattle coming up the Chisholm Trail.

As herd after herd reached Caldwell in 1872 and 1873, the busy trail town began to take shape. Herds were driven north beside the eastern edge of town. The growing cluster of buildings along Main Street stood atop a little hill overlooking Chisholm Street.

Caldwell's first hotel went up on Main Street early in 1872.[2] A two-story, frame structure, the City Hotel was built on the southwestern corner of Main and Fourth, facing east. The City Hotel also would be known as the Caldwell House, while the Haines Hotel of G. W. Haines would provide good meals.

The double line of commercial buildings facing each other across Main Street expanded steadily. Most were one-story frame structures with false fronts, the brave facades popular in western towns as a device to make a building seem more imposing. If a building still appeared insubstantial, at least its false front provided a signboard to advertise the commercial enterprise housed inside.

Several of these little buildings housed saloons, which often changed owners and names. There were general stores, drug stores, and restaurants or "hash houses." Within a few years Main Street would boast meat markets, barber shops, and hardware and dry goods stores. During the 1870s an almost solid line of commercial buildings filled both sides of Main Street between Fourth on the north, and Sixth on the south. Fifth and Main became the central intersection of Caldwell. Just south of this intersection a public well was placed in the middle of Main Street, which was one hundred feet wide.

On Main Street, beyond the two-block cluster of business structures, were scattered a few other commercial buildings, as well as a growing number of dwellings. Businesses and residences also went up here and there on other streets. G. D. Freeman's first blacksmith shop was located on Fourth Street less than a block west of Main, facing south. A livery stable

Looking south on Caldwell's Main Street in 1879, a year before the arrival of the Atchison, Topeka & Santa Fe caused these ramshackle buildings to be replaced by permanent structures. Note the well in the middle of Main Street, and the City Hotel at the intersection of Main and Fourth streets. (The City Hotel burned in 1885.) —Courtesy Border Queen Museum

stretched for an entire block, between Main and Chisholm on the north side of Chestnut, at the south end of town.[3]

Some of the merchants had wives and children, and families lived on homesteads near town. Women and children were civilizing influences on any frontier community. On September 5, 1872, School District No. 20 of Sumner County was formed for Caldwell and vicinity. The first meeting of District No. 20 was held on September 21 and featured the election of officers. A. E. Badger was elected Director and T.H.B. Ross was named clerk. Thomas Hart Benton Ross was a recent arrival in Caldwell. A Union veteran of the Civil War, Bent Ross had worn a deputy sheriff's badge in Cowley County. He would serve the school district for nearly a decade, and was a key law enforcement officer throughout Caldwell's cattle town period. School District Treasurer J. C. Sister failed to qualify, and on October 21 Dr. B. W. Fox was appointed to replace him. A one-room frame school, costing $1,200 and measuring twenty by thirty feet, soon was built. "The new school house is just completed and it is quite an ornament to the town," proclaimed the *Wichita Eagle* on February 20, 1873. The school building doubled as a multi-purpose civic center, being utilized for weddings, dances, political meetings, and community-wide Christmas Eve parties. Each year there were two school terms for a few months each. Homesteader Eli Sewell moved his family more than twenty miles into Caldwell "so that the little Sewells may have the benefit of our shool."[4]

The same forces that pushed for schools also organized churches, and denominations alertly sent missionaries to the new communities. On April 24, 1873, Rev. J. P. Hansen ventured to Caldwell and organized the First Presbyterian Church. Caldwell's first wedding united George Graul and Christena Reid on August 13, 1872. Rev. J. R. Rideout had come with his family from Maine a year earlier as a Presbyterian missionary and homesteaded a claim eight miles east of Caldwell. On Sundays he rode one of his plow horses—without saddle—on a day-long circuit preaching to small rural congregations. Rev. Rideout was named pastor of the First Presbyterian Church of Caldwell. There were just eleven charter members, and when Mrs. Rideout started a Sunday School the only two children were her own. It would take several years for the town's first congregation to raise enough money to erect a church building, and by then other denominations would be ready to build their own churches.[5]

The Rideouts, with four children, soon moved into

Caldwell, renting a one-room house for eight dollars per month. But after receiving a quarterly payment of $125 from the Presbyterian Board of Home Missions, as well as a mission box of clothing, the Rideouts bought a two-room home. Some of the Presbyterian men repaired an old saddle so that their pastor would not have to ride his circuit bareback.

"The town was at this time a very rough and wicked place," described Mrs. Rideout. "Two saloons were kept blazing with quarrels and blasphemy day and night.... One night, very soon after dark, I sent my little boy to the post-office, and in a moment after he had left the house I heard most dreadful screams and oaths, and several shots were fired. I ran to the door and said, 'O dear! I will not let Winnie go anywhere another night after dark;' and as I looked out I heard a ball whistle past my head." Caldwell would prove to be a fertile mission ground indeed for the Rideouts.

A stagecoach line from Wichita reached Caldwell in 1872, then was extended 180 miles to Fort Sill and to trading posts in southwestern Indian Territory. Passing through Caldwell three times a week, the Southwestern Stage Company carried mail and passengers, and in November 1873 a daily run began between Caldwell and Wellington.[6] In the spring of 1873 one passenger, Dr. O. G. Given, reported on the drive from Wellington: "An afternoon's ride over the beautiful prairies of the southern part of Summer County landed us in Caldwell in time to see the king of day sink himself beneath the western horizon."[7]

His stagecoach soon pushed through Caldwell and into Indian Territory. Dr. Given was not impressed with the ramshackle little community, particularly after the driver explained the "First Chance–Last Chance" sign. "Caldwell is truly a frontier town, as a sign on the last house we passed before passing into the Indian Territory would indicate." The doctor added that "I saw nothing very inviting about the appearance of the house or the surroundings." Moments later, in the fading light, Dr. Given saw the seven-year old Chisholm Trail. "We entered the territory on the old cattle trail, which is a very wide, well beaten road, and seemed to be as much traveled as any other road in the states."

A few months earlier another visitor also was impressed with the surrounding countryside. In September 1872 the editor of the new *Wellington Banner* rode to Caldwell in a buggy with three other gentlemen, and "we found it as nice rolling fertile looking prairie land as we have seen in Kansas, on which is growing an exuberant crop of prairie grass." Unlike Dr. Given, the editor expressed enthusiasm for Caldwell. "Instead of finding the people a set of outlaws, it has never been our lot to be among a more get-up active business-like and gentlemanly people than we met here. Improvement seemed to be the order of the day."[8]

The county seat newspaperman may have indulged in a degree of boosterism, but he left a valuable description of Caldwell in its second year. There was praise for the new Haines Hotel, "and travelers will be surprised at getting such good accommodations so near the border of civilization." He mentioned Stone's grocery, Dr. Fox's drug store, the store of J. M. Thomas, the dry goods establishment of a merchant named Reynolds, the saloon operated by a "Mr. Jones," and the large livery stable under construction on Main Street. "We put up at the Caldwell House where our old friend Charley Sieber is ever ready to give his guests as good 'hash' as the country affords."

That same month Dr. Fox chaired a political meeting of Republicans to support the re-election of President Grant.[9] C. H. Stone continued to work to attract a railroad to Caldwell. In anticipation of the 1873 cattle drives, Stone opened a "trading post" on Pole Cat Creek in Indian Territory, "which he will supply from his store at Caldwell." In 1874 the enterprising Captain Stone built a store on the state line west of Caldwell where a branch of the Chisholm Trail entered Kansas en route to Ellsworth.[10]

There were new buildings in Caldwell as the trail town prepared for a busy 1874 season. Early in March a Caldwell correspondent to the *Sumner County Press* declared that "in a few weeks the music of the "Cow Boys" song will be heard on trail as he brings the long horned bovines from their native pastures in Texas. Then will business in earnest begin.... Merchants, mechanics, farmers, in fact, all are setting things in order." The Caldwell House, a boarding hostelry, was purchased by a Wichita businessman, who soon sold it at a profit. Dr. B. W. Fox spent the winter in Illinois, but rented his drug store to a dry goods merchant from Newton. "Several new buildings are contemplated and material is on the ground for two business houses."[11]

J. M. Thomas restocked his store with dry goods. Dave Terrill, who had purchased the First Chance–Last Chance from Curly Marshall, sold the notorious dive to A. C. McLean and opened a restaurant in town, "named after his old home in Texas, Fort Worth." The mood in Caldwell was festive and a May Day party was staged. On Friday evening, May 1, "the

---

Rattlesnakes

Early settlers found the Caldwell region teeming with rattlesnakes. Reverend and Mrs. J. B. Rideout and their children came from Maine as Presbyterian missionaries. Rev. Rideout staked out a homestead claim eight miles east of Caldwell.

"After we moved into our cabin we were frequently visited by large snakes," wrote Mrs. Rideout in her striking reminiscence, Six Years on the Border. "My husband killed one almost seven feet long. They often came into the cabin, and even dropped down from the roof to our table. One night I felt

(cont. next page)

something crawl over my bare foot; the next morning I killed it. It was a rattlesnake with four rattles."

Newspapers referred to numerous people bitten by rattlesnakes, but Mr. Rideout pointed out that death rarely resulted, "as most persons kept an antidote always at hand. I became so accustomed to the peculiar buzz of the rattlesnakes that it did not alarm me very much. I have often killed them, and have laughed to see ladies just from the East run and scream when meeting a snake of the most harmless kind."

Mrs. Rideout learned of a unique baby

(cont. next page)

young folks, assisted by the old ones, enjoyed themselves until the wee small hours, tripping the light fantastic."[12]

Cowboys began to gather in Caldwell in hope of being hired to finish a drive to Wichita. But once a herd reached Caldwell the drive was only a few days from the railhead. Rather than hiring new drovers, many trail bosses paid off part of their crew in Caldwell and finished the drive with a few of their best men. The herds were passing through the trail town by May, and cowboys who did not complete their drives went on their sprees and spent their pay in Caldwell instead of in Wichita. All of Caldwell's saloons charged "the usual price—fifteen cents a drink, two for a quarter, cash down and no stand off."[13]

Although there were no shootouts in 1873, the 1874 season would not be so peaceful. There was a painless preview around the first of March. "A shooting scrape occurred at Caldwell last week," reported the *Sumner County Press*. "Nobody hurt."[14]

The next month, Dan Polk, a visitor to town, imbibed "a lot of buzzard juice." Showing off his revolver, Polk fired a shot over his shoulder—and hit an unlucky stage line employee known as Pony Marshall. The bullet tore a hole in one of Marshall's legs and imbedded itself in the other. Marshall was laid up for a month before he began limping around town. In June Josh Baker, another visitor to Caldwell's saloons drunkenly lunged at a Texan. The Texan knocked Baker to the floor, but he scrambled up and came at Johnny Blair. A charter settler of Caldwell, Blair bloodied Baker's nose and blackened an eye. Baker stubbornly picked up "a good sized stone," so Blair blacked his other eye and ended the fight.[15]

More menacing were known horse thieves Hurricane Bill Martin and Alex Watkins, who were seen in town in May. Soon there were complaints of stock theft. "Several horses and mules have lately been stolen in the southwestern portion of this county, and the people of that locality are organizing for self-defense against the gangs of thieving desperadoes that infest the border," reported the *Sumner County Press*, which added prophetically: "We expect to hear the lively times down there in case a few more horses are stolen."[16]

Stock theft in the Caldwell region was exacerbated when Vail & Co. outbid the Southwestern Stage Company, $11,000 to $17,000, for the mail contract from Caldwell to Fort Sill that rendered the stagecoach route profitable.[17] But the Southwestern Stage Company allegedly paid men to steal Vail livestock so that their contract could not be fulfilled. The most notorious of these men was William L. Brooks, often called "Buffalo Bill," because he was a buffalo hunter, and "Bully" because of his tough nature. Bully Brooks had driven a stagecoach between Newton and Wichita before being hired as Newton's first city marshal. Wounded in an 1872 shootout, he moved to Dodge City, where he killed two men in three gunfights in 1872 and 1873. In 1874 Brooks moved with his wife to Caldwell and led a band of thieves against Vail & Co. livestock.

"Bully" Brooks came to early Caldwell with a reputation as a killer and stock thief. In 1874 Brooks was captured by a large posse in Caldwell, then lynched near Wellington. —Courtesy Boot Hill Museum, Dodge City

rattle. *"A lady who lived near us saw her baby, about nine months old, playing with a bottle; on picking it up she saw a little rattlesnake coiled up in it. Upon inquiring how it came there, the older boys said they drove it into the bottle and corked it up, for they knew it would amuse Frankie; and then they told their mother they had several 'lariatted' out in the field."*

★★★

"Brooks told me that they, (the horse thieves) had taken the contract to run [ruin?] that mail line and that they intended to do it." This revelation was made by Brooks to Southwestern stagecoach driver Burr Mosier. "He said that they were employed by the South Western Stage Company to prevent Vail & Co. from fulfilling the mail contract, at all hazards; that they were to steal their stock and prevent, by any means, the transmission of mails on the route from Caldwell to Fort Sill. That they (Brooks & Co.) were paid six hundred dollars by the South Western Stage Company for clearing the road, i.e. stealing the stock and stopping the mails.... I was also told by Brooks and others to charge up their board to the S.W. Stage Co., as that company was to pay all expenses of the raid...."[18]

Moser was a longtime acquaintance of A. C. McLean, who now owned the First Chance–Last Chance and who belonged to the gang. Another gang member, "Jasper Marion alias Granger," revealed to Mosier other stock thieves: "Red," "Bob," "Jim" (all aliases), Bully Brooks, "One-armed" Charley Smith, Henry Hall, Jerry Williams, and L. B. Hasbrouck. Hasbrouck was Caldwell's first attorney, but he had turned to the other side of the law. In 1872 he was accused of stealing a cow, and in 1873 he became "the legal adviser" of the gang of stock thieves. Jasper Marion told Mosier that a mule theft on June 29, from Vail & Co. stations in Caldwell and Skeleton Creek, had been committed by himself and these men. Soon Mosier saw these stolen animals being herded by Marion and Brooks. "Five or six days afterward I saw the mules and horses, ten in number."[19]

There had been no vigilante activity around Caldwell in more than a year, but such a brazen crime wave would not be tolerated for long. Caldwell still was a village. Everyone knew everyone in town and the surrounding countryside. Gossip was a popular sport, especially in saloons while the liquor flowed. News about stock thefts and rumors about horse thieves—such as Bully Brooks and Lawyer Hasbrouck—raced from person to person. Interest was further stimulated by a $300 reward offered by Vail & Co.

Dr. P.J.M. Burkett, successor to Dr. B. W. Fox as Caldwell's physician and druggist, heard a good deal about "the wholesale theft of Vail & Co.'s mules" from a suicidally indiscreet A. C. McLean. Dr. Burkett confided this information to A. M. Colson in secrecy. But Colson promptly rode north out of Caldwell to the Chikaskia River, where he enlisted several of his old neighbors. Pursuing a trail of stolen stock to the northwest, Colson and his men were joined by Sheriff John G. Davis and a couple of deputies. The posse was out for a week, once mistaking a camp of buffalo hunters for their prey. Six mules and two horses were recovered, but no thieves were captured.[20]

On Sunday, July 26, 1874, a weary Sheriff Davis rode back to Wellington. But shortly after arriving he was presented by Justice James A. Dillard with arrest warrants for the Caldwell stock thieves named by A. C. McLean. Knowing that the mood of the people had reached an explosive level, the sheriff determined to make a large-scale sweep against the nest of desperadoes in Caldwell.

"Horses and cattle by the thousands have been spirited away during the past three years...," stated the *Sumner County Press* in a summary of the activities of the thieves. "If pursued they fled for protection and shelter to the Indian Territory where our citizens could not follow them.... Desperadoes became more frequent, and no farmer's stock was safe. This was the condition when the people began to organize for self protection. Vigilance committees were formed, composed of men fearfully in earnest...."[21]

Early in July a teamster named Pat Hennessey was brutally slain in Indian Territory, and there were sudden fears of raids by war parties. Settlers were not the only people frightened by the possibility of warrior attacks. "The Indian scare had driven most of the horse thieves operating down in the Territory to Caldwell," recalled peace officer Joe Thralls. "They were worse than the Indians and when we found a bunch of them eating breakfast at Caldwell it made us want to turn the Indian hunt into a horse-thief capturing expedition."[22]

Confident that he could raise a large number of exasperated citizens, Sheriff Davis made plans and began spreading word for the congregation of a small army. On Monday afternoon, July 27, the sheriff rode out of Wellington with a hand-picked posse. Arriving late at night outside Caldwell, Sheriff Davis sent a scout forward while waiting for reinforcements. His scout "reported that the parties named in their warrant were armed and evidently preparing for a desperate resistance." Meanwhile armed riders "began to arrive from all quarters until at two A.M., he entered the village with one hundred and fifty men." Mrs. J. B. Rideout "looked out her window and saw armed men coming into the town from every direction."[23]

With such a large force, Sheriff Davis was able to surround Caldwell before advancing, while dispatching parties to specific locations. A. C. McLean was arrested at his "neat log house" near the First Chance–Last Chance. Jud Calkins "surrendered

> **Rogue's Gallery**
>
> From the first-person perspective of a minister's wife, Mrs. J. B. Rideout described each of the men who were arrested by the large sheriff's posse:
>
> A. C. McLean: "a man of some property, lived in a neat log house one mile from town; he was a large fleshy man, but crippled with rheumatism. He had kept a dance house, but it was burned by the citizens and he barely escaped with his life."
>
> Dave Terrill: "a saloon-keeper whose wife was a Catholic." The couple sometimes attended Rev. Rideout's services, but when he paid a visit, Mrs.
>
> (cont. next page)

quietly" at the City Hotel. L. B. Hasbrouck tried to escape the dragnet by running into a corn field, but he was found at daybreak. Several possemen arrested Dave Terrill at a dugout three miles northwest of town. Charley Smith had ridden into Indian Territory earlier in the day, but Sheriff Davis sent fifteen men in hot pursuit.

Bully Brooks and two confederates forted up in his dugout on Fall Creek and defied the posse. "You will never take me alive," declared Brooks. The desperado was afraid of being lynched, but Sheriff Davis insisted that "I will defend you from the mob and you shall have a fair trial." After a siege of "several hours" (probably until daylight) the three gunmen surrendered. All three men were disarmed, but there was a warrant only for Brooks, so his two companions were released.

With Brooks, Hasbrouck, McLean, Terrill, and Calkins in custody, Sheriff Davis left Caldwell with his heavily-guarded prisoners. Within a short time a number of hardcases—clearly intimidated by the impressive force that followed the sheriff—departed Caldwell, and many did not return.

Arriving at Wellington at three o'clock Tuesday afternoon, Sheriff Davis presented the prisoners to Judge Dillard for a preliminary hearing. Dave Terrill was released from custody, while Jud Calkins, who operated a Caldwell livery stable, was permitted to post a $500 bail prior to appearing in court the next day. Brooks and Hasbrouck were thrown into the county jail, but McLean would spend the night elsewhere while under guard. Rev. Rideout, knowing that the prisoners might be lynched, rode to Wellington to "befriend them as much as he possibly could."

In Indian Territory the fifteen-man posse detachment located Charley Smith's camp. The one-armed desperado was gathering firewood when he found himself confronted by armed men. The posse headed north with their prisoner and, pushing hard, reached Wellington Tuesday night. Smith—the brother of Tom Smith, who was lynched in 1871—was tossed into jail with Brooks and Hasbrouck.

On Wednesday warrants were issued for the arrest of Dave Terrill and Jud Calkins, "who were yet supposed to be in town." But the two horse thieves prudently slipped out of Wellington and made a dash for safety. Although two posses searched for them, the outlaws made good their escape and thereby saved their lives.

A report described all of these events in a long article, headlined "ARREST OF SUSPECTED HORSE THIEVES" and scheduled for publication on Thursday, in the July 30, 1874, issue of the *Sumner County Press*. In summing up Tuesday's events the reporter concluded: "Considerable excitement prevailed, and grave fears that an attempt would be made to lynch the prisoners, was entertained by not a few. These fears were shared by the prisoners, to their evident discomfort."

But the nervous prisoners lived through the night. Many "country people" who had stayed in town to see a lynching left for home on Wednesday. Mrs. Bill Brooks set out on foot from Caldwell to see her husband. County officials worked during the day to organize a trial, and the *Sumner County Press* reporter added to this article that evidence was likely "that will prove the existence of an organized band of horse thieves extending all along the border." But the escape of Dave Terrill and Jud Calkins probably helped to solidify a public conviction that an object lesson in swift justice was needed. Apparently sensing the mood around town, the reporter ominously closed his article with an italicized statement: "*The end is not yet.*"

Another article would have to be dashed off before the newspaper could go to press on Tuesday. The headlines were spectacular:

DEAL! DEAD!! DEAD!!!
The Vigilantes at Work
Three Men Hanged by the Neck Until They Are Dead.
A Fearful Retribution.
The Beginning of the End.

A large mob quietly gathered on Wednesday night. There were as many as three hundred armed men, and most of them were mounted. It is likely that some of the vigilantes were men who had ridden over from Caldwell. A full moon rose in the cloudless sky, and at midnight the mob marched to the jail.[24]

"Halt!" shouted a guard. The jail was well-guarded, but throughout the West guards rarely offered more than token resistance to lynch mobs. Jail guards almost always were greatly outnumbered by the mobs, and vigilantes often were their neighbors. About fifty of the mounted men surrounded the jail, then dismounted and disarmed the guards. The jail was opened with the key and the three prisoners were brought outside. A rope was draped around the neck of each doomed man.

"During all this time, not a word was spoken," reported the *Sumner County Press*. "The silence was oppressive."

This ominous silence continued as the prisoners were

Terrill "told him that he had better not call again, as her husband did not like preachers."

Jud Calkins: "a hotel-keeper, a very bad man; his wife was a very bad woman. Both drank whisky and used profane language, and quarreled constantly, not only with each other, but also with their neighbors."

L. B. Hasbrouck: "a young lawyer about twenty years of age, and considered the most handsome young man in that country. He had been educated in the city of New York, and ... had more than usual ability as an attorney.... But he was not a good man; he

(cont. next page)

marched through Wellington and to the State Creek bridge, just below town. "Not even a dog barked."

The ends of the ropes were tossed over the limb of a big elm tree. Hasbrouck requested a drink of water, which was brought to him from the stream in someone's hat, and he asked that his parents never be told his fate. The three men were hoisted in the air, and Bully Brooks struggled the most painfully. The bodies were left hanging overnight, and the next morning a coroner's jury went through the motions. "Believing as we do," stated the *Sumner County Press*, "that the actors included many of our best citizens, we cannot and will not attempt to condemn their act." The corpses were cut down and laid out in the courthouse. Rev. Rideout was praying over the bodies when the wife of Bully Brooks entered the building and fell weeping beside her husband's corpse. A diminutive woman with "large bright eyes and short curly hair," Mrs. Brooks had stayed with her husband throughout the siege in the dugout, then hiked all the way to Wellington hoping to find him alive.

L. T. Williamson, agent for Vail & Co., hosted a banquet in Wellington honoring Sheriff Davis and the nine men who had ridden with him, shortly before the lynching, to recover six mules and two horses. The honorees included A. M. Colson and other men from the vicinity of Caldwell. Williamson divided the promised $300 reward between the honored.[25]

Dr. P.J.M. Burkett, apparently fearing for his life if he remained in Caldwell, moved his family to Wellington. For nearly two years in Caldwell "he engaged in the sale of drugs, purchased property and did a lucrative business." But suddenly Dr. Burkett "deemed it prudent to change his location," and he transferred his professional activities to the county seat.[26]

If Caldwell was deprived of a physician and businessman because of the invasion and multiple arrests of July 28, the trail town also lost a number of horse thieves and other riffraff. Permanently removed from Caldwell—by lynching—were L. G. Hasbrouck, lawyer and "legal advisor" to the gang; Bully Brooks, gunman and stock thief; and Charley Smith, stock thief and, like his brother, bad seed of an honorable family. Jud Calkins would not return to his Caldwell livery stable, and Dave Terrill would not return to his Caldwell restaurant. Caldwell's honest citizens regarded these desperadoes as good riddance. And three weeks after the triple lynching in Wellington they would find themselves driven to take similar action in Caldwell.

Frederick Ricer had opened a shoe shop in Caldwell in

---

kept bad company and spent more money than he could honorably earn." When Rev. Rideout spent an evening with him, "he seemed very amiable, but did not want to talk on the subject of religion."

Charley Smith: "said to have been the son of an ex-governor, but very much degraded on account of strong drink; his right arm had been amputated at the shoulder. . . . During the previous winter he sat day after day in front of the saloons dressed in the same old brown suit; his hair was long and matted; he slept wherever night found him—in the stable, on the saloon

(cont. next page)

March 1874. Ricer was a young widower with two small children. The shoemaker was "given to getting on a spree every now and then," and on Monday evening, August 17, he found a drinking companion in L. L. Oliver. Oliver, twenty-four, drifted into Caldwell about a month earlier and spent considerable time in "carousing alone." The two inebriated men apparently had a "disagreement," perhaps because the shoemaker "used unbecoming language to some ladies at the hotel." G. D. Freeman heard that later Ricer and Oliver quarreled over the price of a pair of boots.[27]

Oliver brooded over the discord, and on Thursday, August 20, he bought a revolver. Continuing to drink, Oliver loaded his gun at the hotel and told a boy "that the shoemaker had only five minutes to live." Soon Oliver peered into the window of Ricer's shop. Spotting the bootmaker working at his bench, Oliver fired a fatal round, and the unsuspecting victim collapsed onto the floor.

The murderer tried to flee but quickly was seized by furious townspeople. There was talk of hanging him from a signboard, but cooler heads pointed out that women and children were present. Oliver was hustled into a room and armed guards went on duty. But late at night a large mob emerged and took possession of Oliver. The killer was taken to Spring Creek, just east of town, and hanged from a cottonwood tree. The next morning the body was cut down, placed "in a rude box," and buried in the boot hill north of town. The cold-blooded murder of an inoffensive citizen had triggered prompt reprisal by the victim's fellow townspeople.

In 1871, 1872, and 1874 eight men were shot to death in and around Caldwell. But during this same period Caldwell vigilantes executed seven badmen. Although Caldwell was branded a "rough town," criminals and gunmen realized that in Caldwell vigilantes had developed a hair trigger. The violent trail town abruptly settled down, and for the next few years there would be little gunplay and less outlawry. And during the respite from violence Caldwell would mature into a community that no longer was a raw frontier outpost. There was a lively schedule of social events and of school and church activities. The town's business section boasted a variety of specialty shops among the saloons and general stores and hostelries. The Border Queen was becoming a community.

---

floor, and doubtless many a time on the cold floor."

Bully Brooks: "He had lived at C[aldwell] but a short time, and was doubtless a bad man; he was very large, and about thirty years of age. The day before the arrest he was in the town with a rifle looking for another desperado that he might kill him; at the same time the other was lurking around and dodging from place to place, seeking an opportunity to kill Mr. B[rooks]. He lived in a dugout, half a mile from town."

From *Six Years on the Border*, 94-98.

★★★

CHAPTER FOUR

Caldwell Becomes a Community

"Only one dance last week."
—Merchant J. H. Sain

During the week before Christmas 1874, Bent Ross hosted not one but two dances in Caldwell. Festivities continued a week later, when New Year's Day was celebrated with a masquerade ball in the evening.[1] The masquerade ball was a favorite in social circles of the era, with men as well as women devising elaborate costumes. In western cities such as Denver, there were professional costumers who rented colorful and historic outfits for the numerous local balls, and who traveled to smaller cities such as Cheyenne to supply their masquerade balls. No costumers assisted with little Caldwell's 1875 masquerade ball, but the revelers who staged the New Year's event were willing to piece together homemade party outfits.

Social life in early Caldwell centered around crude saloons. But within a few years the men and women who were putting down roots in the community began to enlarge their recreational possibilities. Almost any occasion provided a reason to stage a dance. In May 1875 John Adkins, "one of our heavy cattle dealers," sold his herd and prepared to return to Texas. "Our citizens gave him a farewell dance last Tuesday evening."[2]

Dances became so frequent that in October 1875 a Caldwell newspaper correspondent lamented, "Only one dance last week." The next month the Thanksgiving Ball "was well attended, and all present enjoyed themselves hugely." One Christmas there was a "grand Christmas Ball," and the next night, while Rev. Rideout was conducting Christmas services, "a number of their friends" slipped into their house and set up "a long table loaded down with bread, pies, cakes, chickens." When the Rideout family returned home they were surprised with a feast, and afterward "vocal music was the order of the evening."[3]

Early in 1876 "Washington's birthday was duly celebrated by a grand hop in the town hall." Local folk musicians put on a

"Jew's harp serenade," and there was an attempt to organize a brass band. That spring J. H. Sain, proprietor of the Mammoth Cave Drug Store, completed a new building and christened it with a dance: "Come one, come all."[4]

A dance was held each Saturday night in the school building. "The board of trustees were ungodly men," complained Mrs. J. B. Rideout, whose husband preached in the school on Sunday mornings. The Saturday night revelers would dance "until nearly daylight, and on Sunday mornings the schoolhouse would be in a condition not very befitting a place of worship. The seats would be all thrown out and piled on the ground, the stove put in one corner of the room and the floor covered with dirt." In his sermons Rev. Rideout "reproved their wickedness." The school trustees responded by locking the school after a dance, but Sunday morning churchgoers protested so vigorously that the trustees reopened the school to religious services.[5] When Caldwell was overrun with horse thieves and murderers, good citizens acted as vigilantes. Not long afterward, when the public school was closed to church services, good citizens firmly—if less violently—prevailed for the cause of religion.

Texas cowboys in full regalia were a common sight in Caldwell during the 1870s and 1880s.
— Author's collection

Religion exerted an increasing impact upon the life of Caldwell. For years Rev. J. B. Rideout was Caldwell's only pastor. He constantly distributed Presbyterian literature and visited newcomers. He preached regularly on Sunday mornings in Caldwell's school building, and he held prayer meetings on Wednesday evenings. Sunday School was conducted by Mrs. Rideout at three o'clock on Sunday afternoons in the schoolhouse. Rev. Rideout continued to ride his circuit on Sunday afternoons, preaching to rural gatherings before returning to Caldwell for evening services. Periodically he held "protracted meetings," nightly preaching services that customarily went on for two weeks.[6]

"Strong men wept in every part of the house" remembered Mrs. Rideout about one protracted meeting. "Several little children arose and said they wanted to love Jesus and go to heaven." At the first protracted meeting, one of Caldwell's most hardened sinners stated, "This town has been run by the devil long enough, and I think it is time the people began to repent and do better." Unfortunately this reform proved to be temporary.[7]

"Our little church at C[aldwell] was all this time gradually increasing in numbers, interest and usefulness," recalled Mrs. Rideout. "But in such a border village, where the only church is composed of members from nearly every Christian denomination, the pastor, and his wife," had to proceed tactfully. Rev. Rideout was unable to persuade his mixed congregation to fund the erection of a church building, or even to provide their pastor with any regular support. Following a revival one worshipper suggested paying a regular salary. "Mr. Rideout has preached and labored among us all these years, and we have paid him but a mere trifle." The Rideouts constantly were called on for charity, for food or lodging, to unfortunate families. When the Presbyterian Board of Home Missions was compelled to reduce the annual allotment for the Rideouts from $500 to $300, the family suffered severe privation. Wedding fees as much as five dollars helped sustain the household, and nuptials often were held in the Rideout home. Weddings also were conducted at the school or a hotel or a private home. On Saturday, December 7, 1875, the school was packed as Mr. Rideout married blacksmith O. G. Wells and Miss Lou Devore, followed by a "magnificent supper" at the Haines Hotel and a late-night dance.[8]

In order to keep their homestead, the Rideout family had to move back to the country to erect the required "twelve by fourteen" residence, although they later were able to return to their Caldwell home. Sadly, one of their four-year-old twin sons fell ill and died, and a short time later their youngest child, Laura, also died. (Another child had died while they still lived in Maine.) The bereaved and overworked minister developed a hacking cough, and on the advice of a physician the Rideout family moved to Colorado. Their Caldwell ministry had produced solid results, and Mrs. Rideout soon penned a striking memoir, *Six Years on the Border*, that was published in 1883 by the Presbyterian Board of Publication.

By the time the Rideouts left Caldwell in 1878, other ministers were active in Caldwell. In addition to the "flourishing" Presbyterian Sunday School, a Union Sunday School was organized in 1877. Rev. W. N. Neal, who began preaching in Caldwell in 1876, "delivered a very interesting sermon" on Sunday evening, February 25, 1877, "to the largest audience that we have ever seen in Caldwell." Baptists staged a revival in November 1877, and by the following spring Caldwell was on a Methodist circuit, with Rev. A. Ryan preaching every other Saturday evening.[9]

Revivals and protracted meetings, as well as regular Sunday services, provided social and even entertainment experiences to the urban pioneers of Caldwell and to nearby homesteaders. Churchgoers lingered after services to visit with each other. Homestead families came "six or eight" miles in a wagon for the morning service and afternoon Sunday School for the children. They often ate with the preacher: "I generally prepared dinner for from six to twelve besides my own family," reminisced Mrs. Rideout. Rev. Rideout rode his circuits on Sunday afternoons, leaving Mrs. Rideout with "guests" who stayed until evening services: "and thus the day which was given for rest was often for me the hardest day of the seven." In addition to socializing with other churchgoers, members of the congregation enjoyed the emotion-charged preaching and praying. The occasional church picnic offered another entertainment option.[10]

While professional entertainers performed throughout the West, the absence of a railroad decreed that troupes rarely would appear in trail town Caldwell. But on Saturday night, October 9, 1875, a band of "Negro minstrels" played to an appreciative audience. The entertainment was regarded as "excellent," and was enjoyed by all present. "Let's have some more of them." There would be few more, however, until a railroad reached Caldwell. Any performers who ventured overland to the little trail town with no entertainment hall were bottom-of-

Soldiers in Caldwell

Late in 1874, because of a recent Indian scare, an army company established a border camp just outside Caldwell. There were no fortifications at Camp Caldwell, but an army presence was a boost to the economy of any frontier village, especially for a trail town during winter months when there were no herds. Soldiers had money to spend in saloons, while the encampment would need to purchase a variety of provisions for soldiers and animals.

In November 1874 a soldier suffered frozen feet and had to be taken to for

(cont. next page)

the-bill acts. Almost a year later, in August 1876, the Great Western Minstrels came to Caldwell, but the audience was disappointed. "We often see better performances on our streets." The troupe went on to Wellington and played two nights in the county seat. Then the performers slipped out of town leaving a trail of unpaid bills. "The whole outfit is a first class fraud," grumped the newspaper.[11]

By 1877 America's first team sport was being played in Caldwell. Baseball evolved from the English game of rounders and prior to the Civil War was played primarily in the eastern cities. During the war thousands of soldiers learned the game at hundreds of army camps, and after the war these young veterans brought the sport home to a multitude of towns and country villages. Baseball exploded in popularity, and in 1869 the Cincinnati Red Stockings barnstormed across the country, earning nearly $30,000 in gate receipts. In 1876 the eight-team National League was founded.

Caldwell's population included a number of Union veterans who had been exposed to the sport, and baseball began to be played on an open field in town. On Saturday, February 3, 1877, a cold weather game was played "between the Blatherskites and the Hoodlums." Frontier "base ball" in the 1870s required nothing more than a bat and ball and bases—there was no catcher's equipment and no one had gloves. After another Saturday game on February 10, "some of the boys are carrying their fingers in a sling," and merchant Johnny Blair "had a fine limp."

Before the month ended, a "base ball club" was organized, with a captain, president, vice president, and Johnny Blair as secretary-treasurer. Styling themselves the "Lightfoots," the Caldwell nine accepted a challenge to play the Oxford Base Ball Club in Wellington, and tried to arrange a match for the Fourth of July.[12]

As early as 1876 a primitive form of "foot ball" had become "a very popular game with the boys of this town." A milder form of exercise permitted interplay between the sexes. "The croquet players are out in full bloom," observed Caldwell's newspaper correspondent in the spring of 1877. Horse racing was a perpetual sport in western communities, with wagers adding to the zest. "Several horse races last week," reported the Caldwell correspondent in November 1877.[13]

Caldwell's school teachers held spelling bees for the pupils, but literate adults wanted to compete. A "spelling school" was staged in May 1875, "and the citizens are rejoicing over it." Adult contestants, as well as spectators of every age, gathered at the school on a Wednesday evening, "and the house was filled to its utmost capacity.... We only recollect a few of the words that were missed." J. H. Sain inserted an extra "e" in a word; Mrs. Thomas—wife of the merchant and a charter settler—missed "potatoes;" and Mrs. Haines—wife of the hotelkeeper—"acknowledged that thanksgiving was too much of a mouthful for her."[14]

School is an essential center of any community, and frontier towns wasted little time in putting up a school house and finding a teacher. Caldwell was only a year old when the first frame school was built. "Frontiersmen believed that schools were the salvation of democracy and ladders to personal advancement," explained frontier historian Ray Allen Billington. "The principal hope of all pioneers was self-betterment, and this meant equipping the children to rise in the social scale."[15]

School trustees found a succession of unmarried young ladies to try their hands at teaching before they became wives. Miss Carrie Dixon began her third term in September 1875, and the following February she was succeeded by Miss Lizzie Wendels. In April 1876 "Miss Alice Sieber returned home ... from Emporia, where she has been attending Normal School." Having thus completed teacher training, Alice soon took over the Caldwell School for the three-month term. In 1878, when Caldwell's population began to mushroom, Alice opened her own school, following the example of Mrs. Hall. These private schools charged tuition and probably were conducted in the home of the schoolmistress.[16]

For the fall of 1876 Miss Jessie Donaldson would preside over a new school house. It is not known what happened to the "old" building, erected less than four years earlier. Perhaps both buildings were used to accommodate a growing student population—within two more years ninety-six pupils were enrolled in the Caldwell School. The new school was erected as a community project in a single day, on August 17, 1876, in the same way that pioneers would gather to build a cabin or a barn for a new neighbor in a day-long effort. "On Thursday last," reported J. H. Sain, owner of the Mammoth Cave Drug Store, "all turned out, both old and young, to assist in erecting a school house. While the men were at work on the building, the ladies prepared a most bountiful repast, in a grove near by. Too much praise cannot be awarded to Miss Donaldson, for the highly creditable manner in which she managed the affair, making it an occasion to be remembered by all."[17]

The fall term of 1877 began on Monday, October 8, with

amputation. The next month Dr. A. N. Ellis was stationed at the little outpost, and army surgeons traditionally provided medical services to citizens in town. "The Doctor is a pleasant and agreeable gentleman and is already very popular among soldiers and citizens." A few weeks later, unfortunately Dr. Ellis was transferred to Fort Leavenworth.

In February 1875 the stagecoach from Wichita "was so heavily loaded with soldiers and their baggage, that an extra span of horses had to be attached ... to complete the trip to Caldwell." Soon the encampment would be

(cont. next page)

Caldwell Becomes a Community 51

discontinued, but a decade later Camp Caldwell again became a military outpost.

Military travel to and from forts in Indian Territory along the Chisholm Trail offered Caldwellites the opportunity to see frontier celebrities. Colonel Ranald Mackenzie, a "boy general" during the Civil War who had formed the Fourth Cavalry into the army's best Indian-fighting regiment, was in Caldwell in April 1875. Two months later the German sisters, captured during a vicious Cheyenne raid in Kansas in September 1874, passed through Caldwell,

(cont. next page)

"Prof. J.V. Ratliff" as teacher. In December J. H. Sain and J. D. Kelly, president of the Caldwell school district, visited Ratliff's classroom "and were much pleased with the way the exercises were conducted." Sain was impressed by the instructor: "As an educator, Prof. Ratliff has few equals." Male teachers customarily were referred to as "Prof." or "Professor," while females were known universally as "school marms." There was a difference in pay, too, in part because men had families to support. Prof. Ratliff, for example, was paid $75 per month, and another male teacher, S. S. Clark, received $65 monthly. But school marms Fannie Warrington and Mary Clark were paid only $35 per month, while Emma Salmon received just $25. Teachers, of course, received pay only for the six or seven months they taught each year.[18]

The school was jammed with an estimated three hundred

Ranald Mackenzie, a "boy general" during the Civil War and colonel of the crack Fourth Cavalry during the Indian Wars, was one of numerous military celebrities who passed through Caldwell. —Courtesy National Archives

people on Christmas Eve 1877, a Sunday night. Mrs. J. B. Rideout remembered that "there was a present for every child that belonged to the school, and candy and popcorn for every one in the house." By 1876 Christmas shopping already was counted on by businessmen such as J. H. Sain, who "has ordered his Christmas goods direct from St. Louis."[19]

Despite the increasing enjoyment of Christmas in Caldwell, the Fourth of July remained a special holiday. In 1875 an elaborate celebration was planned, with more than forty men and women serving on committees: Committee on Speakers, on Grounds, on Finance, on Music and Singing, on Refreshments, and Committee on Flag. The county tax assessor had just listed the Caldwell Township population at 184, so one out of every five citizens volunteered to work on the Fourth of July project. Since the Fourth fell on a Sunday, it was decided to hold the celebration on Saturday. Five hundred people came to Caldwell on Saturday. Although the scheduled speaker from Wellington did not arrive, a cattle buyer from Texas, Dr. B. D. Norton, substituted "in an excellent manner."[20]

The next Fourth, in 1876, celebrated the centennial of the United States. "The Centennial Fourth was celebrated here in grand style, anvils, torpedoes and firecrackers." The Presbyterian Sunday School scheduled a picnic, and at 10:30 on the morning of the Fourth "the Sabbath School scholars" assembled at the school house. Flourishing flags and banners, and clutching candy, raisins and nuts donated by the merchants, the children "marched to a lovely grove by the side of a sparkling little stream [Fall Creek]." A large crowd gathered, Rev. Rideout prayed, then there was singing, a reading of the Declaration, a few brief speeches, and dinner. That evening about fifty couples danced at the school house until a late hour. The picnic on Fall Creek, the reading of the Declaration, vocal and instrumental music, orations, and an evening dance and fireworks became the standard Fourth of July in Caldwell.[21]

Fourth of July picnics. Community-wide Christmas trees. Baseball games. Spelling bees. Christian fellowship at regular church services. Dances and balls and hops at holidays from Christmas to George Washington's birthday, from Thanksgiving to New Year's. Frequently and in a broad variety of events the people of Caldwell interacted with each other. Caldwell's men acted together as vigilantes on several occasions to curb violence and criminal activity in their town. Men and women coordinated their efforts to organize a Fourth of July for Caldwell and the surrounding region. Townspeople worked

---

staying with Rev. Rideout.

In February 1878 Lt. Col. Fred Grant, son of President Ulysses Grant, stayed overnight at the City Hotel on his way to Fort Sill. Because of overcrowding Grant was asked to share his bed. Instead he slept beside the store in the bar room, and probably was eager to resume his journey the next morning.

See the Sumner County Journal, November 26, December 17 and 31, 1874; February 18, April 15, and June 10, 1875; August 3, 1876; and February 28, 1878.

★★★

Caldwell Becomes a Community   53

Fourth of July Program

In 1875 Caldwell staged a Fourth of July celebration which attracted a crowd of 500, almost triple the population of the township. The program was listed in the **Sumner County Press,** *July 8, 1875.*

- *Singing,* Star Spangled Banner, *by the choir*
- *Prayer, by Rev. J. B. Rideout*
- *Reading the Declaration of Independence, by John T. Showalter*
- *Reading, by John T. Showalter, of an oration delivered by General Devons, at the centennial celebration of the*

(cont. next page)

side by side to build a school in a single day. An undeniable sense of community was evolving in Caldwell.

Following the flurry of lynchings in 1874, badmen prudently avoided Caldwell. For a few years there was little gunplay, although the general tranquility of Caldwell during this period occasionally was broken by a brawl. In September 1876, for example, Johnny Blair "dissolved partnership" with a tobacco salesman with his fist and boot, resulting in a swollen hand and a sore toe. One year later two Texas cowboys "got on a bit of a jamboree" and menaced J. M. Thomas and his wife. Thomas took a chair to one of his assailants, while "Asa Overall knocked the other one into the street with a sap elm board." The Texans were arrested and fined five dollars each and costs. They paid a total of nineteen dollars, and the next morning "started rejoicingly on their way to Texas." The next year, in July 1878, there was a "lively scrimmage" with modest damage: "Two broken glasses, some whiskers extracted, pants torn and one eye dressed in mourning."[22]

J. M. Thomas and Asa Overall were friends and fellow businessmen in Caldwell. Thomas and Overall served together on the committees which arranged the big Fourth of July celebration of 1875. When Thomas and his wife were accosted by two drunken cowboys, Overall did not hesitate to arm himself "with a sap elm board" and charge to the rescue. Men who were the urban pioneers of Caldwell supported each other, recognizing that if the community flourished they would prosper and achieve local prominence.

John H. Sain operated the Mammoth Cave Drug Store. Late in 1874 he became a correspondent for Caldwell Items in the *Sumner County Press,* writing under the pseudonym of "Don Carlos." For years Don Carlos regularly informed readers of happenings in Caldwell, including information about the latest goods in the Mammoth Cave Drug Store ("Almanacs for 1875" and "the largest and best selected stock of candies ever brought to Sumner County"). When Sain erected a new building for his drug store he staged a "social dance." He played a prominent role in the Fourth committees and served as Caldwell's postmaster. When the Gooseberry Bachelor Club was organized in 1877 Sain was selected secretary, but in November 1878 he returned to his home state of Illinois long enough to marry Miss Clementine Wamsley, "a woman of fine figure and presence... [who] will adorn any circle or position into which her new life may lead her."[23]

Johnny Blair was a charter citizen of Caldwell who arrived

"with very limited means." He clerked for Cox & Epperson, worked as a cowboy, clerked for C. H. Stone in Caldwell's first store, then purchased the building and business from Stone. Blair became "a very popular man" and constantly was mentioned in the Caldwell Items of the *Sumner County Press*. A progressive merchant, in 1875 he moved Blair & Co. out of the old log building, and the next year he had Caldwell's first structure torn down to clear off the corner lot on Main Street. Blair served as postmaster until October 1876, earned the title of "Judge" as a busy justice of the peace, and enthusiastically played baseball. ("Johnny Blair has a fine limp and makes a good cripple.") In 1876 he built an addition to his home; two years later he focused on the grocery and hardware business; and later he dealt in cattle, enjoying "almost phenomenal" success. "He now lives in Caldwell in a fine home of his own," wrote G. D. Freeman, "where he and his family live in luxury and ease, holding the confidence and esteem of all who know him."[24]

While Capt. C. H. Stone sold his store to Johnny Blair, he maintained his residence in the town he founded, erecting an addition in 1876. Stone became a full-time cattleman, riding to Texas to buy herds to drive through Caldwell to Kansas. His activities often were reported in the *Sumner County Press* ("Mr. C. H. Stone bought five hundred head of cattle last week"), along with the travels of his wife to visit friends in Wichita or relations in Illinois. Stone fenced in a quarter section of land in 1877, but by the end of the year he moved back to Wichita. Perhaps he finally gave up on luring a railroad to Caldwell, or perhaps his wife wanted the amenities of a much larger town. "We regret to lose them from our midst," lamented Don Carlos J. H. Sain, "but our loss will be a valuable addition to Wichita."[25]

G. D. Freeman also moved, although he would return within a few years. The blacksmith-homesteader-constable rented his father's farm in Butler County in the spring of 1874. But Kansas was stricken by drought that summer, and in early August farmers were devastated by a massive infestation of grasshoppers. Freeman remembered that "the sun was darkened by the clouds of grasshoppers." The voracious insects destroyed crops and fruit trees and gardens.[26]

"About this time the grasshoppers came down upon us," described Mrs. J. B. Rideout, who was living on a homestead a few miles from Caldwell. "The air was darkened, and in a short time after they commenced to fall I could not find room for the soles of my feet on the ground without crushing vast numbers of

Battle of Bunker Hill
• **Oration, by Dr. D. B. Norton**
• **Singing, America, by the choir**
• **Dinner**
• **Dance at the school house**

★★★

them. The roof, and also the walls, of our cabins were darkened. The roar of their wings was like the sound of distant and continued thunder. In less than three days every green thing had disappeared: they devoured even the leaves of the trees.... I had never seen such a storm of living creatures before. They swirled in the air, and came down 'heaps upon heaps' until the very earth seemed to throb with life."[27]

The devastation was so severe that the United States Congress passed a bill permitting homesteaders in affected regions of Kansas, Nebraska, and Wyoming to be absent from their claims until May 1876 so that they might seek temporary employment. Many settlers, however, had nowhere to go. Food and clothing were collected in large amounts and distributed county by county. The Sumner County Relief Committee doled out great quantities of corn, pork, beans, flour, corn meal, and syrup through committees of distribution from sixteen townships, including Caldwell.[28]

Although many homesteaders gave up their claims, many others tenaciously remained, including several who were members of Caldwell's community life. I. N. Cooper farmed a homestead claim half a mile southwest of Caldwell on Fall Creek. He had volunteered his wagon and team and drove prisoner Tom

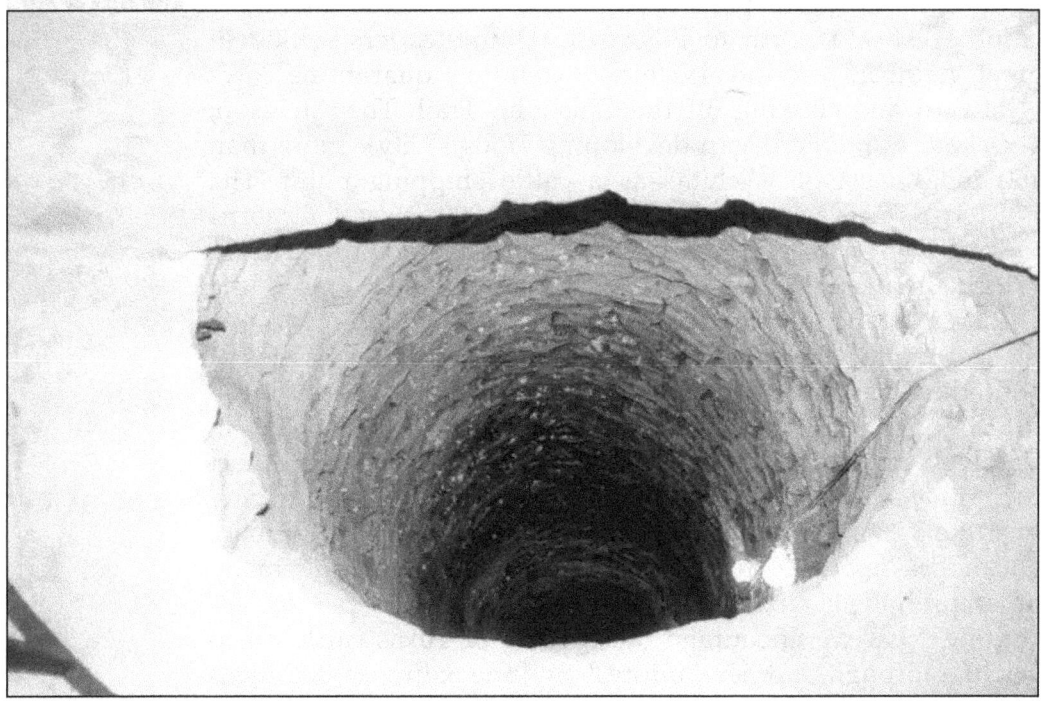

Early-day well in the basement of a commercial building on the east side of Main Street. The contemporary owner of the building, David Mardis, permitted me to inspect and photograph the well.

Smith toward incarceration in Wellington. (The 1872 incident ended with the lynching of Smith). Cooper bought and sold cattle; in 1877 he was complimented on "a couple of the finest hogs we ever saw;" and the next year he claimed "the best field of wheat in Sumner County." He was active in local politics as a Republican, he served on a committee to bring a railroad to Caldwell, and he made Cooper's Grove on Fall Creek available for the local Fourth of July picnic and celebration.[29]

Hank Zuber's claim also was near, and it was news when he "treated himself to a new sulky plow," remarking "that walking is good, but riding is better." Zuber was active in community events, and he provided a useful service by developing an ice house. In one week in January 1875 Zuber harvested and stored fifty tons of ice, and two winters later he put up one hundred tons. T.H.B. "Bent" Ross—lawyer, notary public, and secretary of the school board—harvested twenty tons so that he could have ice cream in the summer.[30]

Such enterprise characterized Caldwell businessmen in the mid-1870s. Business was hurt in 1874 by the drought and grasshopper plague, as well as by a decline in traffic on the Chisholm Trail. From more than 400,000 head in 1873, the number of cattle the next year dropped to 166,000, then to 151,000 in 1875. Many of these did not pass through Caldwell, instead taking the cutoff west and north to Ellsworth. Homesteaders settled in great numbers around Wichita, extending quarantine laws westward and choking off the Chisholm Trail. The Atchison, Topeka & Santa Fe began developing Dodge City—more than 160 miles west of Wichita—as a cattle shipping point. The Western Trail was opened, funneling 322,000 Texas longhorns toward Dodge in 1876. Only 12,000 cattle were shipped from Wichita that year, and in 1877 quarantine laws closed the Chisholm Trail at the Kansas line.

Despite the drought conditions and grasshopper hordes of 1874, the Chisholm Trail remained opened—even if in decline—in 1875. In February 1875 a "Mass Meeting" was held in Caldwell by businessmen and area cattle buyers "to protect their interest derived from their trade with drovers, driving over the Texas cattle trail." J. M. Thomas was elected chairman, and addresses were made by Thomas, J. H. Sain, "and many other prominent citizens." Four resolutions were passed, including "that we encourage the driving of Texas cattle on to Wichita through Sumner County." By June Sain was delighted to report that "A large number of cattle men are making Caldwell their headquarters." A few weeks later "Plenty of

Caldwell Becomes a Community 57

Doctors in Caldwell

No urban pioneer could become as beloved in a frontier community as a doctor. Frontier doctors birthed babies, tended sick children, patched up bullet wounds, made house calls to homesteaders on horseback or in buggies, and accepted payment in corn or eggs or firewood or chickens.

Dr. B. W. Fox was Caldwell's first physician. Dr. Fox also served as a justice of the peace and otherwise immersed himself in community life. Late in 1874 he returned to his home in Illinois "for the winter," but he was in failing health and

(cont. next page)

Texas men" remained in town, and on Sunday, June 27, a herd of 3,800 longhorns passed through Caldwell."[31]

With the population of the trail town approaching 200 in 1875, there was more growth during the cattle season. Before the season began inquiries arrived by mail regarding the price of Main Street lots and the availability of rent properties. The Haines Hotel was jammed with thirty-three guests on a Friday night in March, and George Haines hastily commissioned an addition to his building. New structures were built, along with boardwalks between stores. "The sound of the carpenters' hammers reminds us that Caldwell is improving." T.H.B. Ross and a partner erected a restaurant on Main Street, sixteen by forty feet, and in March a billiard saloon was opened with "a free 'set up.'"[32]

Once again Caldwell's saloons, restaurants, hotels, and streets teemed with cowboys visiting their first town since Texas. Inevitably a few drunken incidents occurred. A cowboy known as "Texas Bill" went "on a bender," brandishing his revolver and guiding his horse onto the boardwalk in front of the Haines Hotel. Mrs. Haines angrily charged outside, prompting Texas Bill to dismount. The redoubtable woman seized his firearm and ordered his arms tied. Texas Bill was tossed into a vacant room, "where he took a good sleep."[33]

On Thursday, April 24, 1875, "a party of Texas cattle men and the citizens of Caldwell" quarreled, and the Texans began firing their revolvers. When the citizens returned fire, the Texans retreated on horseback. The citizens mounted and gave chase, and there was a running fight. The Texans finally were cornered and surrendered, but they "were magnanimously released, upon a promise to leave the city in double-quick time." Both parties must have been drinking heavily, because no one was even wounded during the "brisk fusillade."[34]

Results were deadlier six months later. On Saturday night, November 11, a fight erupted between two African-American bullwhackers in a freighter's camp half a mile south of Caldwell. A drunken Henry Hopkins threatened to kill Henry Colbert, then pulled him out of his wagon and began beating him. Colbert shot his assailant in the chest, killing him immediately. Colbert was arrested and George Haines, acting as coroner, empanelled a coroner's jury which included J. H. Sain, Johnny Blair, Hank Zuber, and J. M. Thomas. The jury went to the camp and held an inquest over the corpse, soon deciding that "Colbert was compelled to shoot in self-defense."[35]

Almost a year and a half passed before serious gunplay again erupted in Caldwell. On Tuesday, February 13, 1877,

Hiram Jones and gambler Charles Lyons argued over a revolver scabbard. When the quarrel became heated, Jones shot Lyons in the knee. The bullet was embedded in the knee joint, and on Wednesday Lyons was taken to Wellington for treatment. Two physicians agreed that amputation was necessary, but Lyons died forty-eight hours after the surgery. Caldwell Justice of the Peace J. M. Thomas presided over the preliminary examination which acquitted Hiram Jones.[36]

During a four-year period, 1875 through 1878, Caldwell was the scene of only three shootouts—a street fight which produced no injuries and two fatal shootings. Both fatalities were deemed self-defense; leaders of Caldwell did not feel that the general peace was threatened, and vigilantes were unneeded.

Throughout the 1870s Caldwell businessmen, beginning with C. H. Stone, worked to attract a railroad. There were community meetings and committees, and various railroad lines were contacted with resolutions of support and promises of bond issues. By 1878 it seemed certain that a railroad soon would reach Caldwell, although some early businessmen finally gave up on this old prospect. Early in 1878, for example, Mr. and Mrs. George Haines sold their hotel and left Caldwell.[37]

Far more people were moving in than were leaving. The 1875 population of 184 grew to 253 one year later, then almost doubled by 1878. In October 1876 twenty-one persons from Wisconsin (two families, one with twelve children and one with five) settled homestead claims near Caldwell. "A good many new houses are being erected," reported J. H. Sain in December 1876. One year later Sain related, "Not a vacant house in town." In May 1878 several wagons carrying "emigrants from Iowa and northern Wisconsin" arrived in Caldwell. By the summer of 1878 J. H. Sain could report, "A large number of cattlemen were making their headquarters at this place."[38]

In April 1878 a townsite addition was laid out adjacent to the south edge of Caldwell. A steam mill was erected late in 1877, and in February 1878 an employee fell into the engine "and was very badly mangled"—Caldwell's first industrial fatality. Late in 1878, just two years after the revolutionary invention of Alexander Graham Bell, a telephone connection was strung between J. H. Sain's Mammoth Cave Drug Store and N. J. Dixon's Dry Goods and Grocery Store. Two of Caldwell's most progressive merchants introduced a technological wonder to their frontier community, thereby affording "a great deal of amusement" to their clerks and customers—as well as an astounding touch of modernity.[39]

---

died in July 1879.

Dr. W. F. Moore practiced for a time in Caldwell, although soon he moved west to Medicine Lodge. The Caldwell practice of Dr. P.J.M. Burkett was abbreviated when he suddenly moved to Wellington in the wake of the mass arrests and lynching of July 1874. Dr. W. F. Maggard moved his practice and family in July 1877 from Oxford, a Sumner County village. Felix Maggard established his office in J. H. Sain's Mammoth Cave Drug Store. Dentists sometimes visited Caldwell for a few days a week, but Dr. Maggard and

(cont. next page)

other physicians often found themselves extracting teeth. A year after Dr. Maggard moved to Caldwell his brother, a physician in Oxford, persuaded him to move back in a joint practice.

The new doctor in Caldwell was W. A. Noble, who moved his practice and his family in July 1878. Dr. Noble brought lumber from Wichita for a residence in northeast Caldwell. The house was built in less than two weeks (there was no plumbing or electricity), and Caldwell now had a long-term physician who would become an important and

(cont. next page)

The editor of the *Sumner County Press* journeyed with a companion from Wellington to Caldwell in August 1875. The travelers stayed at the Haines Hotel and spent "a most pleasant evening" with J. H. Sain, Caldwell's correspondent to the *Press*. After returning to Wellington, the editor described Caldwell with faint praise: "Caldwell is far from a dead town and local trade is fairly active. Her merchants and hotel men wear smiling faces and a contented air indicative of reasonable prosperity. Since our last visit several good buildings have been erected, and Mr. Haines is building a large barn. A good school house is an attractive feature of the village."[40]

Three years passed before the editor returned to Caldwell, and this time he did not have to force his enthusiasm. He recalled that in 1875 the surrounding countryside "was sparsely settled and farming had only been indulged in as an experiment. The Indian scare, the grasshoppers and drought of 1874, had almost depopulated the southern border, and the transfer of the cattle trade to points further west had left the village with but a precarious trade and little hope for the future." But during 1875 a few homesteaders managed "to prove the wonderful capacity of the soil for the introduction of the staple grains."[41]

The subsequent migration of homesteaders had quadrupled the population of the area within just three years "and still the immigration pours in." There were miles of wheat fields and the countryside around Caldwell was dotted with "unpretentious" residences. "The village itself has recovered from its torpor, and enjoys an active and increasing trade. Several new business houses have been added since the halcyon days of Texas cattle traffic, and stocks of general merchandise have been substituted for the 'First and Last Chance,' where the festive cowboys were wont to imbibe the liquor hall."

The Caldwell business section of 1878 was described in detail. Three merchants, N. J. Dixon, G. G. Godfrey, and Houghton, were praised for their "good stocks of dry goods and general merchandise. J. H. Sain has a neat stock of drugs and notions and runs the post office.... Mr. F. G. Hussen has recently opened a hardware and tin shop and does a good business. Hess and Kelly and two or three other firms deal in groceries and provisions. Hank Zuber has one of the finest rooms in the county, tastefully arranged for a billiard hall and saloon. J. M. Thomas dispenses justice and deals in real estate. Two hotels accommodate the traveling public." The editor singled out the Caldwell House, where he had stayed and dined.

"A steam saw and grist mill supplies lumber and corn meal

to the settlers. The machinery for manufacturing flour is to be added in time to begin work on the new crop of wheat." It was pointed out to prospective homesteaders that "government lands may yet be secured in sight of immense grain fields."

Wheat farming and other agricultural pursuits would prove to be the long-range economic base of Caldwell. But for the short term the editor failed to realize that "the halcyon days of Texas cattle traffic" were about to return, and that a host of Caldwell saloons again would dispense "liquid hell" to rollicking cowboys during the last hurrah of the Chisholm Trail.

colorful member of the community.

See the *Sumner County Press,* **July 29, 1875; February 17, July 6, and December 7, 1876; July 28, August 2 and 16, 1877; March 14, July 4, 11, 18 and August 22 and 29, 1878.**

★★★

CHAPTER FIVE

Boss Town of the Southwest

*"Caldwell the Terminus of the Best Road in the State,
and the future Metropolis of the Great Southwest."*
—Caldwell *Post*, January 2, 1879

"HERE IT COMES!" announced a bold headline in the second issue of Caldwell's first newspaper. "Clear the Track For the Cowley, Sumner & Ft. Smith Railroad!" exclaimed the *Caldwell Post* on January 2, 1879. "Caldwell the Terminus of the Best Road in the State, and the future Metropolis of the Great Southwest—"

The Cowley, Sumner & Fort Smith Railroad was a branch of the Atchison, Topeka & Santa Fe, "the Best Road in the State." The A.T. & S.F. served Dodge City, now the railhead of the Western Trail from Texas. But grazing was "uncertain" in the arid vicinity of Dodge, and many cattlemen "would gladly come further east, where the range is always good, if they can get the necessary facilities."[1] Thousands of cattle already were grazing in the region below Caldwell that would become famous as "The Cherokee Strip." In September 1878, while A.T. & S.F. officials were considering the construction of a branch line from Wichita to Caldwell, executives of the Kansas City, Burlington & Southwestern Railway proposed a line that would cross Sumner County from east to west.

Both lines were expected to collect from the county subsidies of $4,000 per mile of track laid, and a county-wide bond election was set for Tuesday, December 31, 1878. It was legal but fiscally imprudent for Sumner County to fund both railroads, when one line would do. There was a great deal of electioneering, with Caldwell citizens unanimously in favor of the A.T. & S.F. line.[2]

The first issue of the *Caldwell Post* was published three days before the election. J. D. Kelly, Jr., son of Caldwell real estate broker and justice of the peace J. D. Kelly, was listed as "Editor and Publisher," while T.H.B. Ross was "Associate Editor." The *Post* vigorously pushed the A.T. & S.F. line.[3]

On election day Caldwell voters backed the A.T. & S.F., 219-

0, while voting against the rival line, 217-0. The other twenty-two townships voted according to community interests, with Wellington in favor of the A.T. & S.F., 307-1. Overall, Sumner County voted strongly in support of the Cowley, Sumner & Fort Smith. County Commissioners thereupon directed the County Clerk to subscribe to the capital of the line in the amount of $180,000.[4]

"Now that the railroad is coming, there remains but one thing more to do," suggested the *Post*. "Subscribe for the *Post*." The *Caldwell Post*, like most frontier newspapers, unabashedly boosted its home community. An influx of new citizens and corresponding construction activity provided story material.

"And they still come!" the *Post* excitedly reported. "The demand for town lots still increases. Every mail brings letters from parties wanting to buy lots in Caldwell—the boss town of the southwest." Boosterism extended to a salubrious climate: "Doctors have been known to starve out in a week, and go back to the East."[5]

Throughout the 1870s the little trail town had remained unincorporated, with scant legal apparatus. The *Post* pointed out "that life and property are very unsafe at times in our burg." Wasting no time, the *Post* began editorializing for incorporation on January 2, 1879. "Strangers generally give towns unincorporated a wide berth. People who have money to invest go where they are protected by law, and where good society and order reign." *Post* reporters made local inquiries: "The saloon keepers say they would willingly pay license, provided they can have protection.... All license money fees, & c., would go into the city treasurere [sic]."

Within days leading citizens called a public meeting at the school. On Monday evening, January 13, "Squire Kelly was called to the chair, and T.H.B. Ross was appointed Secretary." It was decided to circulate petitions for incorporation, and within a couple of days "every man in town signed them." On Thursday the papers were shipped to state officials in Topeka. In July Caldwell, with 264 inhabitants, was designated a city of the third class (which required a population ranging between 250 and 1,000).[6]

"Not a vacant house in town," reported the *Post* in May. "Tents ornament the prairie on all sides in the immediate vicinity of town, with goods stored away in them, waiting the erection of houses. The Hotels are crowded to their utmost capacity." The need for houses was so great that a one-room "box house" was stolen from the homestead of John Calhoun while he was gone. Calhoun vowed to fashion a dugout and see if the thieves could get away with that.[7]

More than seventy-five town lots changed hands during the month of February. "Carpenters are being over-run by work," stated the *Post* in April. One of Caldwell's "heavy contractors" sent off to Wichita for several more craftsmen. A new merchant, Levi Thrailkill, hauled in lumber for a store building in early April, and within two weeks the structure was "strung together" by a carpenter named Doc McCamnant. By September there were twenty-six business houses fronting the west side of Main Street, with twenty-three more on the east side.[8]

One of the newcomers attracted to the growing community was George Flatt, a hard-drinking Texan who wore two guns. "Flatt was a drinking man and when under the influence of whiskey he was looked upon as a 'holy terror,'" reminisced George Freeman, who knew Flatt in Caldwell. "He proved himself to be a man of down right bravery and a shrewd observer of men and nature. He was very seldom known to be perfectly sober." Although still in his twenties, Flatt had the alcoholic's constant need for liquor, along with a ferocious temper and great skill with handguns. Freeman disapproved of Flatt's companions. "His general associates were a rough class of people as well as a low class of humanity. When his temper was aroused he was ferocious as a tiger.... He was an expert shot with the revolver, combined with great dexterity and alertness."[9]

This dangerous man would find Caldwell a compatible arena for his lethal temperament. Flatt, who may have ridden through trail town Caldwell with Texas cattle earlier in the decade, moved to the presumptive railhead in 1879. "G. W. Flatt has purchased the Occidental Saloon of Jas. Moreland," announced the *Caldwell Post* on February 27, 1879. Perhaps Flatt's financial arrangements fell through, because Moreland soon returned to operating the Occidental. But Flatt—and his revolvers—would return violently to the Occidental, beginning a troubled year that would earn him—and Caldwell—a chapter in the gunfighting lore of western cattle towns.

George Freeman returned to Caldwell early in 1879. The charter settler had left his Caldwell blacksmith shop and homestead to move back to Butler County. The death of his wife left him with four motherless children, but he remarried. Health problems persuaded Freeman to leave farming, and late in 1878 "I purchased a daguerro car and started west, traveling through small towns, stopping several days in a place to take photographs." He and his daguerro car wheeled into Caldwell in

April 1879. Re-establishing his home in Caldwell, Freeman opened the town's first photo gallery on Main Street. Within a month he accepted an appointment as constable, a position he had held during his early tenure in the trail town.[10]

A large part of Freeman's photographic business came from cowboys, who always enjoyed posing in their colorful attire, often while brandishing six-guns. "Some of the boys would wear a large sombrero and have several revolvers hanging from a belt worn around the waist, others would be represented in leather leggins, two large Texas spurs on their boots, revolvers in hand, and looking as much like a desperado as their custom and appearance would admit."[11]

Sometimes Texas cowboys brought the desperado mentality into Caldwell saloons. On Monday afternoon, July 7, 1879, Texans Jake Adams and George Wood, who had just helped deliver a cattle herd into northern Indian Territory, received their pay and rode into Caldwell for a spree. After an hour of heavy drinking in the Occidental Saloon, Adams and Wood weaved into the street and began firing their revolvers. Returning to the saloon, they threatened a patron, Dave Spear, but Jim Moreland intervened.[12]

By this time Constable W. C. Kelly had enlisted half a dozen men, including George Flatt, to help subdue the belligerent cowboys. Armed with two revolvers, Flatt stalked into the saloon and stepped directly to the bar. He downed a drink, yelled out "a Texas whoop," and had another drink. The troublemakers exchanged whoops with Flatt, then suspiciously turned their guns on the posse members and began moving toward the door. Flatt boldly stepped in front of the door, whereupon the two cowboys leveled their guns at him and demanded his revolvers.

"I'll die first," growled Flatt, pulling his pistols. A round from one of the cowboys whizzed past Flatt's head and grazed the temple of posseman W. H. Kiser, who stood behind Flatt. As Wood darted for the door, Flatt triggered two shots. One slug went wild, but the other clipped off the end of Wood's forefinger, tore away the trigger of his gun, ripped through both his lungs, and came out beneath his right shoulder blade. The impact of the bullet rolled Wood into the street, and he died on the spot.

Almost simultaneously Flatt squeezed off a shot from his other gun. Adams was struck in the right side, and the slug tore all the way through his body. He fired back at Flatt, but succeeded only in grazing the wrist of Assistant Constable John Wilson. A sign painter and paperhanger who also was good with a gun, Wilson pumped two slugs into Adams, drilling him in the right hand and stomach. As he went down, Adams shot Wilson in the leg, then breathed his last on the saloon floor.

"Flatt was very much excited after he had shot the men," related George Freeman. Flatt pointed his guns toward the boardwalk and fired several rounds into one plank. Citizens from every direction were hurrying to the scene of the shooting, but "Flatt was so excited that he ran out into the middle of the street and would allow no one to approach him."

Justice of the Peace J. M. Thomas enlisted a coroner's jury of six men and conducted a preliminary inquest. The jury reconvened the next morning at nine o'clock and examined a number of eyewitnesses, then returned a verdict: "That said men came to their death by pistol shots fired from the hands of the officers of the law and their deputies, while in the act of performing their duties."

The bodies of Adams and Wood were buried in the little cemetery north of town. But within a couple of days the corpses were disinterred, at the order of the Sumner County Coroner J. H. Folks. Arriving from Wellington two days after the gunbattle, Coroner Folks insisted upon asserting his authority. He formed another coroner's jury and held another examination. The verdict remained the same, and the two troublemaking cowboys again were laid to rest.

Caldwell's cemetery was dilapidated and neglected. In April the *Caldwell Post* issued a strong plea for "a respectable burying ground." There were about sixty scattered graves, "and in a sad plight they are," reported the *Post*. "Many of them are deformed by coyotes, and trodden upon by the herds." At least twenty children had been buried, but "not one-half of their mothers can go and pick out the grave of their own child." Headboards had "been blackened and burned by the prairie fires." The *Post* published a prophetic call: "Let us adopt some plan by which we may purchase a piece of ground suitable for a Cemetery, survey it into lots and avenues, surround it with a hedge, and soon you will see it ornamented with trees and shrubbery, and decked with marble monuments and tombstones."[13]

Heeding this call, a Cemetery Association was formed late in September. Land was purchased from a corner of a farm owned by J. M Huff north of town. The new cemetery took form west of Caldwell's first graveyard, which then was abandoned and completely neglected.[14]

Caldwell's first election as a city of the third class was held

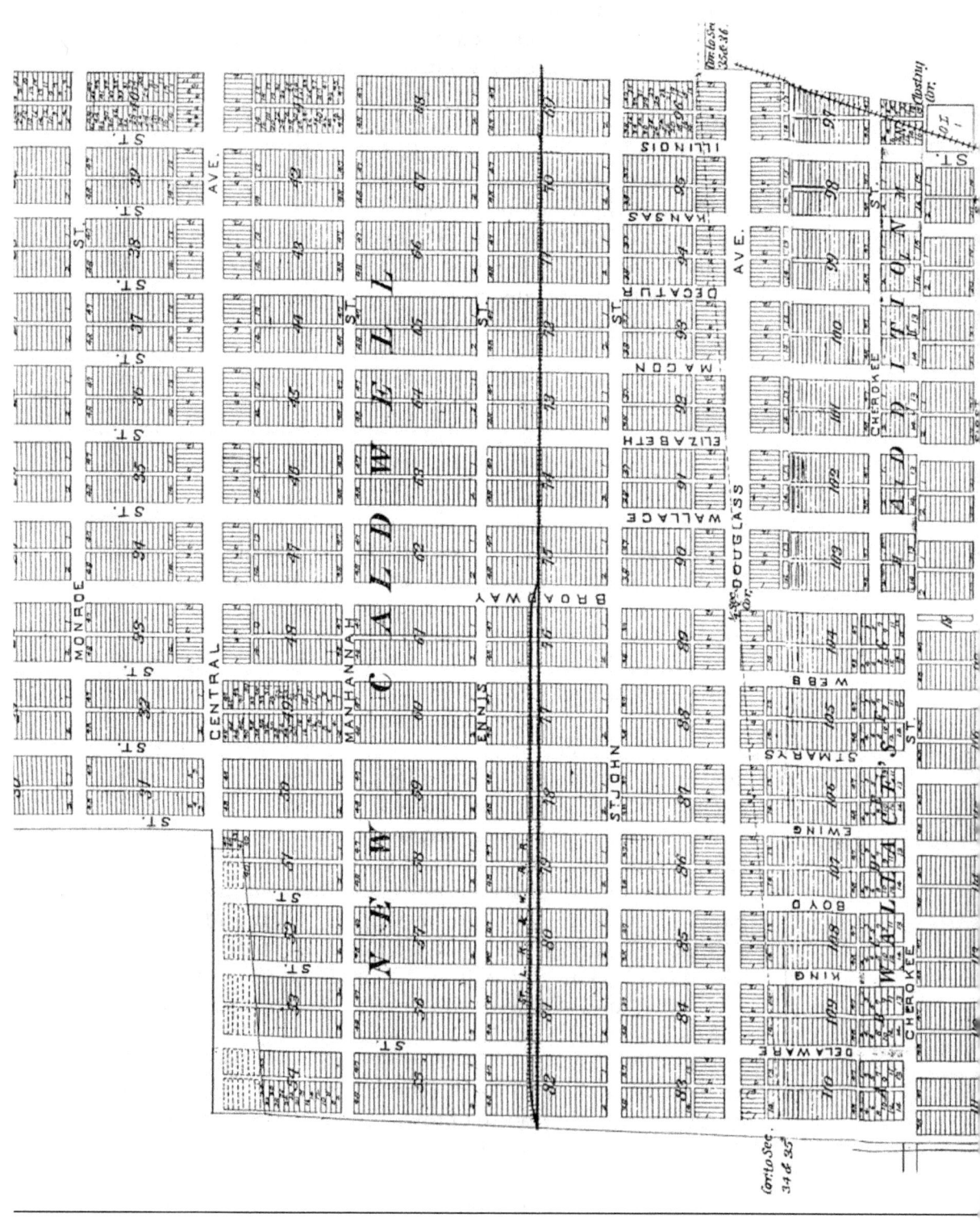

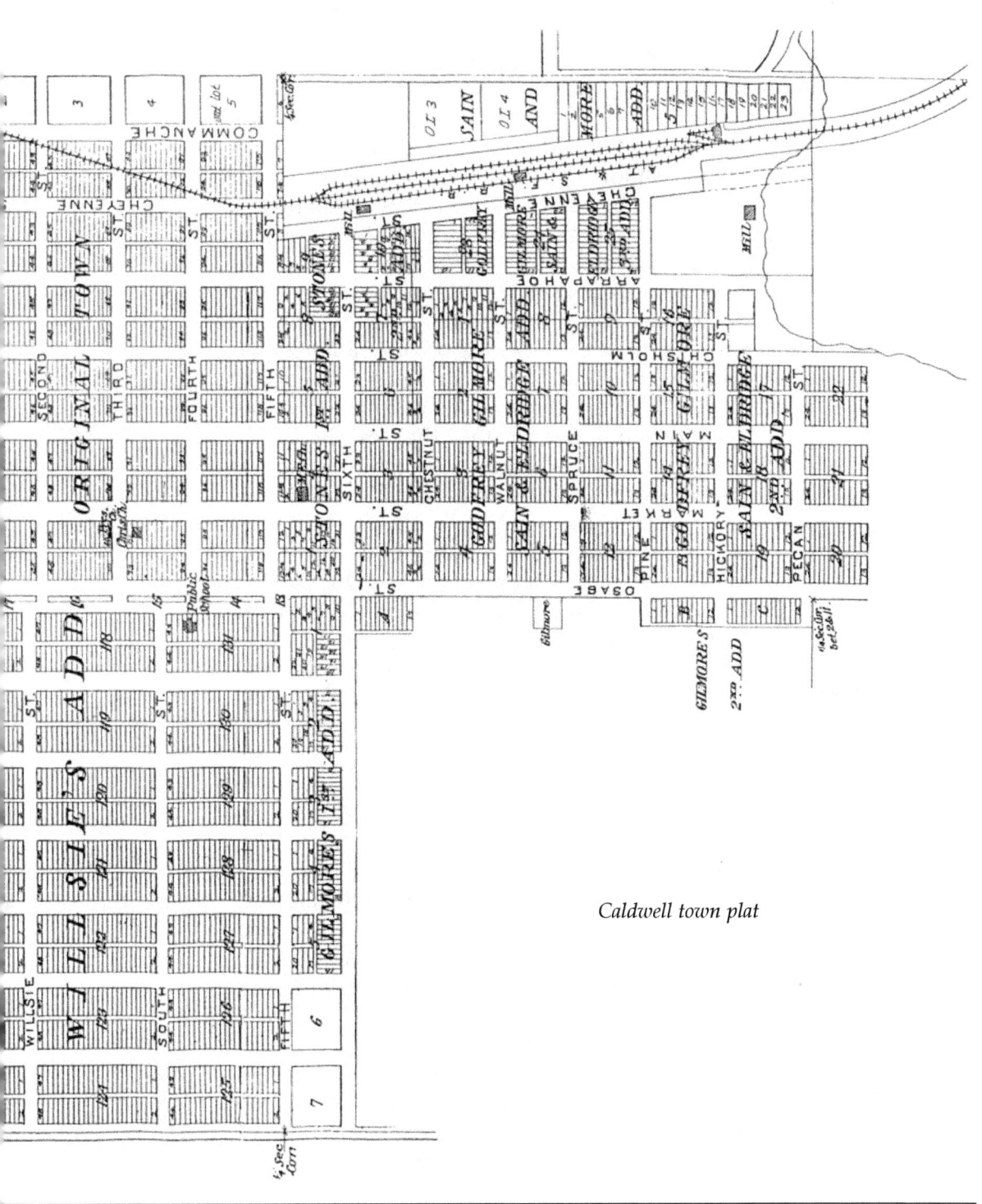

Caldwell town plat

on Thursday, August 7, two weeks after the Order of Incorporation was received. Merchant N. J. Dixon was elected mayor; Justice of the Peace and real estate dealer James D. Kelly was elected police judge; and five city councilmen were elected. J. D. Kelly, Jr., editor of the *Post*, was appointed city clerk.[15]

Also appointed to office was George Flatt, who became Caldwell's first city marshal. Only one month had passed since Flatt and John Wilson had gunned down Adams and Wood in the Occidental Saloon shootout. Wilson already was deputy constable under Judge Kelly, while Flatt's impressive performance in the Occidental made him an obvious candidate for law enforcement. The city council authorized the erection of a jail. "The calaboose was dedicated last night," announced the *Post* on November 6, 1879, "with only one guest."

Marshal Flatt was married to Fannie Lamb on September 16, 1879, at the residence of a friend. "The bride's dress was made of fine Empress cloth elegantly trimmed," and the event was "attended by a goodly number of the elite of the city." Caldwell's "elite" included Mayor Dixon, who gave the couple a lamp. Another guest provided a cow and a calf. The ceremony was followed by an "elegant" supper.[16]

But one week after attending the wedding of George Flatt, Mayor Dixon died. Married and the father of four children, Dixon had been a community leader since Caldwell's earliest days. He was an enterprising merchant, dealing in dry goods and groceries, while simultaneously working as Caldwell's express and stagecoach agent. A few days after the Flatt wedding, Dixon fell ill. He died on Friday afternoon, September 23, 1879, and the City Council issued a series of resolutions praising "our much honored and respected Mayor and fellow citizen." Less than two weeks later, on October 4, Julia Dixon died, leaving four orphaned children, including a baby she named after herself. (The next year little Julia Dixon, only one year old, died at the home of relatives in Arkansas City.) An epidemic of "typhoid malaria" swept the Caldwell area in the fall of 1879. Aside from Mayor and Mrs. Dixon, one of the other victims of the epidemic was Mary A. Colson, nineteen-year-old bride of community leader A. M. Colson. The infant daughter of Dr. and Mrs. W. A. Noble died. Marshal George Flatt became "very ill," but recovered.[17]

At a special election held on Tuesday, October 28, Cassius M. Hollister won the vacated office of mayor by an eleven-vote margin over merchant W. N. Hubbell. A native of Ohio, Cash Hollister migrated to Caldwell in 1877 when he was thirty-one. The next year he married Sarah Rhodes. Soon after their marriage Cash and Sarah moved to Wichita, returning to Caldwell late in 1878. Hollister had a quick temper and he was always willing to resort to fists or guns, but these qualities won respect among the rugged residents of Caldwell.[18]

Indeed, a month after becoming mayor, Hollister quarreled and fought with Frank Hunt, who later would become a member of the Caldwell police force. Hunt filed an assault complaint, and Marshal Flatt was compelled to arrest the mayor. Mayor Hollister pled guilty and was fined one dollar and costs, but he retaliated by filing an assault charge against Hunt, who also was fined one dollar.[19] Although Hollister would choose not to run for re-election as mayor during the annual city election in April 1880, he was appointed to a succession of law enforcement positions. During the next few years, while Caldwell experienced its rowdy heyday as the last railhead of the Chisholm Trail, Cash Hollister served as a brave and efficient peace officer.

By the time that Hollister took office as mayor in late August 1879, the population of Caldwell had tripled from the 264 listed on the application for incorporation in January 1879. "Caldwell has a population of about eight hundred," reported the *Post* on November 6, 1879, "and will no doubt double that within the next twelve months." Although this bold prediction sounded like the usual *Post* boosterism, it would prove accurate.

There were ninety students enrolled in Caldwell's school in February 1879. By December enrollment climbed to 110, and in February 1880 there were more than 160 pupils. The students were divided into primary, intermediate, and advanced grades. By early 1880 students and teachers were in a new building. The latest Caldwell school cost $1,600, a two-story frame structure that measured thirty by forty feet. The old school was purchased and moved to the east side of Main Street for use as a restaurant.[20]

More impressive than the two-story frame school or any other of Caldwell's new buildings was the three-story brick hotel erected late in 1879 and early in 1880. The fifty- by seventy-five-foot structure went up on two lots on the northwest corner of Sixth and Main. A full basement would be divided into a billiard parlor, a barber shop and, in the rear, bathrooms. The main floor would have dining rooms, a kitchen, and hotel offices. The upper two floors would boast forty-six "large and well ventilated rooms," as well as a view that extended two miles to Indian Territory.[21]

Major D. M. Odum built the hotel, then sold it to two part-

The Leland Hotel opened in 1880, with 46 rooms and a windmill in the rear to provide water. The small building at right was a barber shop.
—Courtesy Caldwell Historical Society

ners who would christen it the Leland Hotel. Demand for accommodations in Caldwell was so pressing that the Leland was opened to guests before the third floor interior was finished. A Dedication Ball was held at the hotel on Wednesday evening, February 26, 1880. Five hundred printed invitations were sent to "prominent citizens" in Caldwell, Wellington, and other communities throughout the region. "At early lamplight the sweet strains from Kelly's cornet band began to fill the air from the veranda of the hotel," described the *Post*, "and the joyful crowd commenced to assemble and by 7:30 over sixty couples were

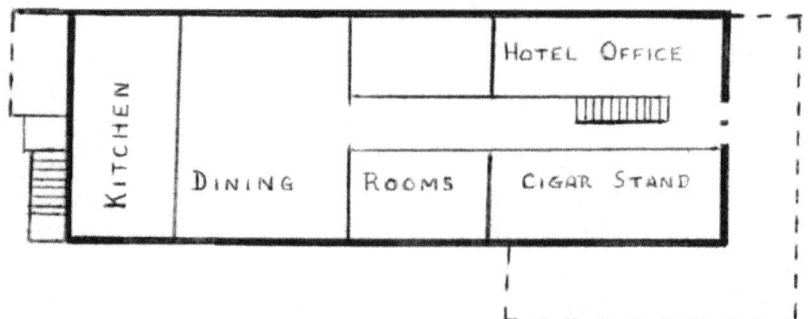

The first floor of the Leland Hotel. A billiard parlor was in the basement, and a frame cupola was atop the roof.
— Author diagram from Sanborn Insurance Map, 1885

The Barber and the Widow

Small-town gossips avidly noted the growth of tender feelings between a Caldwell barber and a local widow. In case anyone remained unaware of the budding romance, the Post published a poem (July 28, 1880) about the prospective couple:

  In Caldwell city a barber dwells,
  And a widow next door to him.
  And, Lord a'massy, how he swells
  When the widow designs to call him.

  Then does his heart with love o'erflow.
  Each wish he fills, if she ask it;

(cont. next page)

And when she whispered—peaches sweet, He fetched her of peaches, a basket.

So at his chair our barber stands. And shaves, and loves and sigheth; But when the shades of evening come, He to his loved one hieth.

Then shines his face with smiles lit up, While o'er the widow cooing, With laughter silent—hid from sight, We watch the barber's wooing.

★★★

South side of the Leland. Note the horse-drawn bus to connect patrons with the depot, located several blocks to the southeast.
—Courtesy Caldwell Historical Society

ready to participate in the 'grand march.'" The *Post* declared the ball "the grandest affair that ever occurred" in Caldwell. "To show the public that Caldwell ladies compare favorably in a dress with some of our eastern cities, we give below a list of some of the styles of dresses worn on that occasion:" The list of twenty ladies included:[22]

Mrs. C. M. Hollister—Black grosgrain silk and velvet with onyx jewelry.
Mrs. T.H.B. Ross—Black cashmere trimmed in velvet
Mrs. Dr. W.A. Noble—Black grosgrain silk and cameo jewelry.
Mrs. Mike Meagher—Pretty combination suit of blue and drab.

But even before the Leland opened it had competition as Caldwell's leading hostelry. The forty-room Central Hotel, "a heavy frame building, substantially built," was the centerpiece of "New Caldwell." Early in 1879, shortly after railroad bonds were voted, a company of investors from Kansas and Illinois began planning a major addition to Caldwell. As the little trail town began to grow, investors quietly worked to purchase land north and west of Caldwell townsite. In May 1879 the development company, "representing a capital of one hundred thousand dollars," announced that "New Caldwell" would be laid out, a 760-acre addition north of the current center of town. Caldwell's north-south streets were extended northward through New Caldwell and renamed, while surveyors platted new east-west streets and lots. Commercial lots were laid out along Douglass Avenue, a wide east-west thoroughfare six blocks north of Fifth Street (Fifth and Main was the central intersection of Caldwell).[23]

The developers of New Caldwell anticipated that the St. Louis, Kansas and Western Railroad would build an east-to-west line parallel to and a block and a half north of Douglass Avenue. Clearly the developers hoped to shift the center of Caldwell northward, into their addition. They offered lots for as little as twenty dollars apiece, and spent $9,000 to erect the Grand Central Hotel on a corner of Douglass and Wallace. By the time the Grand Central opened, early in 1880, there were twenty-five or thirty lesser buildings completed or under construction in New Caldwell.[24] Caldwell was booming, but would there be sufficient population to support *two* business districts?

The growing town was threatened by fire and violent winds. As the sun went down on Thursday, March 13, 1879, a prairie fire appeared northeast of Caldwell. Fanned by heavy winds, with "flames leaping high in the air," the conflagration was "fearful to behold" as it approached the outskirts of town. Caldwell was saved only by a backfire set along a small stream just east of town. "Several of our citizens had narrow escapes from the fire," reported the *Post* on March 20, 1879, "but at 11 o'clock all was pronounced safe."

A few weeks later, on the evening of April 8, a ferocious wind struck Caldwell from the southeast. With "hurricane" power the wind blasted a frame storehouse, "raising it from its foundation and scattering the fragments for two blocks up the street." While Kelly's cornet band was practicing in the school house, "the building was moved about five inches from the foundation by the wind." A new commercial building, seventy feet long, was flattened. Many outhouses, stables, and sheds were demolished.[25]

High winds swept a prairie fire into Caldwell from the west on Thursday, March 4, 1880. The new, two-story school was struck by flames, but the pupils were evacuated and the fire put out with little damage. A barn was destroyed, the engine room of a mill was torn down to save the main structure, and the entire town was in peril. Citizens turned out to fight the blaze. Wells were drawn dry, and wagons and teams were sent to Fall Creek to fill barrels and pails with water. "Men, women, and children all engaged in fighting the fire to save their homes," described the *Post*. After an hour of all-out effort the town once again was delivered from conflagration.[26]

Two months later, on Saturday, May 8, fire broke out beneath a "mansion" on Broadway in New Caldwell. The occupants were all sporting women, and they frantically tried to save their beds and bedding. As smoke billowed from the windows, a large number of men ran up to fight the fire. An experienced firefighter directed the impromptu fire brigade to remove the doors and windows, and the proprietor of the nearby Grand Central Hotel brought over the hotel's modest fire apparatus. The Grand Central was headquarters for the A.T. & S.F. and one of the railroad's civil engineers directed that the burning building should be tipped over on its side. On the second try the men upended the frame structure, and then quickly extinguished the flames beneath. The building was placed back on its foundation, and the doors and windows were put back, while the furnishings were brought inside. "We are informed," related the *Post*, "that the ladies were very grateful for the kind aid rendered to them and extended... a general invitation to the boys to call on them under more favorable circumstances. The loss is quite severe," added the *Post* reporter with tongue in cheek. "So far as we can learn it consists of one smashed stovepipe, one broken window and about fifty cents damage to the floor."[27]

With Caldwell poised to become a railhead for the Chisholm Trail, the presence of sporting ladies was inevitable. Some of the women who set up business in Caldwell undoubtedly had worked in Wichita or Newton, Dodge City or Abilene. "Several ladies of easy virtue now reside in Caldwell," reported the *Post* on November 6, 1876. Also arriving were gamblers who followed the action from one cattle town to another, and bartenders. "Three new saloons will open this week," announced the *Post* on December 4, 1879. "Then we will have six." By the time the railroad arrived seven months later there were eleven saloons, as well as a beer garden two miles south of town. It was estimated that these establishments would provide the city treasury with annual licensing revenue of $2,000.[28]

Destined to attain special infamy in Caldwell was the boldly named Red Light Saloon and Dance Hall. The term "red light houses" came to identify bordellos when railroad men would hang the red lanterns used to signal outside the door when they paid a visit to soiled doves. George and Mag Wood had operated a dance hall-saloon-bordello for several years in Wichita, but in 1879 they decided to move their business to Caldwell. Intending to establish Caldwell's premier entertainment center, George and Mag decided upon a label that would be clear to every potential customer.

George Wood was born in Texas about 1853. Margaret Ann Gillon was born a few years later in Georgia, moving with the family to Kansas when she was about eight. She left home as a teenager, and by 1875 Maggie was linked with George in Wichita. She used his last name without benefit of marriage, so George apparently was her pimp. In 1876 George and Mag established a dance hall near Fort Worth, on the Chisholm Trail. Five bartenders served drinks, and as many as thirty girls brought from Wichita charged fifty cents for a dance set. "Places like that dance hall," reminisced a cowboy customer, "took a fellow's money right away from him."[29]

George and Mag soon returned with their staff to Wichita, where she frequently was fined as a prostitute and George as a "keeper of a house of ill fame." In August 1879 Mag organized a trial run in Caldwell. With civic alarm, the *Post* reported: "Mag Wood, a notorious Wichita prostitute, in company with several pieces of feminine frailty, made a descent from that unchristian city on our little village last week, and temporarily located on the creek, outside the city limits."[30] Mag and her girls operated for several months in temporary quarters. Business was encouraging, and in April 1880 George Wood erected a two-story frame building on the northeast corner of Chisholm Street and Fifth, one block east of Caldwell's Main Street. The front of the ground floor was a saloon owned by George, who painted a sign on the window: "Red Light Saloon." Mag ran the dance hall in the rear. Upstairs were about eight bedrooms. There were several girls to house, as well as bartenders and a handyman and an African-American cook named Becky Banks, a former prostitute. George and Maggie also needed living quarters. George may have built a lesser structure on his property, perhaps a flimsy row of cribs.

The inmates of the Red Light were young. George was twenty-seven in 1880. Maggie, who finally had married George in December 1879, was twenty-three. Becky Banks was twenty-four. The dance-hall girls were in their teens or twenties. Even the bartenders were young men.[31] The Red Light throbbed with youthful energy, and music and loud voices and drunken laughter.

Orderly citizens were horrified by the presence of the Red Light. When the Red Light was about to open, the *Post* protested the establishment of a dance hall. "It is the hot-bed of vice and the favorite place for murders, assault and drunken ribaldry. A gambling room is as moral as a church raffle, and a saloon as quiet as a funeral, when compared with the dance-house." One week later the *Post* published complaints from citizens, including the terse appeal: "Stop that 'dance-house' racket." George Freeman called the Red Light "a house of ill-repute" and "a den of prostitution," and he referred to Maggie as "that notorious character." Freeman was bitter that the Red Light had been permitted to open. "Oh, the deeds of crime which have been committed within its walls of iniquity and shame. Many are the crimes and murders which have been caused by its immoral and vile influence." The Red Light probably was no more "immoral and vile" than dance halls in other frontier boomtowns. But the Caldwell dive would indeed become the site of a startling series of killings.[32]

By the time the Red Light opened for business, railroad tracks were approaching from the northeast. The A.T. & S.F. delayed construction from Wellington to Caldwell until a rival line, the Kansas City, Lawrence and Southern Railroad, threatened to lay tracks from Wellington to the border town. Caldwell city fathers offered the K.C.L. & S. acreage, city lots, and a modest amount of cash ($1,100). It was the prospect of this line that spurred development of the New Caldwell addition. But a better offer, totaling $28,000 from townships to the east of Caldwell, persuaded the K.C.L. & S. to build due south from Wellington. The railhead would plat a railhead community, Hunnewell, on the state line twelve miles east of Caldwell. These two neighboring railheads would immediately become keen competitors for the Chisholm Trail cattle trade.[33]

Railroad trestle built across Fall Creek in 1880. — Author photo

By 1880 railroads were adept at laying track rapidly. The A.T. & S.F. advanced swiftly from Wellington, twenty miles of track on a straight line angling to the southwest. As the tracks advanced more buildings went up in Caldwell, more people flocked into town, and more businesses started. A large stockyard complex began to be built on the state line about two miles southeast of Caldwell.[34]

A.T. & S.F. tracks reached Caldwell on Tuesday, June 2, 1880. The *Post* reflected the excitement of the community. "Besides the many advantages which Caldwell will reap from being a cattle market, the fact of being the terminus of the road makes it a distributing point for a vast amount of government supplies which will be shipped to this place to be hauled here to the different posts and agencies in the territory." Furthermore, on three sides Caldwell was surrounded by farms which produced "wheat, corn and other produce." The railroad brought boundless promise. "Well may Caldwell look forward with reason to many years of glorious prosperity."[35]

An early AT&SF train at the Border Queen.
—Courtesy Caldwell Historical Society

CHAPTER SIX

Last Railhead on the Chisholm Trail

"It was just as natural in those days for us to go in and shoot up a town and raise hell generally as it is nowadays to go to see a football game or play a game of golf."
—Charles Colcord, former cowboy

Although tracks of the Atchison, Topeka & Santa Fe reached Caldwell on the first day of June 1880, the Kansas border town was not yet a livestock railhead. Located two miles southeast of town on the Kansas state line, the stockyard complex was designed to accept cattle from Indian Territory, then funnel the animals onto stock cars without violating Kansas quarantine laws. Tracks still had to be laid to the stockyards, including tracks across Fall Creek and Bluff Creek. A depot had not yet been built; the depot agent established his office in a freight car until the structure—112 feet long with a 150-foot platform—was completed at the end of June.[1]

At last, on Wednesday morning, June 16, the first carloads of cattle were shipped from the Caldwell stockyards north toward Kansas City—"thus winning the race," crowed the *Post*. The "race" was between the A.T. & S.F. and the Kansas City, Lawrence & Southern railroads. The K.C. L. & S., of course, had built due south from Wellington to the state line, while the A.T. & S.F. raced to Caldwell. Caldwell was a long established town on the Chisholm Trail, while newly platted Hunnewell would rise fourteen miles east of the main trail. "Caldwell is ahead," boasted the *Post*. "Hurrah!"[2]

But even though the first cattle shipments of 1880 were along the A.T. & S.F. instead of the K.C.L. & S., the "race" between the two lines continued throughout the shipping season. The railroads competed for business with a rate war which delighted cattlemen. But railroad officials could not long tolerate such losses, and by September 1880 the A.T. & S.F. completed negotiations to buy the K.C.L. & S. The A.T. & S.F. soon began constructing a roundhouse south of their new depot in Caldwell.[3]

After absorbing the K.C.L. & S., the Atchison, Topeka & Santa Fe controlled shipping from Dodge City, Caldwell, and Hunnewell, striving to achieve a balance in future seasons that would best serve the railroad. This regulated competition with Dodge City and, especially, nearby Hunnewell, reduced to some extent the traffic that railhead Caldwell should have enjoyed.

Nevertheless, during the early 1880s a tide of Wild West excitement inundated Caldwell. Caldwell teemed with important cattlemen, who were not, as in earlier years, simply passing through on their way to Abilene or Newton or Wichita. Now Caldwell was the destination. In hotel lobbies, restaurants, saloons, and at the stockyards, cattlemen made deals with other cattlemen and with eastern cattle buyers.

Joseph G. McCoy had created Abilene as a cattle town and opened the Chisholm Trail in 1867. A giant in the Kansas-Texas cattle trade, "Colonel" McCoy became a familiar figure in railhead Caldwell. When he was in town on business in November 1880, *Post* editor J. D. Kelly, Jr., reacted with obsequious awe: "The Colonel is the kind of man that we are always glad to have around, not only on account of his pleasant and social ways, but for his highly educated conversational qualifications, that are always interesting and entertaining." The following June in Caldwell, McCoy bought "a neat span of ponies, a new set of harness and comfortable top buggy," then drove south to visit roundups in Indian Territory. He returned by the end of the month, but in August went back into I.T. "for an extended trip down among the cattle men."[4]

Cattle being loaded from the Caldwell shipping pens in 1882. The men prodding them along demonstrate the origin of the term "cowpoke."
—Caldwell Historical Association

Also present in Caldwell in August 1881 was legendary Texas rancher Shanghai Pierce, who sold "a bunch of yearling steers." The six-foot-four Shanghai rode his big mount, Old Prince, in constant search of deals. "I am Shanghai Pierce, Webster on cattle, by God, sir," he liked to announce in his booming voice. He and his brother had built El Rancho Grande in South Texas. After Shanghai led the lynching of five rustlers in Texas he spent a year and a half in Kansas while legal troubles were alleviated. But even after returning to Texas, Shanghai was in Kansas for most of every shipping season. Before leaving Caldwell after selling his herd in August 1881, he visited the editor of the *Post*, loudly expressing concerns about the tardiness of other trail herds from Texas. "Shanghai has dwindled away to a mere skeleton," facetiously observed editor Tell Walton,

"*I am Shanghai Pierce, Webster on cattle, by God, sir.*" *The flamboyant Texas cattleman was in and out of Caldwell throughout its cattle town years.*
— Author's collection

"and his gentle voice can scarcely be heard in the adjoining county, by reason of his anxiety."[5]

Although not as colorful or as loud as Shanghai, David T. Beals was just as large an operator. Beals, a wealthy Boston shoe manufacturer, decided to increase his fortune in the West. A cattle ranch in Colorado was profitable, but an influx of homesteaders caused him to look for more isolated range. In 1877 Beals and W. H. Bates, a fellow Bostonian, founded the LX Ranch in the Texas Panhandle. Within a few years the LX ranged as many as 50,000 head of cattle, and in September 1881 Beals was in Caldwell awaiting the arrival of 5,000 head being trailed from the Panhandle ranch.[6] Beals acquired a holding spread a few miles south of Caldwell, and he started an LX horse ranch four miles east of town. Like J. G. McCoy and Shanghai Pierce and other successful cattlemen, Beals traveled constantly, visiting cattle towns and roundups and his ranches, as well as buyers and potential investors in the East.

Along with McCoy, Pierce, and Beals, other prominent cattlemen in and around Caldwell included Texas brothers Dudley and John Snyder; Col. B. H. Campbell, commonly called "Barbeque" Campbell—because of his brand—in Caldwell as well as Texas; Print Olive, whose move from Texas to Nebraska involved a lynching which branded him with the unwanted nickname, "Man Burner;" and dozens of other ambitious ranchers and trail drivers. Capt. C. H. Stone, founder of Caldwell,

The historic LX Ranch headquarters was built in the 1880s. Located two miles east of Caldwell, the LX currently is owned and managed by Carson Ward.
— Author photo

Texas Cowboy/Caldwell Merchant-Bridegroom

Charles Siringo cowboyed for two of the notable Texas cattlemen who frequented Caldwell, Shanghai Pierce and David T. Beals. A cowboy since childhood in South Texas, Siringo began working for the dynamic Pierce as a teenager. Wiry and athletic, Siringo was a superb rider who reveled in the colorful life of a cowboy. He hired on with Beals on the vast LX Ranch in the Texas Panhandle, where he met Billy the Kid and other New Mexico outlaws, including Henry Brown.

(cont. next page)

now was a cattleman and often was in and out of town. Several local men—most notably Ben "Circle Bar" Miller, A. M. Colson, and Asa Overall—now were busy cattlemen.

For several months each year Caldwell hosted large numbers of cattlemen. They were restless, ambitious, confident, energetic, and Caldwell was enlivened by their presence. Stockmen began to hold meetings in Caldwell—in September and in October of 1881, for example, to organize winter "pools." A meeting of stockmen who held cattle in the Cherokee Strip was scheduled to convene in Caldwell on March 1, 1882, when the spring roundup would be organized.[7]

As they had done the previous year, Caldwell businessmen planned a ball and banquet during the convention to welcome the cattlemen back to town. "Show the stockmen that we appreciate their coming to town to hold their conventions," urged the *Post*. A planning meeting was held at the York-Parker-Draper Mercantile Company, and committees were formed. Eight hundred of "the toniest invitations that have ever been sent out

Charlie Siringo was a Texas cowboy who drove a herd of LX steers to Caldwell in 1882, then took over the LX horse ranch near town. But Siringo soon bought lots in Caldwell, built a house, brought his mother to the Border Queen, and found a teenage bride. He quit cowboying and opened a popular shop.
—Courtesy Caldwell Historical Society

in this county" were distributed locally and to incoming cattlemen.

"When Caldwell goes at anything," observed the *Post*, which printed the invitations, "nothing but the best answer her tastes."[8]

Each season Caldwell sent representatives down the Chisholm Trail to attract herds to the railhead that now styled itself the "Queen of the Border." Early in 1882 Ben Miller and Asa Overall planned to head a delegation to attend the Texas stockman's convention in Austin.[9]

Caldwell citizens often visited nearby roundups to watch the excitement, and sometimes offered their help. In June 1881 Harvey Horner rode out in his buggy to a roundup on Pole Creek in Indian Territory. There were numerous other men from Caldwell present, including Dr. W. A. Noble and his father, who was visiting from Missouri. Tell Walton, editor of the *Post*, rode into the roundup camp on Thursday evening, June 9, and he took a two-hour shift as a night hawk. "Our saddle was very tired, and needed rest." Walton gratefully climbed into his bedroll, but the camp was up at four o'clock. The editor viewed the day's activities, and wrote a lively account of the roundup for *Post* readers. On Friday afternoon Walton "turned our horse's head homeward," arriving at Caldwell "just as the shades of night were falling, tired sore, hungry and dusty, but well pleased with our trip to the roundup."[10]

The *Post* devoted a major amount of copy to livestock trans-

Beals acquired a small ranch a couple of miles southeast of Caldwell, primarily to winter his cow ponies. When Siringo arrived in November 1882 with a herd of LX steers, Beals placed him in charge of the horse ranch.

Impressed by growing Caldwell, Siringo purchased lots, contracted to build a house, and made plans to move his widowed mother to the Border Queen. He journeyed by train to Texas and brought Mrs. Siringo to her new home late in 1882.

At the ranch Mrs. Siringo had about two hundred "fat ponies," and almost every evening he

(cont. next page)

House on Osage Street built in 1882 by Charlie Siringo. — Author photo

galloped into town to check on his mother "and to see my sweethearts."

The principal sweetheart was fifteen-year-old Mamie Lloyd. "It was a genuine case of love at first sight," said the smitten cowboy. After a whirlwind courtship Charlie and Mamie were married in Wellington in March 1883.

A few days later Siringo and a crew of cowboys drove a horse herd to the LX in the Panhandle, then worked the spring roundup. Siringo next led a herd of "eight hundred fat shipping steers" to Caldwell.

Following a brief reunion

(cont. next page)

actions, trail news, and cattlemen. "STOCK TRANSFERS, SHIPMENTS AND ARRIVALS" was a feature which detailed the number of cars of cattle shipped on the railroad. For the week of August 12-18, 1881, for example, the biggest shipper was Hewins & Co., which steadily shipped large numbers of "cars of cattle to Chicago:" Sunday—29 cars; Saturday—40 cars; Sunday—84 cars; Monday—48 cars; Tuesday—43 cars; Wednesday—none; Thursday—25 cars. The total for the week for the Ed Hewins cattle company was 219 cars shipped from the Caldwell stockyards. The *Post* also included all of the smaller operators, such as, on Sunday: "A. M. Colson, 3 cars cattle to Kansas City;" on Wednesday, "W. R. Terwilliger, 5 cars ponies;" and on Thursday, "Lem Hunter, 24 cars cattle eastern market."[11]

A regular column, "Local Stock Notes," listed various items of interest to stockmen. On September 22, 1881, for example: "Ben Miller brought in 240 fine wintered beeves from the Miller Company ranch Monday, and sold them to Joe R. Murray. Joe shipped them from Hunnewell [unwelcome news in Caldwell] Tuesday. Price paid, private." In addition to news of cattle and cattlemen, there also were items about other livestock, such as sheep and horses. On September 8, 1881, J. G. McCoy shipped "one car of hogs." The *Post* also reported in detail on local stock conventions and related gatherings, and there was regular news from Texas during the trail season. For instance, on September 29, 1881, the *Post* stated: "The number of cattle passing Ft. Griffin up to Sept. 1st was 214,228. There were fully as many more passed through other parts of Texas enroute for ranches and Kansas of which no record was kept."

On the eve of the 1882 season, in the March 30 issue, a *Post* headline announced: "Caldwell the Best Stock Market in the West." The following story pointed out that, as "the terminus of the great Chisholm trail," Caldwell was "easily accessible to the great distributing points, Kansas City, Chicago and St. Louis, by rail and by telegraph." At Caldwell eastern buyers could "procure any and all classes of cattle desired." The *Post* extolled Caldwell's hotels and banking facilities, and pointed out that the stockyards were being remodeled. "Cattle drovers, drive to Caldwell," implored the *Post*. "Cattle buyers, come to Caldwell to purchase."

Cattle buyers could find two banks to facilitate financial transactions in Caldwell. Caldwell's first financial institution was the Merchants & Drovers Bank, organized in 1879, with an experienced banker, J. S. Danford, as president. It was a noteworthy event in town when the bank's big safe arrived. In 1880, with the coming of the railroad, business boomed. The bank added staff and built a two-story masonry structure, transferring the safe to the ground floor and renting out the second-floor offices. Late in 1881 President Danford and his cashier slipped out of Caldwell with the bank's cash, although a flurry of telegraphs resulted in their arrest in Wichita. A large group of the bank's creditors brought the thieves back to Caldwell, where they attended the arraignment and began legal pressure to seize Danford's assets.[12]

Caldwell's second bank was organized by enterprising stockmen—including Ed Hewins and Ben Miller—at the same time the Merchants & Drovers Bank was undergoing failure. The Stock Exchange Bank was chartered by the State of Kansas on November 12, 1881, and opened for business on December 24—in the recently emptied Merchants & Drovers building. But these quarters were only temporary. The Stock Exchange Bank launched construction of a two-story stone building on the southwest corner of Main and Sixth—just across the street from the Leland Hotel. The Stock Exchange opened the doors of its new home (where it remains located today) on Monday, May 1, 1882. Also in the spring of 1882 the Caldwell Savings Bank came into existence. The Stock Exchange afforded cattlemen a financial institution in which they could trust, while the Caldwell Savings Bank afforded the town a second bank.[13]

Caldwell's best hotel was the Leland. From its top floor cattlemen could see into Indian Territory, perhaps catching a glimpse of their herd grazing near the stockyards. If a livestock deal was struck in the lobby of the Leland, the cattlemen could walk across the street to the Stock Exchange Bank and finalize financing. When "Mrs. Gov. [John P.] St. John and her daughter, Lutie, of Topeka," traveled in the area to visit relatives, they dined at the Leland.[14]

The only hotel large enough to compete with the Leland was the two-story frame Grand Central. The Grand Central Hotel was the centerpiece of New Caldwell, the northerly addition which anticipated the arrival of the K.C.L. & S.—which laid track instead to Hunnewell. One by one the buildings clustered near the Grand Central were moved south to less isolated parts of town. The Grand Central loomed empty, except for a few people who lived there. The manager occasionally drummed up a little business by staging a dinner dance. In late November 1880 there was an effort to raise money among the business community to move the big structure to Main Street. But follow-

with his bride in September 1883, Charlie was told to take the outfit back to the Panhandle. But while supplying the chuckwagon at a Caldwell store, he abruptly quit and turned the outfit over to his Number Two. The next day he rented a commercial room on Main Street, donned a pair of suspenders—"the first I had ever worn"—and opened a tobacco shop which soon was expanded to an ice cream parlor and lunch stand.

The gregarious Siringo knew hundreds of cowboys and ranchers, who provided excellent patronage when they were in town. Prospering as

(cont. next page)

a businessman, in his spare time he began writing his reminiscences as A Texas Cowboy.

Taken from *A Texas Cowboy* and the Caldwell *Post*, November 9, 1882, and September 3, 1883.

★★★

ing a dance on Thursday night, December 2, a fire broke out on the roof. Considerable furniture was carried outside, but the Grand Central Hotel burned to the ground. The building was insured for $3,500, which may have been the financial objective of the hotel's ownership.[15]

The Leland remained unchallenged as Caldwell's finest hostelry for three years, 1880-1883, until the Southwestern Hotel was erected on the northwestern corner of Main and Fourth.

The Stock Exchange Bank opened in 1881. The Cherokee Strip Live Stock Association headquartered upstairs in the front suite of offices. The lower photo shows the bank interior. —Courtesy Caldwell Historical Society

Like the Leland, the Southwestern was a three-story brick hotel. The Southwestern opened in November 1883, with thirty-eight rooms, as well as a ladies' parlor on the second floor. "Next to a good newspaper," remarked the *Post*, "nothing speaks better for a town than a hotel properly conducted, and in both respects Caldwell is now well supplied."[16]

In addition to two three-story brick hotels, Caldwell enjoyed a number of other upgrades along Main Street. The ramshackle, false-front, single-story, frame commercial houses of the 1870s were replaced during the early 1880s by two-story brick or stone structures. Banker J. S. Danford, before disgracing himself, built "Danford Hall," an "opera house" with a stage twenty feet wide and fourteen feet deep. Danford purchased a set of scenery for $1,000, and the drop curtain was adorned with "a very artistic scene." Five hundred chairs were placed in the hall. "Professor E. C. Taylor, the great illusionist" was the first act booked, for a week during October 1881. Most of the chairs were moved out in late November for a Thanksgiving ball, the first of numerous dances held in the hall. A popular play of the period, *The Union Spy*, was presented by amateur performers from Wellington. A professional troupe brought *Uncle Tom's Cabin* to Caldwell. After Danford ruined the Merchants & Drovers Bank, new management of the opera house continued to enliven Caldwell's en-

Built in 1883, the Southwestern Hotel boasted 38 rooms and a second-floor ladies' parlor.
—Courtesy Kansas State Historical Society, Topeka

tertainment scene with performances and balls. In January 1882 the Kendall Combination attracted good crowds during a nine-day engagement in which they presented such plays as *Jane Eyre*, *Yuba Bill*, and *Cinderella*. And during this long run the men of the company were taken on a hunt into Indian Territory.[17]

With handsome, substantial brick buildings up and down Main Street, other improvements were made. Boardwalks were extended throughout the business district. Streets were graded. "Sixth street is being graded," reported the *Post* in the spring of 1882, "and the small duck pond that used to be there after each rain, is a thing of the past." A street sprinkler was used to keep down the dust. An iron bridge was built across Fall Creek.[18]

Telegraph lines reached Caldwell, of course, with the railroad in 1880. A more recent communications breakthrough had hit town in 1878, and telephone service was expanded in June 1882. J. C. Lyeth, station agent for the A.T. & S.F., ran telephone connections from the depot to the stockyards and to the City Drug Store downtown. "Telephones are all the rage now," stated the *Post*. Publisher-editor Tell Walton ran a line to his residence. From Horner's Drug Store phone lines were strung to the homes of proprietor Harvey Horner and Dr. W.A. Noble, who worked out of the drugstore.[19]

Caldwell's Methodist and Presbyterian congregations, which had met in the school on Sundays, finally were able to erect proper church buildings. The Presbyterians built a thirty-by fifty-foot frame structure with a corner bell tower. The building cost $1,450, along with donated labor, lumber, and furniture. At the same time that the Presbyterian Church was dedicated, in October 1880, the trustees of the First Methodist Church began accepting bids for a brick church. There were delays, but carpenters completed their work in August 1881. But on Thursday night, September 29, a ferocious storm flooded Caldwell, destroying several residences, blowing over outhouses and windmills, washing away a small railroad bridge, and knocking the new Methodist steeple through the roof. After repairs were made, the Methodists purchased an organ. By 1882 a Christian Church had been formed, and the congregation bought one of the old frame school buildings for a meeting house.[20]

The Caldwell Public Schools soon built a two-story brick school. There had been a succession of frame school buildings. But with a swelling student population and a progressive atmosphere in Caldwell, voters—including women—approved a $10,000 school bond on July 1, 1881. In 1882 Caldwell students moved into an impressive red brick school, topped by a cupola, located two blocks west of Main Street. "There are a number of stockmen who are holding cattle in the Territory," observed the *Post* hopefully, "who will move their families to this point if we have good schools."[21]

Caldwell's population reached 1,100 during 1881 and continued to climb. The permanent population, as well as the numerous seasonal residents, were served by two banks, two three-story hotels, three churches, two newspapers (the *Post* and the *Commercial*), an opera house, a brick school, and a number of law and medical offices. (In September 1881 a dentist, Dr. N. A. Scribner, joined Caldwell's medical community: "Filling, cleaning, extracting and regulating done in scientific manner. Artificial teeth a specialty.")[22]

The most popular commercial establishment was A. S. Groh's Cheap Cash Chicago Store; the proprietor journeyed to Chicago a couple of times a year to buy merchandise. The Chicago Store catered to cowboys, and so did the Lone Star Clothing House. Other prominent businesses included H. A. Ross & Co. Dry Goods, the City Drug Store, Horner's Drug Store, W. N. Hubbell & Co. Gen'l Mdse, Hulbert's Gun Shop,

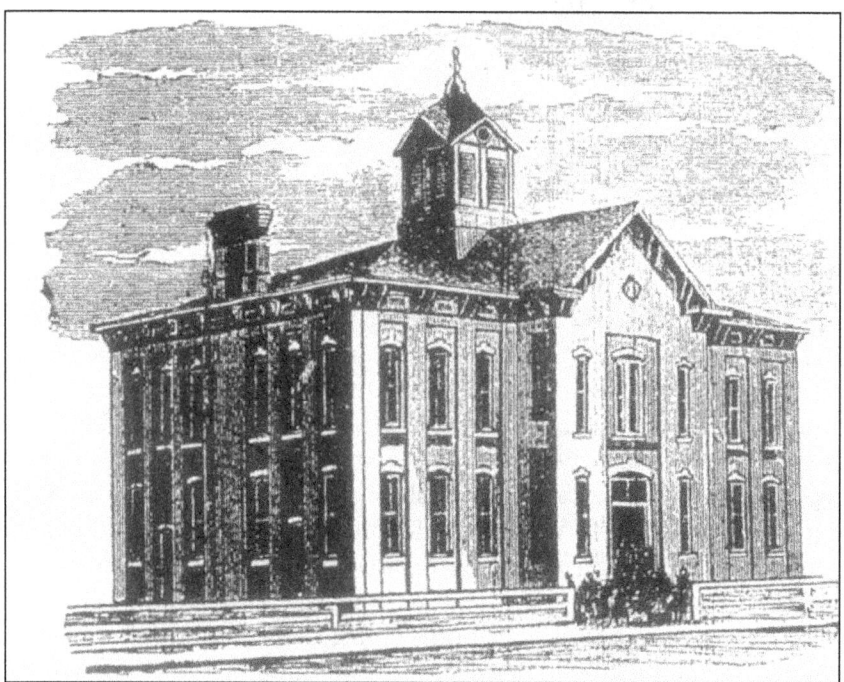

In 1882 Caldwell students moved into a two-story brick school located two blocks west of the business district. The eight rooms soon were crowded to capacity. The fence was built to keep wandering cows out of the schoolyard.
—Caldwell *Journal*, March 3, 1887

Hockaday's Tinware and Hardware, Levi Thrailkill's, Smith & Ross' Grocery Store, Charles H. Fay's Grocery, the Morris Grocery, and York-Parker-Draper Co. There were livery stables, restaurants, lumber yards, jewelry stores, tonsorial parlors, ladies' millinery, a bookshop, a photo gallery, and a Chinese laundry.

A dozen saloons flourished, including the Moreland House, the Occidental, Fitzgerald's, the Red Front, Moore Brothers Saloon, the Golden Wedding, the Kentucky Saloon, Phillips', the Exchange, Robison's Saloon, Flatt and Horseman's, and—of course—the Red Light. The Red Light offered fun-seeking customers liquor and gambling and girls, and drovers also drank, gambled and roistered in other saloons. After a long drive from Texas, or a shorter drive from the Cherokee Strip—following a long winter in a lonely Indian Territory line camp—cowboys came to Caldwell for a spree.

"It was just as natural in those days for us to go in and shoot up a town and raise hell generally as it is nowadays to go see a football game or play a game of golf, and there was no more evil intent than there is in these relaxations of today," reminisced Charles Colcord. "It was just the wild spirit of unrestrained youth taking its relief and change from the monotony of their harsh, daily life on the range." Looking back on his career as a cowboy, Colcord rationalized that cattle town revelry "was an essential part of the life, the place and the times."[23]

Colcord became a Texas cowboy at thirteen in 1872. "Every range rider in Texas was ambitious to make at least one trip up the trail with one of the north bound herds."[24] The teenaged drover first went up the Chisholm Trail in 1875. Later he ranched in Texas and in Kansas with his father, and he spent long winters in the Cherokee Strip. He was a pioneer settler in Oklahoma City, where he served as chief of police, county sheriff, and deputy U.S. marshal. He became wealthy in real estate, building the first twelve-story skyscraper in Oklahoma City. But during his cowboy years he was in and out of Caldwell: "Caldwell at that time was one of the worst towns in the country."[25]

In old age Colcord wrote his autobiography, reflecting thoughtfully and in depth on his cowboy experiences. Contrary to later theories that most cowboys did not carry or use guns, Colcord insisted that the gun culture was part of the way of life on the cattle frontier. "Everybody carried six-shooters and Winchesters in those days, and ... if a man had to make a choice he would just as soon leave off his pants as his six-shooter."

Colcord emphasized the point: "One's most constant companion was his gun. He wore it everywhere—almost slept with it. It was perfectly natural that the gun retained its essential place when we were on our outings." Target practice was a welcome recreation around a bunkhouse or line camp. "I suppose I have seen a carload of cartridges fired in my time on the range.... For years I spent most of my wages on cartridges."[26]

Colcord reflected on the early cowboy's "hard and lonely life; rough and violent most of the time. Those who read about the old days and the tough manner in which the boys had their 'good times' when they got into towns ... would find it easier to understand if they would think of the weeks and months that these young, active men spent in lonely solitude; in constant contact with the most violent forces of nature; drenched by the rain and buffeted by the winds and storms; having to deal constantly with the cussedness of half wild cattle; with wild cattle and wilder Indians.... When we were off duty with money to spend our relief often just naturally took violent form, constant with the life we lived every day."[27]

Colcord described a spree that included a shooting scrape and which probably took place either in Caldwell or Hunnewell. Colcord and a dozen other cowboys had completed a winter at a Cherokee Strip line camp and had a week of "vacation" before the spring roundup began. "We had several months of pay in our clothes and rode up into one of the Southern Kansas towns to spend it in some way that would give us amusement. We rode up to the hotel, went into the bar and lined up for drinks all around...." Colcord soon quarreled with the bartender, who lunged for his revolver on top of the bar. Colcord palmed his Colt .45 and triggered a round that tore through the bartender's gun hand. "Damn you, you've ruined my hand," shouted the bartender. Two of the cowboys took him to a drugstore, where his wound was dressed. The next morning the injured man took a train to Wichita for treatment at a hospital, where Colcord paid his expenses.[28]

"That was all that was ever done about it. It was just an example of the type of thing that happened over and over when the cowboys were in town. They were easily angered, quick to act and very dangerous in action," explained Colcord.

"We stayed in town several days having a good time in various ways, most of which were plenty rough and often accompanied by harmless shooting." Colcord realized that these cowboy antics "must have been rather trying to the nerves of the residents." Finally mounting up to leave town, "in accordance

---

Cowgirl from Caldwell

Texan Samuel Dunn Houston was trail foreman in 1888 for a herd of 2,500 steers headed out of New Mexico for northern Wyoming. Shorthanded, Houston bedded the herd down near Clayton, New Mexico, and went into town. He hired a drover named Willie Matthews, who "was nineteen [?] years old and weighed one hundred and twenty-five pounds. His home was in Caldwell, Kansas, and I was so pleased with him that I wished many times that I could find two or three more like him."

Houston assigned the new

(cont. next page)

hand to the horse herd and put his wrangler with the cattle. "The kid would get up on the darkest stormy nights and stay with the cattle until the storm was over. He was good natured, very modest, didn't use any cuss words or tobacco, and always pleasant."

The slow trail herd took a couple of months or more to reach Hugo in northern Colorado, near the Wyoming line. At lunch Willie approached Houston and asked to quit. "He insisted, said he was homesick, and I had to let him go."

At sundown Houston and his crew were sitting around

(cont. next page)

with cowboy custom [we] began riding our horses at a run up and down the main street of the town. We'd had some drinks, but all of us were sober enough not to shoot anybody."

As the cowboys lined up for their final run back toward Indian Territory, "the city marshal got out in the street and headed us off." The peace officer reached for Colcord's mount, "grabbing the left side of the horse's bit with his left hand. I swung at him with my gun, reaching over my horse's neck, but the blow fell short and he pulled down with his gun, jabbing it against my breast solidly and snapped it." The lawman's revolver twice failed to fire, and one of Colcord's companions clubbed him over the head with butt of his Winchester. The marshal collapsed and dropped his six-gun. "The boys all gathered around and eventually we made peace with the marshal and rode on off."

The cowboy attitudes and practices described by Charles Colcord were carried out in Caldwell. On September 8, 1881, for example, the *Post* reported a spree that would have been familiar to Colcord. "Two of the boys got on a hurrah Monday night, and turned their six-shooters loose about a dozen times within the city limits, contrary to a certain ordinance ... for which they were fined in the sum of $20 and costs, which they refused to pay, whereupon they took a rest in the cooler."

Like other cattle towns, Caldwell prohibited by city ordinance the discharge within city limits of "any gun, pistol, or other firearms," subject to a fine of twenty-five dollars. Another ordinance prohibited the carrying of "any deadly or dangerous weapon, such as firearms, slung shot, sheath or dirk knife, brass knuckles or any other weapon." Ordnances also established a police force, headed by a city marshal, and in August 1880 the City Council provided "neat badges for the police force."[29]

Despite efforts of Caldwell's community leaders to enforce order, there were frequent violations of firearms ordinances. There were sprees and "hurrahs" in the streets of Caldwell the railhead just as there had been during Caldwell's unregulated trail town days. And violence often was directed against those commissioned to maintain order in Caldwell.

Caldwell's first city marshal was George Flatt, appointed at a salary of $33.33 per month. On October 29, 1879, reported the *Post* the next day, John Dean rode into town and soon became drunk and disorderly. Dean was armed, a violation of city ordinances, and Marshal Flatt and his deputy, Red Bill Jones, marched to arrest him. Dean suspiciously mounted his horse and began riding out of town, firing into the air—like Charles

Colcord's cowboys. Flatt ran toward Dean, declaring him to be under arrest. Dean snapped a shot at Flatt, then spurred away. The two lawmen pursued on foot, emptying their pistols as they ran, but Dean galloped to safety.

The hard-drinking George Flatt soon was dismissed from the marshal's office. With Fannie Flatt expecting a baby, George entered into a saloon partnership with William Horseman, and worked as a range detective. Flatt also continued to drink heavily, often expressing bitterness against city officials.

William Horseman succeeded Flatt as a city marshal on April 12, 1880. His assistant marshal was Dan Jones, and James Johnson was appointed policeman—then was replaced by Frank Hunt. "Our city police are vigilant as hawks," praised the *Post*, "and we cannot enough praise them for their efficiency." In May Horseman and his officers twice subdued saloon brawls involving hard-drinking cavalrymen encamped south of Caldwell. The next month Marshal Horseman, Deputy Hunt, and John Meagher (brother of Mayor Mike Meagher) tracked down a pair of horse thieves hiding along Fall Creek, arresting the felons and recovering the stolen horses.[30]

Former marshal George Flatt was murdered in the same month. On Friday, June 18, 1880, Flatt spent the evening becoming increasingly inebriated and raucous, and he had trouble with Frank Hunt and others. An hour after midnight, C. L. Spear and Samuel H. Rogers persuaded Flatt to leave for home, although he insisted on first stopping by Louis Segerman's restaurant to eat.[31]

As they walked toward Segerman's, a rifle exploded from above and behind Flatt, slamming into the base of his skull and severing his spinal cord. Flatt dropped dead, but a fusillade of shots from across the street spattered around him and three more slugs ripped into his body. Doctors Noble and Macmillan examined the corpse. Flatt was buried in Caldwell's new cemetery, and four days later Fannie Flatt gave birth to a son.

The coroner's inquest indicated that Flatt was gunned down "by members of the police force, whose lives he had been threatening for some time." Marshal Horseman, Frank Hunt and James Johnson, Dan Jones, Mayor Mike Meagher, and two other suspects were arrested and taken to Wellington. Horseman, Hunt, Johnson, and Jones all were bound over for the next term of the district court. The city council relieved the police force of its duties, appointed a new slate of lawmen, then reinstated the policemen they had relieved. Marshal Horseman again was relieved in August 1880. Tried in April 1881, Horseman

---

their camp. "I saw a lady, all dressed up, coming toward camp, walking." As she approached Houston stood up to receive his guest. "Our eyes were all set on her, and every man holding his breath."

The men were "dumbfounded" when they realized the young lady was Willie. They crowded around her, shook her hand, and brought a tomato box for her chair. She explained that her father was "an old-time trail driver from Southern Texas" who took a job on a ranch near Caldwell. She grew up listening to his tales of the long drives, and when she was

(cont. next page)

won acquittal. The identity of Flatt's killer never was determined.[32]

Meanwhile, Deputy Frank Hunt found himself at the center of gunplay. Cowboy W. F. Smith, who recently had "hurrahed" Hunnewell, roared into Caldwell on Thursday, September 2, 1880. Smith "liquored up pretty freely," rode around town brandishing a forbidden six-gun, then visited the Red Light. Afterward, he remounted his horse and "commenced firing a salute." Policeman Hunt approached with a shotgun and ordered Smith to halt. The drunken cowboy leveled his revolver, but Hunt triggered the shotgun. One buckshot lodged in Smith's knee; the rest killed his horse. Smith was hauled to the police court, where he pled guilty to disorderly conduct, paid a fine, then was turned over to Dr. Noble. "A great deal of sympathy was expressed for the horse," submitted the *Post* before offering an editorial view. "We are very sorry that some of the cow-boys who come in here allow whisky to get the better of them.... We expect them to have all the fun they can get, but they must acknowledge that the citizens of our town have a right to insist upon a strict compliance with the city's laws."[33]

A month later, on Thursday evening, October 9, there was a disturbance at the Red Light. Deputy Hunt arrived on the scene and tangled with a sporting lady and her customer. Keeping an eye on the situation, Hunt took a turn on the dance floor while

> a teenager she read in the newspaper that herds would pass through Clayton. "Donning a suit of my brother's clothes and pair of his boots," she left home for New Mexico, where she was hired by Houston.
>
> That evening the trail boss took Willie into Hugo to catch a homebound train. Later he received correspondence from Willie, and a letter of gratitude from her father.
>
> From *Trail Drivers of Texas*, 75-77.

★★★

Georgie Flatt was born on June 23, 1880, only four days after the assassination of his father. Fannie Flatt later married a Caldwell man named Muntzing, but she lost little Georgie, who died on March 2, 1883. Georgie was buried at the City Cemetery. —Author photo

City Marshal James Johnson and Special Policeman Dan Jones entered the premises. Hunt sat down beside a window, but within moments a shot exploded from outside. "I'm killed!" shouted Hunt. "He did it out there."

Mortally wounded, Hunt fell writhing to the floor, while the other officers dashed outside. No one could be found in the darkness. Hunt was placed in the Leland Hotel and a brother from Missouri was summoned. Still in his twenties, Frank Hunt died on Monday and was taken to Missouri for burial. Young Steve Spears was arraigned for his murder, but soon released.[34]

The following year, Red Light proprietor George Wood was killed in Caldwell's most notorious establishment. In the spring of 1881 Wood opened a Red Light in Hunnewell. Fred Kuhlman, a one-time Caldwell saloonkeeper, managed Hunnewell's Red Light, but he was slain there in an altercation over one of his soiled doves in June 1881. Less than two months later, on Thursday night, August 18, Wood quarreled in Caldwell's Red Light with a young man named Charlie Davis, who wanted to liberate one of Maggie's girls. Davis angrily drew a Colt .45 and shot Wood. The heavy slug went in above Wood's navel and tore out his back. Wood seized the gun and grappled with Davis. The revolver went off again, harmlessly, then Davis broke away and ran into the night.[35]

Wood staggered toward the rear of the Red Light, but collapsed. Writhing in agony, he was placed on a cot. Maggie came to his side. Dr. Noble was summoned, but could do little. Wood died after half an hour. Although Davis quickly was captured, he escaped almost as quickly and disappeared from Caldwell. Maggie buried George beside Fred Kuhlman in the Caldwell Cemetery, and she placed a common stone to mark their graves.

Before the end of the year a wild street fight in Caldwell resulted in the death of one of the most widely respected of all cattle town lawmen. Mike Meagher was an Irish immigrant and Civil War veteran who pinned on the city marshal's badge of Wichita in 1871. He was not a short-termer, like Wild Bill Hickok in Hays City and Abilene, or like almost all of Caldwell's city marshals.

Meagher was the chief peace officer of raucous Wichita from 1871 through 1877, with the exception of 1874, a year in which, among other adventures, he worked as a deputy U.S. marshal. Reappointed city marshal of Wichita in 1875, Mike soon married; Jenny Meagher would bear him a son and a daughter. Mike's younger brother, John, served as one of his deputies before winning election as county sheriff. Another deputy, in 1875 and 1876, was Wyatt Earp. The deputies followed the example of Marshal Meagher who "by his consummate coolness and wonderful bravery, preserved the lives and property of our people." The editor of the *Wichita Eagle* flatly stated that "Mike Meagher did not know the meaning of fear."[36]

Marshal Meagher distinguished himself by making arrests, sometimes in the face of drawn guns, without violence and by frequently preventing bloodshed. But on New Year's Day, 1877, a drunken troublemaker named Sylvester Powell opened fire while the marshal was occupying an outhouse. Although wounded in the lower leg, Meagher barreled out of the flimsy structure and, after a scuffle and pursuit, shot Powell to death.[37]

With Wichita in decline, Meagher moved his family to Caldwell in 1880, the year the tracks arrived. He opened the Arcade Saloon on the west side of Main Street, midway between fifth and sixth. The noted peace officer briefly wore the marshal's badge, and in April 1880 Meagher became Caldwell's third mayor. Although he was out of office when trouble struck town late in 1881, Meagher did not hesitate to support City Marshal John Wilson.

Jim Talbot was a shady character from Texas whose real name was James Sherman. Arriving in Caldwell with a trail herd, by November 1881 he installed his wife and two children in a rented house on Chisholm Street just north of the Red Light.

Mike and John Meagher were in Caldwell together, after serving as law officers in Wichita. Mike was Caldwell's mayor in 1880, but he was killed the next year by Jim Talbot during a street battle. —Courtesy Kansas State Historical Society, Topeka

Talbot spent the next month on an extended spree, "gambling, drinking, bullying, and attempting to bulldoze every one," according to *Post* editor Tell Walton, who was threatened by the "outlaw." George Freeman regarded Talbot as a "desperado" who "loved to be feared." Talbot threatened the city lawman and former mayor Mike Meagher. Meagher, of course, had received countless drunken threats during his years as marshal of Wichita. Unintimidated by Talbot, Meagher must have longed for a chance to slap down the bully, as he had done to scores of rowdies in Wichita.[38]

Talbot and a crowd of fellow ruffians frequented the Red Light, and when carousing around Caldwell they brought along the sporting girls "and made disturbances by using loud, obscene language in the presence of the ladies," related a disapproving George Freeman. On Friday night, December 16, 1881, Talbot drank his way around town with Bob Bigtree, Tom Love, Jim Martin, Bob Munson, Dick Eddleman, and George Spears, the new manager of the Red Light. These roistering pals swaggered into the Opera House, where they loudly disturbed a performance of *Uncle Tom's Cabin*. An irritated Tell Walton told Talbot to "desist from his obscenity," triggering a murderous threat in response.

The sprees continued through the night, and at dawn on Saturday the revelers discharged their pistols. During the morning Talbot repeated his threat against the *Post* editor, while Tom Love fired his revolver in Moore's Saloon. Mike Meagher, with his trained lawman's ear for trouble in town, went to John Wilson's house and awakened the marshal. Wilson and Meagher went to Moore's Saloon and arrested Love. Love was marched past three or four of his friends, each armed with revolvers and rifles. But as Wilson and Meagher neared Judge Kelly's police court with the prisoner, James Talbot and his confederates hurried to intercept them. There was a confrontation at the intersection of Main and Fifth, where a barrage of drunken threats was directed primarily at Meagher. Characteristically unarmed, Meagher backed up the outside stairs to the second floor of the Opera House, his retreat covered by a gun-wielding Marshal Wilson.

The situation cooled off for a few hours until shortly after mid-day, when Marshal Wilson arrested Jim Martin for carrying a gun. Judge Kelly fined Martin, who had no money on him. Six-foot-four Deputy Marshal Bill Fossett accompanied the prisoner as he went to obtain funds, but once again Talbot and his pals intervened. As a crowd gathered, Talbot urged Martin not to pay the fine. Someone handed Talbot a revolver and he opened fire, warning nearby children, "Hide out, little ones."

A flurry of pistol shots scattered the crowd, although Mike Meagher and other citizens armed themselves to support their law officers. Talbot led his men downhill to his house, just over a block away, where their rifles were stored. These heavily armed men then emerged and moved back toward Main Street, and gunfire erupted in downtown Caldwell.

"The bullets flew thick and fast," remembered George Freeman. "Those who were unfortunate enough to be in the city shopping hurried themselves to a place of safety, some taking refuge behind dry goods boxes, while others in their fright, rushed hither and thither looking for a better place to hide and escape the stray bullets, which were crashing through the glass front windows of the stores and tearing through doors and windows of the dwelling houses, damaging pictures, breaking mirrors, and defacing the walls of the buildings." Indeed, more than a decade later Sam Ridings opened an office in the old Opera House, noting that "there remained several large places where the bricks were shot out on the corner at the east or rear end of the building" — where Mike Meagher had stood while exchanging shots with Jim Talbot.[39]

Talbot had moved south on Chisholm Street, taking cover behind a shed. Looking northwest he spotted Meagher at the rear corner of the Opera House building. Talbot fired a rifle shot which chunked the masonry near Meagher's head. The two adversaries exchanged rile fire for a few moments, then Meagher decided to flank Talbot. Moving to the front of the building, he raced south down Main Street, then slipped through an alley to the east. But while Meagher was on the move, Talbot changed positions, shifting north to Fifth Street near the rear of the Opera House.

When Meagher emerged from the alley into the open, Talbot triggered a Winchester round. The slug perforated Meagher's right arm, tearing through both lungs and out the other side. Meagher dropped his rifle and six-gun, and gasped, "I am hit, and hit hard."

Marshal Wilson helped him to sit down on a box, then returned to the fight. Ed Rathbun dashed to Meagher's side and blurted, "Good God, Mike, are you hit?"

"Yes," Mike managed to reply. "Tell my wife I have got it at last." Carried to a barber shop, Meagher died within half an hour. He was thirty-eight.

When Meagher fell, Jim Talbot led a flight out of town.

Merchant W. N. Hubbell, who had succeeded Mike Meagher as mayor for several months, was one of several citizens who joined Marshal Wilson and Deputy Fossett in raining fire upon Talbot and his retreating confederates. According to Sam Ridings, who was a teenager at the time of the shootout, Hubbell hurried out the back of his store at the southeast corner of Main and Sixth. Armed with a Winchester, he took up a position in the blacksmith shop of Lengthy Jones, located at the southwest corner of Sixth and Chisholm. Hubbell began firing at the horses tied near the Red Light.

George Spears was saddling one of these horses when he was fatally wounded by Hubbell or another citizen. The Talbot faction hurried under fire to Kalbfleisch's Livery Stable, located on Chisholm Street a block north of the Red Light. Horses and saddles were commandeered, and Talbot led Bob Bigtree, Jim Martin, Bob Munson, and Doug Hill in an escape to the east. Talbot's horse was shot, but he clambered up behind Hill. The fugitives rode across the railroad tracks, then cleared town and headed southeast toward the border. When Dick Eddleman and Tom Love entered the livery stable, they were met with defiance, then placed under arrest.

Officers organized a pursuit posse, and after a twelve-mile chase Talbot and the others were found at an old stone dugout in Indian Territory. Cattleman W. E. Campbell, who joined the chase after the fugitives stole mounts from his horse ranch east of town, was wounded in the wrist. But the citizens imposed a siege without suffering further casualties. Reinforcements arrived, including a posse from Wellington led by Sheriff J. M. Thralls. During the night, however, the fugitives slipped away into the darkness. During their subsequent flight they entered the line camp of Charles Colcord. "They told me they had been in a shooting scrape up at Caldwell," recalled Colcord, who noted that they had taken punishment in the scrape: "Jim Martin with his right thumb shot off, Doug Hill shot through the right leg and Bob Bigtree wounded in the hip."[40]

Sheriff Thralls had been notified by telegraph of the battle in Caldwell's streets, and the same story was wired on to Wichita. In an evening edition that day, December 17, the *Wichita Times* announced to its readers: "As we go to press, hell is in session in Caldwell."

Mike Meagher was taken to Wichita for burial. Caldwell Mayor Cass Burrus offered a reward of $500 for the fugitives, Sheriff Thralls added $200, the wounded W. E. Campbell added another $200, and J. M. Steele of Wichita posted an additional

$200—"dead or alive."[41] Dick Eddelman and Tom Love were jailed in Wellington. In January Love was acquitted at the preliminary examination. Four days later Eddleman escaped jail and stole a horse, but was chased down by Sheriff Thralls and a posse. Doug Hill, placed on trial in 1887, pled guilty to manslaughter and was sentenced to six months in the county jail. Talbot finally was located in California. Tried in Kansas in 1895, he was found not guilty, but the next year he was assassinated in California. Some suspected his wife's lover, but another rumor held that John Meagher avenged his brother's killer.[42]

In the meantime, hell remained in session in Caldwell. George Brown was a bachelor in his late twenties. His sister, Fannie, kept house for him on east Fifth. Previously offered the position of city marshal, he finally accepted by early 1882. Marshal Brown was conscientious in his duties, collecting regular fine money from drunks, gamblers, and prostitutes.[43]

City Marshal George Brown was shot to death in the Red Light in 1882.
—Author photo

Marshal Brown experienced no serious trouble until Thursday morning, June 22, 1882, with Caldwell in the midst of its third shipping season. Herds were encamped for miles south of town, the streets teemed with cowboys and cattle buyers, and the stores and saloons were thronged with customers. Marshal Brown was on the street collecting signatures to two petitions regarding board elections. He responded promptly when informed that an armed man had entered the Red Light. Accompanied by Constable Willis Metcalf, Brown marched upstairs to the second-floor bagnio of Caldwell's most notorious establishment. At the top of the stairs stood three men, one armed with a revolver. Brown grasped his arm and told him to surrender his gun.[44]

"Let go of me," snarled the armed man, as Brown pinned him against the wall.

Metcalf's throat was seized by the second man, and the third produced a six-gun and leveled it against the constable's head. Then another man emerged from a bedroom and shouted at Brown, "Turn him loose!"

Brown shifted his attention, and at that moment his adversary twisted the gun and shot the marshal in the head. Brown was killed instantly. The culprit and his friends sprinted outside and were last seen headed for Indian Territory. Fannie Brown was convulsed with grief when informed of her brother's death. When Brown was buried, every business house in town closed.

Two of the perpetrators were identified as brothers Steve and Jess Green, cowboys who had been in Caldwell the past three summers. The Governor of Kansas offered a reward of $500 apiece for the arrest and conviction of the Green brothers, who had escaped from Texas after shooting a peace officer. In October 1882 the fugitives were mortally wounded in a hail of bullets from a Texas posse.[45]

In Caldwell Fannie Brown was consoled by "kind and loving friends." Within a week after her brother's death, Fannie married Caldwell merchant Samuel Swayer, and in the years to come the couple would prosper in the Border Queen.[46] But if Fannie found solace and happiness in the wake of the killing, Caldwell had suffered another black mark against its tattered reputation. The city marshal had been slain in the most notorious dive on the cattle frontier. In the midst of its third season as the railhead of the Chisholm Trail, Caldwell keenly needed the taming hands of stalwart peace officers.

CHAPTER SEVEN

The Town Tamers

*"Marshal Carr and Henry Brown, the assistant,
made a different town of Caldwell."*
—G. D. Freeman

Within less than two years, in addition to other gunfight fatalities, four of the Border Queen's chief representatives of law and order were gunned down in the center of town. Former city marshal George Flatt was the victim of midnight assassins on Caldwell's Main Street in July 1880. Fewer than three months later Assistant Marshal Frank Hunt was murdered in the Red Light. In December 1881 former mayor Mike Meagher was killed during the wild street fight with Jim Talbot's "gang." Six months later City Marshal George Brown was slain by two troublemaking Texans in the Red Light.

"Life was becoming perilous to live; the officer and citizen were in suspense and anxiety," observed former Constable G. D. Freeman. "Who would be the next to die at the hands of an assassin?" The county seat newspaper, Wellington's *Sumner County Press*, criticized the "flagrant violations of the laws of the state" which were rampant in Caldwell, and Caldwellites must have recognized the bad light cast upon their growing town by the repeated assassinations of city officials.[1]

Long pressured by Caldwell citizens offended by the indecency and notoriety of the Red Light, Mag Wood put her establishment up for sale. A local committee quickly raised $400, and Mag left Caldwell for Wichita. The two-story frame building was sold for use as a warehouse and moved from its corner lots on Chisholm Street, and the proceeds were split up among the committee members. (The *Post* wondered in print what men from Wellington "who visit Caldwell for recreation will do with themselves.") With the infamous Red Light shut down, Caldwell's leading citizens focused on upgrading law enforcement.[2]

When Marshal Brown was killed on June 22, 1882, Caldwell was busily engaged in its third shipping season. Herds were encamped for miles south of town, the streets teemed with cowboys and cattle buyers, the stores and saloons were thronged with customers—and the death of yet one more law officer had rendered the police force vacant.

Like any important cattle town Caldwell needed efficient policing. Eastern cattle buyers might shun a town in which violence and outlawry were rampant, hardly desiring to become a victim of thievery or homicide. Railhead city councilmen readily employed gunmen—Marshal Wild Bill Hickok of Abilene, for example—to curb rollicking cowboys, hoping to achieve an atmosphere sufficiently menacing to discourage shootouts, but sporting enough to attract spendthrift cowboys of robust appetites.

Such efforts were far more successful than Western legend suggests, and under the authority of gunslinging law officers, rip-roaring cattle towns hosted hard-drinking cowboys and sported saloons, dance halls and red-light districts—but enjoyed a modest homicide rate which would be the envy of modern American cities.[3] The trick seemed to center around the employment of non-puritanical lawmen who would tolerate roistering, gambling and whoring, but who were sufficiently feared as gunmen to stifle petty crooks and outbursts of shooting, and who were good enough not to be killed when gunplay erupted.

Within a week and a half of the death of George Brown the vacated marshal's office was filled and reinforced by a deputy. On Monday night, July 3, 1882, Mayor A. M. Colson and the Caldwell City Council appointed B. P. "Bat" Carr as City Marshal and "Henry Brown, formerly marshal of Tascosa, Texas, as Assistant City Marshal." Carr had been recommended to Mayor Colson and the city council "as a good man" for the marshal's office, and they considered him "a necessary evil to straighten out the lower class of humanity which paraded the streets of Caldwell."[4]

Henry Brown also would prove to be a necessary evil. Brown had not served as marshal of Tascosa, although he had worn a deputy's badge in the "Cowboy Capital of the Panhandle." If Brown exaggerated his role in Tascosa, he avoided all mention of other elements of his background. The *Post* apparently heard one accurate rumor about Brown: "We have a new Assistant Marshal on the police force now—Mr. Henry Brown—and it is said that he is one of the quickest men on the trigger in the Southwest."[5]

The *Post* also exhorted the citizenry to "back the officers." A number of citizens offered tangible support after the new lawmen had been on the job a little over a week. On Wednesday

---

Border Queen Police Dockets: 1879-1885

Caldwell historian Rod Cook compiled a comprehensive study of the police dockets from 1879 through 1885. James D. Kelly was the police judge during most of these years, although T.H.B. "Bent" Ross served a term abbreviated by his untimely death.

Judge Kelly was elected soon after Caldwell's incorporation in 1879, and a short time later George Flatt was appointed city marshal. The first recorded arrest was made by Marshal Flatt on September 6, and Judge Kelly fined J. G. Wendels

(cont. next page)

three dollars for "speeding" his horse.

During the six years there was a total of 240 "drunk," 113 "fighting," 146 disturbing the peace or disorderly conduct or profanity, 56 assaults, 55 carrying "a sixshooter" or "concealed weapon," and 17 "did shoot off a sixshooter."

"Indecent exposure" caused one arrest. Another offender was "Confined for swearing in court." Frank Pratt was arrested for riding his horse on the sidewalk. "Prisoner was committed to the new city prison but escaped through the bars."

★★★

morning, July 12, Main Street businessmen subscribed $75, and Colonel Jennison bought a brace of six-guns and presented them to Marshal Carr.

"Mr. Carr," stated Jennison, "in behalf of the citizens and business men of this city, I present you with these weapons, not that we would encourage the use of them, but that you may better protect the rights of property and life, and maintain the dignity and honor of the city and your office as Marshal. It is not for the intrinsic value of the present we offer you, but it is our appreciation of your services as an officer. I request that you accept these pistols from the citizens of this city as a light token of their confidence in your ability to protect the same from being used for any purpose other than the defense of the city and maintaining the peace and quiet in the same."[6]

Henry Brown also wore a two-gun rig while in Caldwell. For a time, however, shooting was not necessary. Carr and Brown, "both of whom always seem to be in the way when any fun is going on," were active and diligent in enforcing city statutes. The new marshal was from near Colorado City, Texas, where he had been an early settler and became known as "Captain Battie." Carr was a curious combination of "the polished gentleman and the daring frontiersman." He had a pleasant, courtly personality and was a favorite of children and ladies, often escorting them across Main Street. Carr usually was nattily dressed in a navy blue uniform with brass buttons and a gilt trim. Pinned to his breast was a silver star inscribed "Bat Carr, Marshal," and he sported a walking cane and a jeweled ring. But beneath his refined exterior was a primitive need "to be feared by men," and he strove to have "his name looked upon with terror and dismay by the cowboy and desperado." Carr was a rugged, two-fisted brawler who took seriously his commission to tame Caldwell.[7]

During the second week of his tenure he encountered an African-American who was wearing a gun in violation of a city ordinance, and the man was ordered to hand over the weapon. The lawbreaker tried to outdraw Carr, but the marshal palmed a .45, disarmed the man, and marched him to city court where he was fined $12.50. A week or so later Carr tangled with a high roller who was trying to bilk a cowboy. When the gambler back-talked Carr, the marshal hurled his stocky five-foot-eight, 180-pound frame at the gambler, knocking him off his feet.[8]

Carr's readiness with his fists apparently intimidated Caldwell rowdies to the extent that gunplay was unnecessary. By the second month of the new police regime, a local newspaper happily observed that "the Winchester and self-cocker have given place to nature's arms, good 'bunches of five,' and perhaps a stick." Carr and Brown had established "a new order of things that makes the six shooter in this community of no more account than a toy pistol."[9]

These observations were made in a story describing two disturbances in August 1882, either of which might once have erupted into a shooting during a previous year. One disagreement was a Saturday night squabble over money, and was settled with fists instead of bullets. The other problem arose out of a prayer meeting conducted on Wednesday night, August 23.

In the congregation was a local ruffian who had never received religious instructions. He heard for the first time that Jews had killed Jesus more than eighteen hundred years earlier, and throughout the night he brooded over the murder of the Savior, deciding to exact vengeance in direct Western style. Early the next morning he encountered a Jewish merchant on Main Street and lit into him in a "mad endeavor to avenge the wrongs of eighteen centuries standing."

Bat Carr and Henry Brown rushed to break up the fracas, and promptly hauled the vengeful convert to the city court of Judge James D. Kelly. After hearing the complaint, Judge Kelly glared at the defendant and asked, "What have you to do with Christ anyhow?" A fine of five dollars was levied, and hopefully

A bird's eye view of the author's scale model of Caldwell looking at Main Street from the east. The Southwestern Hotel is at upper right, and the Leland is at extreme left. The model is housed in the Main Street museum of the Caldwell Historical Society. —Author photo

the offender channeled his religious impulses into more constructive activities.[10]

On Monday, September 4, a cowboy named William St. John rode through town, whooping it up and practicing his roping skills on the sheep in Dr. W.A. Noble's yard. But his celebration ended abruptly when Carr rode alongside, seized the drover's six-gun and hauled him off to Judge Kelly's court.[11]

After just two months in office, "Marshal Carr and Henry Brown ... made a different town of Caldwell." When a man began to cause trouble, the officers were ever-present to back him down "at the muzzle of a cocked six shooter," and within a few weeks "quietness reigned supreme in the city of Caldwell."[12] Brown was recognized as a significant member of the law enforcement team; indeed, he had become so widely respected as a lawman that the Cherokee Strip Live Stock Association hired him as a strongbox guard.

In the fall of 1882 the Association needed to ship a considerable sum of money—probably $50,000—to Cherokee representatives in the Strip to complete lease arrangements. A buckboard driver was employed, and Brown's services were secured to discourage any would-be highwaymen. The cash was delivered without incident, but after Brown met an outlaw's end, the buckboard driver claimed to cowboy Joe Wiedeman that he had become "suspicious" of the quiet gunfighter and "would not make another trip with Henry for all the Strip lease money." The fact remains that Brown ignored the relatively easy chance to steal the money. At this point Henry Brown was respected as a pillar of the law, and his neat dress and gentlemanly manner won him friends throughout town. But he still was reserved and "seldom smiled;" consequently women and children did not warm to him as they did to Carr. Carr dominated newspaper accounts and public attention. At this time in his life, Brown seemed to want his own place of prominence, and he became restless in a Caldwell dominated by his superior, Carr.[13]

In mid-September Brown temporarily resigned his position and joined a posse headed into Indian Territory to track down the killers of Mike Meagher. In mid-September 1882, Sheriff Thralls received information "from a reliable source" that "The Talbot Gang" was herding rustled horses and cattle in southwestern Oklahoma. Henry Brown eagerly enlisted in the Thralls posse; $1,100 in rewards had been offered "for the outlaws, dead or alive."[14]

Thralls led his men out of Caldwell on Tuesday, September 19, and the party rode southwest, through the Cherokee Strip, to

Cantonment on the Cheyenne-Arapahoe Agency, a journey of nearly eighty miles crosscountry. For more than two weeks the posse scoured the region, fruitlessly following a succession of leads before deciding to head home. Sheriff Thralls, Brown and the others rode into Caldwell on Thursday, October 5, having been on the trail for seventeen days. Brown wasted no time in telling his story to a local reporter, then he was reappointed to his position as assistant city marshal.[15]

Meanwhile, Carr had begun to arrest card sharks, having them fined for carrying derringers. Then he ran several professional gamblers into Judge Kelly's court, seeing to it that fines were levied in an attempt to curb "low down thieving games, such as nine dice, three card monte, etc." The Caldwell establishment was so pleased that another presentation was made to Carr. Several businessmen and cattlemen contributed more than $75, and "the handsomest badge we ever saw" was ordered from a local jeweler. A solid gold shield was suspended by two gold chains from a gold plate, with black enamel lettering on the shield which read: "Batt Carr, City Marshal, Caldwell, Kan.," and an inscription on the backside of the shield proclaimed: "Presented by the Citizens of Caldwell."[16]

Carr was so pleased that he made plans to return to Texas, show off his badge and guns, sell his property in Colorado City and reinvest his capital in Caldwell. Carr left for West Texas on

Five Beans in a Wheel

Bat Carr, Henry Brown, and George Flatt were among the men who wore two guns on the streets of Caldwell. The two-gun practice became common before the Civil War because it took a dangerously long time to reload cap-and-ball revolvers, and during a hot fight a shootist needed a backup gun.

After the war metallic cartridges rendered cap-and-ball pistols obsolete, and the most popular handgun became the Colt .45 single-action six-shooter. But the Colt single-action revolver had no safety, causing many men to leave

(cont. next page)

Caldwell was served by several livery stables. Note the windmill behind the barn.
— Courtesy Caldwell Historical Society

the hammer resting on an empty cylinder to avoid an accidental discharge. This practice, known as carrying "five beans in the wheel," meant that in a shootout a man could fire only five loads—unless he carried a second pistol.

★★★

October 16, 1882. He offered six Colorado City houses for sale, closed to his affairs, and was back in Caldwell on November 2, 1882.[17]

During Marshal Carr's two-and-a-half-week absence, Henry Brown was appointed acting city marshal. A newspaper remarked that in the past Brown had demonstrated "ample evidence" of his law enforcement abilities, and that he was "all business, yet withal quiet and unobtrusive." The rowdy cattle-buying season was waning and Brown's lethal talents were not immediately tested, but one significant event took place: Brown appointed, as his assistant marshal, a tall, sinister Texan known as Ben Wheeler. Carr resumed the marshal's post when he returned, Brown again became assistant marshal, and Wheeler temporarily left the police force. But in the future Brown and Wheeler would prove to be a formidable team of gunmen.[18]

When Carr returned to town he presented to Mayor Colson "a splendid gold-headed cane," and renewed his campaign against gamblers and troublemakers. Within days he personally escorted Robert Gillman, a hard-drinking gambler and "odorous citizen," to the depot and put him aboard a train headed for Dodge City. Soon afterwards he arrested, or ran out of town, a dozen members of "the slick-fingered gentry." Two weeks later he jailed seven more gamblers within a single evening, and several days after that, he apprehended an African-American who had stolen a pair of shoes from a cobbler. Henry Brown competently backed Carr, especially in the curtailment of gambling, and thereby increased his skills as a peace officer while gaining the respect of the community.[19]

In mid-December Bat Carr again journeyed to Texas. He may have had further business to conclude, and it was rumored that he intended to return to Caldwell with a bride. But Caldwell oldtimers G. D. Freeman and Joe Wiedeman suggested a different motive—one that may have involved Henry Brown. Freeman hinted that there were deep "peculiarities" in Cart's "enigmatic" [sic] personality, and he said that the marshal "was removed from office" on December 2, 1882.[20]

Wiedman flatly stated that an ambitious Henry Brown had approached Carr and insisted that Carr resign, so Brown could take his place. Carr declined this request, but later in the day Brown supposedly encountered the marshal in the street and jerked the fancy gold badge from his vest.[21] Although he was an effective fist-fighter, Carr never had fired his guns in anger while in Caldwell, and Brown was sufficiently menacing to run the Texan out of town without gunplay.

There was no mention of such an incident in the Caldwell newspapers. Brown may have tried to pressure Carr in private, but if he had confronted the marshal on a public thoroughfare and ripped his badge off, surely the event would have been reported.

Whatever the reason, Bat Carr left for Texas during the second week of December and he never returned to Caldwell. On Thursday night, December 21, 1882, the city council met and elected Henry Brown to the office of city marshal. Brown had served on the police force for twenty-two weeks, and would reign as marshal for more than sixteen months—sixteen busy and violent months in the life of Caldwell.

CHAPTER EIGHT

Caldwell's Outlaw Marshal

*"He begged me not to give him away as he intended
to reform and lead an honorable life."*
—Charlie Siringo

The pseudoscience of phrenology made an appearance in Caldwell early in 1884. German anatomist Franz Joseph Gall (1758-1828) claimed that each of the mind's functions had its specific location in the brain, and a person's mental and moral characteristics could be determined by examining the shape of the head. Gall insisted that he could feel the "organ" of *tune* in musicians, or the organ of *number* in the mathematically gifted, or the organ of *reverence* in the devoutly religious. According to Gall, a certain bump indicated a criminal, while another bump could identify a poet. Traveling phrenologists provided entertainment to Europeans and Americans during the nineteenth century.

A blind phrenologist scheduled Caldwell on his 1884 tour. Posted circulars attracted an eager crowd to the Leland Hotel. The elderly professor stood in the center of the Leland's largest parlor, holding the back of an empty chair while he explained phrenology. "He was a fine looking old man," observed one spectator, "regardless of the fact that both eyes were out."[1]

When the phrenologist asked for someone to come forward to have his head examined, the crowd loudly called for the popular and respected city marshal, Henry Brown. "Brown hesitated quite awhile" before taking his place in the empty chair. "But it was soon made plain by the color of his face that he regretted going," as the phrenologist announced "some very uncomplimentary remarks" about Caldwell's chief law officer. "I knew that the phrenologist was telling the truth," reminisced Caldwell merchant and former cowboy Charlie Siringo, "because I had known Henry Brown when he was a member of the notorious 'Billy the Kid's' outlaw gang."[2]

After the phrenologist released Brown, he also had unkind remarks for his next subject, hulking Ted Baufman. Then the audience called for Siringo's sixteen-year-old bride Mamie. "Here is a good-natured little somebody who cannot tell a lie or do wrong," said the phrenologist. When the audience next called for Siringo, the professor detected "a large stubborn lump" and announced to immediate laughter, "ladies and gentlemen, here is a mule's head."[3]

Although the crowd was entertained by an evening of phrenology, Marshal Brown was visibly uncomfortable. As the only person in the Leland parlor who knew Henry Brown's past, Siringo may have been overly alert to his reactions to the phrenologist. But without question Caldwell's city marshal did not want his past known around town.

Henry Newton Brown was born in 1857 near Rolla, Missouri. Following the death of both parents when he was a little boy, Henry and his older sister Ellen were shuttled between the homes of various relatives. By 1875, like many other adventurous teenagers of this period, Henry headed West to become a cowboy. In 1876 Brown pumped three slugs into a fellow cowboy in a cattle camp in the Texas Panhandle. Charles Siringo heard about Brown's first killing in 1878 when he worked for the LX Ranch in the Panhandle.[4]

After killing a man in Texas, Brown gravitated to turbulent Lincoln County, New Mexico. Brown hired his guns to both factions in the growing conflict in Lincoln County. He was present when John Tunstall was murdered and was an all-out participant in the ensuing Lincoln County War. Brown was one of three men indicted for murdering Sheriff William Brady and Deputy Sheriff George Hindman. He was part of the Regulator posse when Frank Baker, William Morton, and William McCloskey were killed, and he participated in the Blazer's Mill shootout with Buckshot Roberts. Brown fought in the five-day Battle of Lincoln, and after a narrow escape he leagued with Billy the Kid and other fugitives who formed a band of stock thieves.[5]

In the fall of 1878 the Kid, Brown, Tom O'Folliard, and two other rustlers moved a herd of stolen horses from New Mexico to the Tascosa area of the Texas Panhandle, where Charles Siringo encountered the gang. By October the Kid and O'Folliard were ready to return to New Mexico, even though they were wanted by the law there. The others wisely decided to stay away from Lincoln County, and Brown elected to remain in Tascosa. By now an expert gunman, Brown was appointed a deputy sheriff of Oldham County, but soon he was fired because he "was always wanting to fight." He hired on as a cowboy for cattleman George Littlefield, but in 1881 he was discharged "because he was always on the war path." Brown then was employed on a ranch in the Cherokee Strip by foreman Barney O'Connor—who would reappear dramatically in his life three years later.⁶

When Brown heard about the vacancies on Caldwell's police force he decided to give law enforcement another try. He was working out of a Cherokee Strip cattle camp with Charles Colcord, whose father, William Colcord, along with another prominent rancher, Major Andrew Drumm, gave Brown a recommendation because of his "great nerve and fearlessness."⁷ While applying at Caldwell Brown apparently exaggerated his office in Tascosa, from deputy sheriff to city marshal. Although Brown carefully avoided details of his background as a gunman, his long history of shootouts made him confident of handling any trouble he might encounter in Caldwell.

After pinning on a badge in Caldwell Brown grasped at the opportunity to redeem himself and escape his outlaw past. By the time that Charles Siringo arrived in Caldwell, Marshal Brown had established himself as a formidable lawman, and the officer approached his old acquaintance from the Texas Panhandle. "He begged me not to give him away as he intended to reform and lead an honorable life,"⁸ related Siringo. In Caldwell Brown dressed neatly, and he did not drink, smoke, or gamble.

"Mr. B. is a good one," declared a newspaper when announcing his appointment "and will have the moral as well as physical support of our citizens running the city as it should be."⁸ The twenty-five-year-old Brown received the backing of the community, which had become strongly committed to quality law enforcement during the past several months. As recently as July 1881, the city council had cut wages for the marshal from $60 to $50 per month, payable only in city scrip, which normally had to be redeemed at

Marshal Henry Brown killed two troublemakers during 1883. Brown excelled as a frontier peace officer, but he had a fatal flaw.
—Courtesy Kansas State Historical Society, Topeka

a discount. But when Carr and Brown were hired, the city had supported them in every way, including the payment of their salaries in cash. City Marshal Brown was paid the rather handsome salary of $100 per month. Brown's deputy was paid $75 monthly, a fifty percent increase over the 1881 marshal's salary.[9]

Marshal Brown's deputy and right-hand man was Ben Wheeler. G. D. Freeman's impression of Wheeler was that he leaned to the "desperado style," and "although he was gentlemanly in deportment and dress, he bore the rougher marks of humanity, by expression and carriage of form."[10] Freeman's observations proved perceptive.

"Ben F. Wheeler" was an alias used by an extremely tall, somewhat sinister Texan who was born Ben Robertson in 1854 in Rockdale, some sixty miles northeast of Austin. The Robertson family was respectable and law-abiding, and one of Ben's brothers eventually became general land agent for the state government. But Ben's nature revealed itself in 1878, when he seriously wounded an adversary in a shooting scrape, then fled the country, abandoning his wife and children. Robertson headquartered for two or three years in the vicinity of Cheyenne. Finally he trailed a cattle herd several hundred miles southeastward to the small Nebraska town of Indianola. There he met a young lady named Alice Wheeler and stayed to woo the frontier belle, neglecting to mention to her his wife and children in Rockdale. His courtship was successful, and "Ben F. Burton" and Alice M. Wheeler were married in the Indianola home of her parents, in November 1881. Alice soon became pregnant, and in the spring of 1882 Ben traveled from Indianola to Caldwell, perhaps on cattle business.[11]

Once he arrived in the bustling railhead he stayed, forgetting his expectant wife and assuming a new alias—"Ben Wheeler."[12] It was during this period that he served as a temporary deputy to Acting Marshal

Ben Wheeler, Henry Brown's deputy and accomplice.
—Courtesy Kansas State Historical Society, Topeka

Henry Brown and it was also during this brief time that Henry Brown recognized in Wheeler a kindred spirit. Brown and Wheeler both had quiet and restrained personal habits, both had desperate backgrounds which they wanted to keep hidden, and both could handle a gun. Wheeler was Marshal Brown's first choice as deputy. Moreover, it was observed during his initial tenure on the police force that "Mr. Wheeler has the sand, so the boys say, to stay with the wild and wooly class as long as they are on the war path."[13] When Henry Brown was given a permanent appointment as city marshal, Ben Wheeler was named assistant marshal.

A week later Marshal Brown received an expensive and impressive gift. Just as they had done with Bat Carr, local Caldwell leaders raised a subscription to impress upon their new police chief how strongly they supported him and the order he represented. On Monday, New Year's Day, 1883, an unsuspecting Brown was lured into the York-Parker-Draper Mercantile store, where several friends already had gathered. Frank Jones stepped forward, made a speech appropriate to the occasion, and the astonished Brown was presented with a magnificent .44-40 Winchester. The stock had been shaped from polished black walnut and sported a pistol grip, and the butt end was covered with intricately engraved gold plate. The barrel was octagonal, and on the right side of the stock was a plate ornately inscribed: "Presented to City Marshall H. N. Brown for valuable

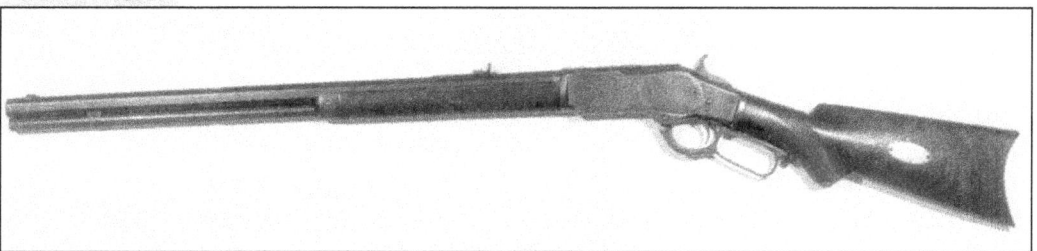

On January 1, 1883, grateful citizens of Caldwell presented Marshal Henry Brown this engraved .44-40 Winchester. Later in the year Brown used it to kill gambler Newt Boyce.

The inscription plate reads: "Presented to City Marshall H. N. Brown for valuable services rendered in behalf of the Citizens of CALDWELL KAS A. M. Colson Mayor Dec. 1882"

—Courtesy Kansas State Historical Society, Topeka

services rendered in behalf of the citizens of CALDWELL KAS. A. M. Colson, Mayor, Dec., 1882." The flabbergasted marshal stammered his appreciation, both for the gun and for the demonstration of confidence. The Winchester was a finer weapon than the six-guns which had been presented to Carr, and it was more useful than Carr's fancy badge.[14]

After Brown and Wheeler had been in charge of policing the town for a month, the marshal decided to take a vacation. Following an absence of nearly a decade, he wanted to visit Phelps County, Missouri, and his relatives, to show them his engraved Winchester and impress them with his respectable position. In mid-winter the cattle buyers were gone and Caldwell was quiet, and Ben Wheeler was obviously capable of policing the town during such a lull. In fact, the *Caldwell Commercial* observed that "Ben is equal to the occasion, being of that class of men who have very little to say but are very prompt when action is necessary." Brown had little trouble in obtaining a month's leave of absence, and he boarded a train at the Caldwell depot on Wednesday, January 31, bound for Missouri. In Rolla he visited his sister, was interviewed by the editor of the *Weekly Herald*, and showed off his rifle.[15]

Marshal Brown's homecoming to Caldwell was welcomed. The week after Brown moved back into his room at the Southwestern, the *Caldwell Commercial* stated: "Since his return, the boys are not quite so numerous on the street at night." Apparently Ben Wheeler had not quite lived up to expectations, but the constant patrol of the steely-eyed Brown quickly settled the local toughs.[16]

Things stayed so quiet for a time that spring promised to be very pleasant. The local schoolmaster, Professor Sweet, organized a local outing to nearby Polecat Creek in the third Sunday in March. A somewhat shy participant in community socials, Marshal Brown went along as "guard" of the group. The picnic was spread beneath the shade of cottonwoods and elm trees which lined the creek banks, and the outing was marked by laughter and horseplay.[17]

The following Thursday the peace was shattered by a shootout. The participants were not rollicking cowboys, but a pair of local citizens. The popular physician, Dr. W. A. Noble, was drinking at Chesney's Saloon when he took offense at a statement made by lunch counter attendant Charles Everhart. Dr. Noble angrily produced a double-action revolver and opened fire. The first shot was wild, but the second slug struck Everhart in the chest. Everhart spun around, just as a third bullet slammed into him. The gunfire ended abruptly when Ben Wheeler burst onto the scene and snatched the pistol from Noble's hand. While other physicians were being summoned, Wheeler marched Dr. Noble to the jail where he posted a $10,000 bond. Everhart recovered and left town, and the case was permitted to lapse.[18]

The *Commercial* editorialized over this incident, concerning itself with Caldwell's image:

> ... can adequate reasons be given why a prominent citizen... in this or any other well organized community in Kansas should habitually carry ... dangerous weapons of any kind? ...
>
> There should be no mawkish sentimentality regarding any man, however high his standing, or whatever his wealth or social position may be, who, habituated to going armed in a civilized community, under a fit of alcoholic insanity makes use of a weapon. The law should be as strictly enforced in this case as in the case of any cowboy who comes off the range ...
>
> Treat all alike, prince or peasant, rich or poor, citizen or stranger, and make no rule in one case that will not be applicable to all other cases under like circumstances.[19]

Early each April the Caldwell city elections were held, and the newly elected city council of 1883 wasted no time in reappointing Brown and Wheeler for the next term.[20]

A few days later the local officers were called to assist in chasing horse thieves. Cash Hollister, a fearless Caldwellite who had been arrested several times for fighting—once while serving as mayor in 1879—had obtained an appointment as a deputy U.S. marshal.[21] Almost immediately he arrested a horse thief, and not long afterward he was approached by another victim of rustlers. On Sunday, April 8, J. H. Herron rode into Caldwell, sought out Hollister and asked his help in capturing a gang of horse thieves he had trailed all the way from Texas. Herron had lost a pair of horses and a pair of mules, and the band had stolen animals from other individuals as well.

Hollister saddled up and rode with Herron toward Hunnewell, twenty miles east of Caldwell. The rustlers were camped a few miles southeast of Hunnewell, but a little scouting revealed that there were too many of them to safely apprehend. They were led by a rogue named Ross, and backed by Ross' two sons. Three females were present—Ross' wife, daughter, and daughter-in-law—and the latter woman had a child. Another group which had accompanied the Rosses was camped nearby. Hollister apparently left Herron to keep an eye on the rustlers, then rode back to Caldwell to enlist aid.

He arrived back in town on Tuesday, and by eleven that night Henry Brown and Ben Wheeler were headed toward Hunnewell with Hollister. In Hunnewell the lawmen added City Marshal Jackson and Sumner County Deputy Wes Thralls, and in the dead of night the posse continued on toward the sleeping camp.

By daybreak the officers had surrounded the Ross camp, and when everyone was in position, the quiet of dawn was abruptly shattered by demands of surrender. The Ross party replied without hesitation, firing their Winchesters and drawing a hail of return fire. For half an hour there was a fierce exchange of shots, during which the older Ross boy was killed and his younger brother hit by two or three bullets. Gunfire from the camp stopped, and the posse moved in on the remaining rustlers. The wounded Ross brother proved talkative, indicating that the gang had headed north from Texas with about forty head of mules and horses, including a prized stallion for which a reward of $500 had been offered. He added that two members of the original gang had driven part of the stolen herd toward Wichita on the previous Sunday.

The dead rustler was left in Hunnewell, and part of the posse escorted the rest of the family to jail in Wellington. Anxious to return to their responsibilities, Brown and Wheeler apparently headed straight back to Caldwell, arriving in town at eleven A.M. on Wednesday, the morning of the shootout. They immediately gave the editor of the *Commercial* details of the fight, just in time for inclusion in the Thursday edition of the weekly.[22]

The next month Marshal Brown found himself in a shootout in Caldwell. Native Americans often came up from their reservations in Indian Territory to Caldwell. "I have seen our little town full of them," said Mrs. J. B. Rideout, "their red blankets flashing in every direction." In September 1880 thirty-eight wagons of Indians came into town to trade hides for supplies. The next December another trading foray brought Caldwell's boys "a new supply of bows and arrows." But Pawnees developed a reputation as beggars: in May 1882 the *Post* complained "that their begging expeditions are getting to be almost a nuisance."[23]

During the second weekend in May 1883, a Pawnee known as Spotted Horse arrived in Caldwell from Indian Territory on one of his periodic visits, during which he would pimp for one or more of his wives. He brought along one squaw, and parked his wagon on a vacant lot located between Main and Market Streets. From this makeshift camp he conducted business throughout the weekend, and on Monday morning he decided to cap off his trip with a little freeloading on Main Street.

Taking his woman in tow, Spotted Horse appeared in the Long Branch Restaurant at about 6:30 A.M. and asked the management to donate breakfast for the two. They were turned down, but, undaunted, Spotted Horse went to the Moreland House, where his begging was rewarded with a sack of bread and cold meat. The two then crossed Main Street, walked a block to Market Street and entered the house of E. H. Beals.

When the Pawnees appeared at their breakfast table, Beals' wife and daughter were shocked and frightened, and Beals sternly ordered the intruders out of his home. Spotted Horse shuffled outside, but then handed his sack of food to his squaw and barged back into the residence. He walked impudently to the table and placed a hand on the Beals' daughter. Beals jumped out of his chair, snarled a curse and demanded in sign language that the Indian leave. Spotted Horse drew his revolver, but Beals implored him to finish the trouble outside. The Pawnee put up his gun and walked into the yard, followed by Beals. When the Pawnee again drew his pistol, Beals armed himself with a shovel. A passerby named Grant Harris ran toward Spotted Horse, verbally assaulting him for attacking an old man. The Pawnee began to curse Beals in English, but Harris finally persuaded Spotted Horse to leave peacefully. Angry words about the incident spread quickly around town, and a messenger was sent to find Marshal Brown and register a complaint against Spotted Horse.

Spotted Horse, trailed by his woman, returned to the Long Branch and entered the back door of the kitchen. The Pawnees began eating their fill, and the only staff member present, Louis Heironymous, made no protest as the intruders ate. Appetites satisfied, Spotted Horse headed up Main Street while the squaw went back to their wagon. The first building north of the Long Branch was Morris' Grocery, and Spotted Horse strolled inside.

In the meantime, Henry Brown had begun searching for Spotted Horse. He found him in the grocery store, and asked that he attend a parlay with a citizen named Covington, who would serve as an interpreter. Brown seized Spotted Horse to move him along, but the Pawnee angrily refused to go and began to grope for his revolver.

Brown instantly drew a six-gun and ordered his adversary

118 *Border Queen Caldwell*

to stop. Spotted Horse continued to fumble in his blanket for a gun, and the marshal fired four rounds at the Pawnee. Despite the point-blank range the first three shots missed, as Brown apparently fired at least two warning shots. Black powder clouded the air with a thick white haze, and Spotted Horse twisted away as Brown hurried his fire. Finally the Indian located his gun and cleared the barrel from beneath his blanket, but at that instant Brown's fourth bullet ended the fight. The slug hit Spotted Horse in the forehead, sending him sprawling onto the floor.

The sound of gunfire attracted a crowd, and upon hearing the commotion, Spotted Horse's squaw hitched the horses to the

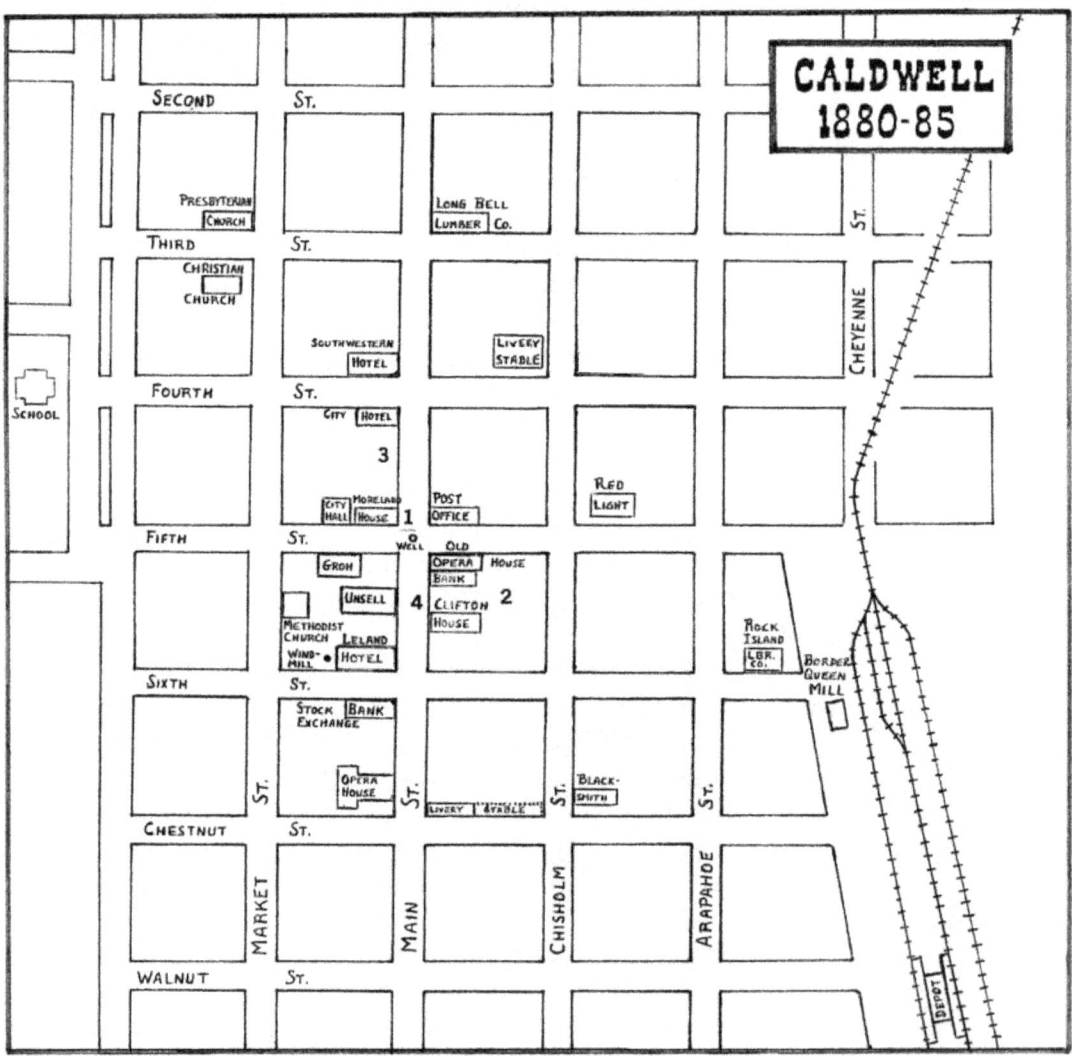

1. Where George Flatt shot Adams and Wood.
2. Where Mike Meagher was shot.
3. Where Henry Brown shot Spotted Horse.
4. Where Henry Brown shot Newt Boyce.

> **Resisting Arrest**
>
> At a farm in Chikaskia township, nine miles from Caldwell, young Chet Van Meter beat his wife and teenaged brother-in-law, fired at neighbors, and threatened to kill them. The next day, Wednesday, November 21, 1883, a complaint was filed in Caldwell, and Deputy U.S. Marshal Cash Hollister was directed by Justice of the Peace T.H.B. Ross to arrest Van Meter and "to get some one to go with him, and to go well armed."
>
> Hollister and Assistant City Marshal Ben Wheeler set out in a spring wagon for the farm of Van
>
> *(cont. next page)*

wagon and whipped them south toward the Territory. Spotted Horse was carried to a warehouse two doors north of the grocery store and doctors were summoned. The Pawnee appeared to be conscious, but remained silent. About two hours after being shot, Spotted Horse quietly died.

The coroner, a man named Stevenson from Wellington, viewed the remains and conducted an inquest that evening. The next morning, Tuesday, May 15, 1883, the coroner's jury declared "that the deceased came to his death by a gunshot wound at the hands of H. N. Brown, and that the shooting was done in the discharge of his duty as an officer of the law." The community vigorously endorsed this verdict, and respect for Brown soared.[24]

Brown's demonstration of his expertise in enforcing the peace—occurring just as cattle herds, cowboys, gamblers, prostitutes, and pickpockets began to converge on Caldwell for the 1883 season—had a dampening effect on the level of violence. The most sensational recent event in town was the shooting of Spotted Horse, and Caldwell's permanent residents eagerly spread the story to the town's visitors. Revelers and ruffians in 1883 were sobered by the knowledge that the marshal of Caldwell had shot a troublemaker in a face-to-face confrontation, and that he and his deputy also were instrumental in the violent capture of the Ross gang during the previous month.

In the middle of the season the *Journal* reported that during a five-month period Marshal Brown and his deputy had generated $1,296 in fines, "being just $421 more than the salary they have received for that time. A very good showing for a quiet town like Caldwell." The five months referred to—March through July—were busy ones in a cattle town. In the late spring high rollers and loose women arrived to host the high-spirited drovers who were looking for excitement. The most common offenses encountered by Brown and Wheeler were fighting, public swearing or otherwise disturbing the peace, prostitution, and the carrying of weapons inside the city limits. The marshal depended upon a "chain lightning" draw which allowed him to fell adversaries by clubbing them in the neck with a six-gun. Brown then would drag his prisoner off to the justice of the peace, who usually would assess a fine of one to ten dollars.[25]

A problem occurred a few weeks after the shooting of Spotted Horse. For three or four days a transient in his mid-twenties named John Caypless had been loitering around Caldwell, and local officers were keeping a watch on him. On Friday night, May 25, a saddle was stolen from a Caldwell store, and the proprietors reported the theft to Brown and Wheeler. The following Monday night Brown, Wheeler and Cash Hollister cornered Caypless and interrogated him. The itinerant came up with a story that some accomplices—who already had left the vicinity—had stolen the saddle. Caypless offered to lead the officers to the spot where they had hidden it. Caypless led them to nearby Fall Creek, and the missing saddle was located in a ravine. The officers reasoned that, since Caypless had managed to transport the saddle to its hiding place, justice demanded that he lug it back to town.

Near daybreak Caypless staggered into Caldwell, stooped and weary under the heavy rig. His captors turned him over to a constable named McCullough and went off to catch up on their sleep. McCullough marched Caypless and his burden to the office of the justice of the peace, T.H.B. Ross. A *Journal* reporter and a curious crowd followed the pair up to Ross' second-floor office, and within moments Caypless was sentenced to the county jail in Wellington.[26]

Henry Brown had been hired to control troublemakers, and in 1883 he did his job so well that the cattle season passed without an incident of any real consequence. On Tuesday, August 7, a trio of high-spirited cowboys left town firing a few rounds into the air. Brown and Wheeler rode after them and apprehended the three revelers. Brown and Wheeler brought the drovers back to Caldwell, where they were fined by Judge Ross. The three subdued wranglers quietly rode out of Caldwell toward camp.[27]

The 1883 shipping season proved to be a disappointment. In 1882 more than 64,000 cattle had been shipped north from Caldwell, but because of drought and market conditions only half that number was shipped out of the stockyards south of town in 1883.

As the weather began to turn cold the cowboys drifted south and most of the seasonal frontier riffraff left town. But a gambler named Newt Boyce had come with his wife to spend the 1883 season in Caldwell, and Christmas found the couple still in town. Later there were rumors that Boyce knew about Brown's disreputable past, and by late in 1883 there was bad blood between the lawman and the gambler.

On Friday night, December 15, 1883, a brawl broke out in a saloon on the east side of Main Street. Boyce had pulled a knife and superficially cut a soldier and one of the saloonkeepers, but Ben Wheeler quickly appeared, disarmed Boyce and ordered him to go home. Shortly afterward, Wheeler met Brown in the Southwestern Hotel. No sooner did Wheeler tell Brown about

---

Meter's father, located seven miles northeast of Caldwell in Falls township. As the two lawmen approached the farm house they discovered Chet outside, Winchester at the ready. The officers jumped out of the wagon, and Wheeler ordered Van Meter to throw up his hands. Van Meter instead snapped off a shot at Hollister, who instantly triggered a barrel of his shotgun. Wheeler also fired a bullet at Van Meter, but even though Chet was wounded, he again tried to work the Winchester.

Hollister and Wheeler each loosed a second round, and Van Meter fell dead in

(cont. next page)

his tracks. His bullet-riddled carcass showed five wounds in the chest, a gaping hole in his right side, a slug in the belly, and one wound in each hand—even his rifle had been struck by buckshot from Hollister's scattergun. Van Meter was dumped in the wagon, and the lawmen drove back to Caldwell. The body was taken to the basement of the Leland Hotel and checked by a physician and a coroner's jury, then picked up by Van Meter's father for burial.

See the Caldwell Post, November 22, 1883.

★ ★ ★

the fight than a man ran in with news that Boyce was back on the street, threatening trouble. The lawmen crossed the street and Brown spotted Boyce inside Hulbert's gun shop. The gambler was paying for a knife and six-gun, which were lying on the counter. Brown approached him and shoved the weapons aside, arrested Boyce, and jailed him for the night.[28]

The following morning Boyce was taken before Judge Ross, who fined and released him. Boyce seemed docile during the brief hearing, but later he began drinking and making threats against Brown and Wheeler. That night Wheeler encountered Boyce dealing monte in the saloon where he had been arrested the previous evening. Boyce looked up from his game and began cursing Brown, belligerently demanding to know where the marshal was. Wheeler withdrew without provoking Boyce; later he told Brown about the incident, warning that the gambler was in a mean mood.

Marshal Brown went directly to the saloon and confronted Boyce. Boyce snarled that as soon as he finished the monte game he would settle with Brown. Marshal Brown pushed matters no further and left the saloon to continue his rounds. Brown found Wheeler inside the Moore Brothers Saloon and told him of the run-in, and remained behind while the deputy left to patrol the streets. Almost immediately Wheeler was accosted by Boyce, who had left his game and now demanded again to know where the marshal was—"he wanted to see the fighting S.O.B."

Site of the Van Meter homestead, located a few miles northwest of Caldwell. On November 21, 1883, lawman Cash Hollister and Ben Wheeler came here to arrest Chet Van Meter, who opened fire and was slain by the officers. —Author photo

Wheeler allowed that Brown was inside the saloon, but advised Boyce to go home to his wife and sober up. At that point a man named T. L. Crist decide to leave Moore Brothers, and as he walked toward the door, Boyce thought that Brown had overheard his threats and was coming for showdown. The gambler retreated into an alley beside the saloon, groping inside his coat for a revolver rigged for a right-handed crossdraw. Wheeler watched Boyce for an instant, but when Crist appeared in the doorway the deputy turned and walked up the street. Boyce stepped onto the boardwalk, cocked his pistol and aimed it at Wheeler's back, but when he saw Crist nearby he held his fire and left.

Crist hailed Wheeler, and while he was telling the lawman what Boyce had done, Brown emerged from the saloon. Wheeler told Brown of the incident and warned the marshal "that Newt Boyce intended to do him some harm." Brown replied that "he didn't want to be murdered by anyone," and said that he was going to get his Winchester.

When Brown reappeared with the rifle, he and Wheeler walked north on the west side of Main Street. Just as they reached H. C. Unsell's Lone Star Clothing House, they spotted Boyce across the street, standing on the boardwalk outside Phillips' Saloon. Readying his rifle, Brown strode into the wide, dusty street toward Boyce, stopping about thirty feet from him. The marshal shouted a warning, and Boyce jumped behind an awning post and plunged his right hand inside his coat.

Brown fired two rounds from his Winchester. One shot missed, but the other hit Boyce's right upper arm, shattering a bone and piercing his side. Boyce cried out for Brown not to kill him, stumbled inside the saloon, and crumpled to the floor.

A crowd gathered and someone went for Dr. W. A. Noble to examine Boyce, but he found that little could be done. The internal bleeding could not be stopped, and Boyce died at about 3:00 A.M. Merchant D. D. Leahy sat up with the body of his former customer.

A telegram was sent to Wellington summoning the county coroner. A reply was received that the coroner was out of town, so Judge Ross began assembling a coroner's jury. After the jury was impaneled the inquest proceeded rapidly, and the verdict was delivered that "the deceased came to his death at the hands of an officer while in the discharge of his duties." The following Tuesday Mrs. Boyce headed for Austin, Texas, the home of Boyce's father, with the remains of her husband.

Despite criticism "in some quarters,"[29] most Caldwellites

held Marshal Brown in awe. D. D. Leahy later reminisced: "The people of Caldwell at that time were very proud of Brown. They said that he was the best officer that they had ever had. He had murdered a few persons ... but the people regarded his bloody disposition as official firmness." Leahy was not one of Brown's admirers, however, stating flatly that Boyce "knew too much and Brown killed him." Leahy offered an interesting insight into the relationship between Brown and Wheeler. According to Leahy, Brown and Wheeler were at odds with one another as a result of a "pretended feud." After each of Brown's killings Wheeler testified in his behalf, "and as they were supposed to be unfriendly, his statements were readily accepted as true."[30]

A month after the death of Newt Boyce the *Journal* suggested editorially that Brown and Wheeler should be elected constables in the election on February 5, 1884. "The boys would make excellent constables," praised the *Journal*, pointing out that holding this office would be a significant advantage when lawbreakers fled the city limits of Caldwell, since Brown and Wheeler held no jurisdiction outside the township. If shooting were involved in an incident of this sort, city policemen could be charged with murder; whereas if they were commissioned as constables, they "could make the arrest legally and be protected by the statutes."[31] Although Brown and Wheeler would have appreciated such protection, they were not elected constables. But the two lawmen enjoyed community-wide admiration—and Henry Brown fell in love.

CHAPTER NINE

Tragedy at Medicine Lodge

*"This is hard for me to write this letter but,
it was all for you, my sweet wife, and for the love I have for you."*
—Henry Brown

Always shy and reserved, Henry Brown had begun his adulthood in Lincoln County and Tascosa, on isolated ranches and in similar frontier locales where eligible girls were scarce and in great demand. He had never enjoyed a meaningful relationship with a young woman, but life in Caldwell was now made complete by Alice Maude Levagood.

Miss Levagood was twenty-two years old, the adopted daughter of Caldwell brick manufacturer Robert Rue and his wife. The Rues sent Maude to "an Eastern seminary," where she received an A.B. degree "with high honors" in June 1882, then returned to Caldwell to become a teacher. In addition to being "a very fine girl," Maude was pretty enough to attract Marshal Brown and at least one other local suitor. Brown's competition was a young man who was a clerk in D. D. Leahy's mercantile establishment. On a Sunday night, the young clerk was escorting Miss Levagood from the Methodist Church to her home when Brown appeared from behind a tree. Henry drew a six-gun on his rival and accused him of a variety of offenses. These accusations planted doubts in Miss Levagood's mind concerning the character of the clerk. It became clear to the clerk that Brown would kill him if necessary.[1]

It was not necessary. The young man prudently retired from the field, and Brown pressed his advantage. Maude accepted his proposal. They traveled to Wellington on Tuesday, March 25, 1884, obtained a marriage license, and were married the following day. The ceremony was conducted by Methodist minister Dudley E. Akin in the home of J. N. Miller, Maude's brother-in-law and husband of her adoptive sister. Brown was reluctant to remove his gunbelt, and strapped his rig back on as soon as he had kissed his bride. A reporter quipped that Brown "did not Lev [a] good girl, but took her unto himself for better or worse... The *Journal*, metaphorically speaking, throws its old shoe after the young folks and wishes them a long and prosperous life."²

The Browns honeymooned for a week at the Southwestern Hotel. The marshal purchased a house on two adjoining lots six blocks north of the business area on Main Street. Brown bought a cow to provide milk, butter, and cream, and staked her behind the house.³ At the age of twenty-six, Henry Brown tried to settle down to enjoy his first real home.

The cost of domesticity was high. The price of his house and lot was $900, and after making a downpayment of $165, Brown was forced to sign a mortgage for $735. Brown had accumulated no savings and it was necessary for him to borrow $300 from the Caldwell Savings Bank. Co-signed by Levi Thrailkill and William Morris, the loan was used to make the downpayment and furnish the house. Brown never had owed a large sum of money, and his obligations of more than $1,000 felt oppressive. He became anxious to settle the debt. In April, Brown was reappointed city marshal, but despite a salary of $125 per month, his income seemed inadequate Soon he was pondering ways to supplement his $1,500 annual salary. The marshal of Caldwell hit upon a scheme to solve his financial problems.⁴

Like a doomed hero in a Greek tragedy, Henry Brown would be destroyed by a fatal flaw. Like Iago, Shakespeare's despicable villain in *Othello*, Brown deceptively presented one image while dark secrets loomed beneath the surface. Marshal Brown had tamed a tough, violent cattle town. Clearly he possessed a gift for frontier law enforcement, and a career as a peace officer might have placed Brown in the upper echelon of Western lawmen alongside Wild Bill Hickok, Pat Garrett, Bill Tilghman, and Heck Thomas. But the same criminal impulses that drove him to kill and steal horses in Lincoln County resurfaced in Caldwell. Marshal Brown had earned respect and popularity—and a fine salary—in the Border Queen, and he had found a bride. Brown's future was full of promise, but his inner demons thrust him back into crime.

Marshal Brown decided to rob the Medicine Valley Bank in Medicine Lodge, seventy miles to the west and twenty miles north of the Oklahoma line. A few years earlier Henry Brown had worked as a cowboy under Barney O'Connor on a Cherokee Strip ranch less than a day's ride below Medicine Lodge. Brown therefore was familiar with the town and surrounding terrain.

In Medicine Lodge business houses which catered to area ranchers faced each other for three blocks along Main Street, and the north end of this thoroughfare was dominated by the finest building in town. The two-story brick structure crowned the northwest corner of First and Main; a boardwalk extended outward from the two street-sides of the building, and an ornate sign above the main entrance boldly advertised, "Medicine Valley Bank." The bank president was the leading citizen of Medicine Lodge, Edward Wylie Payne. In his mid-thirties, Payne had a large family and extensive commercial holdings around town. He owned the newspaper, as well as 3,000 head of cattle. Through Payne's leadership and financial backing, the brick three-story Grand Hotel—which still stands in Medicine Lodge—was under construction.[5]

Henry Brown had little difficulty in recruiting accomplices to rob Wylie Payne's bank. Ben Wheeler was eager to go. Alice M. Burton, Wheeler's most recent wife, had been treated shabbily by her husband. Despite the fact the she was pregnant, Ben Burton deserted her in the spring of 1882 to come to Caldwell. A few months later, after the birth of their child, she joined him in Caldwell. A wife and a baby cramped the style of Deputy Ben Wheeler, and he offered to support her if she would return to her family in Indianola, Nebraska. Considering Wheeler's character, it is probable that the payments were few, small and infrequent. Alice Burton unwillingly lived with her elderly parents and a sister until December 1883, when her father died. Following the funeral, she returned to Caldwell and spent several weeks with Wheeler before he again sent her away. But, as she now was responsible for the financial support of her baby, mother, and sister, Wheeler must have been forced to make considerable monetary pledges before she would leave. In the spring of 1884 Wheeler shared the same financial dilemma as Henry Brown—and the same plan of solution.

Soon the two Caldwell policemen were joined by cowboys William Smith and John Wesley. Smith and Wesley were from Texas and both had found work on ranches in the vicinity of Medicine Lodge, where they had met Henry Brown. It is likely that Brown approached one of these Texas cowboys, who then recruited his friend as the fourth accomplice.

Bank president E.W. Payne was a family man and the most prominent citizen of Medicine Lodge. Payne also was a director of the Cherokee Strip Live Stock Association.

—Courtesy Kansas State Historical Society, Topeka

Billy Smith was in his late twenties and was from Vernon, Texas, where he had come to know Wesley when the latter drifted into town. Smith had proven himself to be such a dependable hand on the T5 Ranch that the owners placed him in charge. But he became dissatisfied with foreman's pay (probably no more than fifty dollars per month) and, like Henry Brown, was eager to improve his financial status. John Wesley had ridden for Treadwell and Clark's Cherokee Strip range during the winter of 1883-1884. He was from the northeast Texas town of Paris, where he was born in 1853. Wesley was a sinister man who sometimes used aliases (most recently "Harry Hill"), and who was never without his six-gun and Winchester.[6]

Another resident of the Medicine Lodge area, "I-Bar" Johnson, was approached to join the band about five weeks prior to the holdup. When Johnson declined he was threatened with death should he divulge the scheme. Nevertheless, Johnson wrote a warning note to Wylie Payne and cashier George Geppert, advising them that if the robbery materialized, they should offer no resistance. But since there had never been a bank holdup in Medicine Lodge, Payne and Geppert ignored the warning.

After weeks of planning, Brown approached Mayor A. M. Colson with a request for a leave of absence for a few days. Brown told Colson that he and Wheeler had learned the whereabouts of a murderer with a reward of $1,200 on him who supposedly was at a hideout not far into the Cherokee Strip. The cattle season was beginning and there was talk of Colson appointing a temporary police chief, even though Brown promised that he and Wheeler would return in a few days.[7]

With leave granted, Brown and Wheeler had their horses reshod and stuffed their saddlebags and cartridge belts with extra ammunition. On Sunday afternoon, April 27, 1884, Brown bade farewell to his bride, who knew nothing about the plan. Brown strapped on his .44 Colts, sheathed the gold-plated Winchester, and mounted up to join Wheeler. The deputy also had a Winchester and a pair of single action .44 Colts, and he rode a fast and newly-purchased horse.[8]

The two "lawmen" took the road west out of town, a most indirect route to the Strip and their supposed prey. They rode to Harper, a small town thirty miles northwest of Caldwell and thirty miles due east of Medicine Lodge. On that same afternoon Wesley told the men at Treadwell and Clark's range that he was going to ride into Kansas to meet Smith, and he headed north on a gray horse to join the T5 foreman.[9]

On Monday, April 28, Brown and Wheeler probably stayed

in Harper. The next day they rendezvoused with their accomplices in the Gyp Hills, south of Medicine Lodge. The men checked their guns, wire cutters, and gunpowder, with which they intended to blow the bank safe. The night before the robbery Wheeler and Smith stayed with settler Ben Harbaugh, while Brown and Wesley remained in the rugged concealment of the Gyp Hills. Harbaugh's place was on Brush Creek, eight miles south of the Lodge and two or three miles east of the Gyp Hills. Following breakfast Smith and Wheeler rode out to meet Brown and Wesley. Wednesday morning, April 30, was overcast and rainy as the four riders headed toward Medicine Lodge.[10]

In Medicine Lodge Wylie Payne breakfasted with his wife and nine children in his home on the north bank of the Medicine River. Payne was preoccupied at the table; that morning he had been scheduled to lead a herd of cattle north to a shipping point. The heavy rain and swelling streams, combined with generally low market prices, caused him to cancel the shipment and spend the dreary day inside the bank.

A big roundup had been set for Wednesday, April 30, at nearby Antelope Flat, but the downpour caused a number of cowboys and ranchers to congregate inside a livery stable across the street from the bank. The riders were restless to leave the confines of the musty barn, and they kept their horses saddled and ready to ride. Barney O'Connor, who had been Henry Brown's foreman two or three years earlier, was among those in the livery stable. At mid-morning he dashed down the street to run an errand.[11]

The bank opened at nine. A lone customer quickly transacted his business and left. The clerk was sent running through the rain with a packet of mail to be sent off to Harper. George Geppert busied himself behind the cashier's window, while Wylie Payne sorted through paperwork at his desk.

A few minutes past nine Henry Brown led his men toward the bank from the west, pleased that the heavy rains were keeping curious onlookers off the streets. The horses were tied in back of the coal shed behind the bank. Smith remained with the wet animals as his three confederates walked toward the bank through the mud. Brown and Wesley entered the side entrance and Wheeler entered by the front door. Holding a six-gun in one hand and a sack in the other, Wheeler advanced to the cashier's widow. Winchester in hand, Brown went to the window opposite Payne's desk and ordered the bank officials to throw up their hands.

Geppert immediately raised his arms, then turned his head to look at Payne, who defiantly reached for a pistol. Brown triggered his gold-plated Winchester and the bullet struck Payne in the right shoulder blade. Payne dropped to the floor in pain. Geppert turned to look at Payne and Wheeler began firing his six-gun. Two .44 slugs struck Geppert in the chest and head, spinning him back toward the vault. He staggered to the safe, fastened the lock, and collapsed to die on the floor of the vault.

Unexpected gunfire resounded throughout the center of the small town. In the commercial building serving as a courthouse, L. W. Moore, the register of deeds, and his sister, Della Moore, heard the gunshots. Moore ordered Della, working as his deputy, to put the record books in the vault. As she bustled about Moore glanced out the rain-spattered window, then turned to slam and lock the vault's door—not realizing that he had shut his sister inside.[12]

Close to the bank, people appeared in doorways and windows. Reverend George Friedley began shouting an alarm, and city marshal Sam Denn raced into the street from beneath the awning of Herrington and Smith's. The short, red-headed lawman had never been in a gunfight, but he drew his pistol and began popping away at Smith. Smith returned the officer's fire, and took wild potshots at anyone else he could see. One bullet ricocheted off the barn and shattered a window in a nearby

The Medicine Valley Bank. Henry Brown fired three Winchester shots at the city marshal from the front door.
—Courtesy Kansas State Historical Society, Topeka

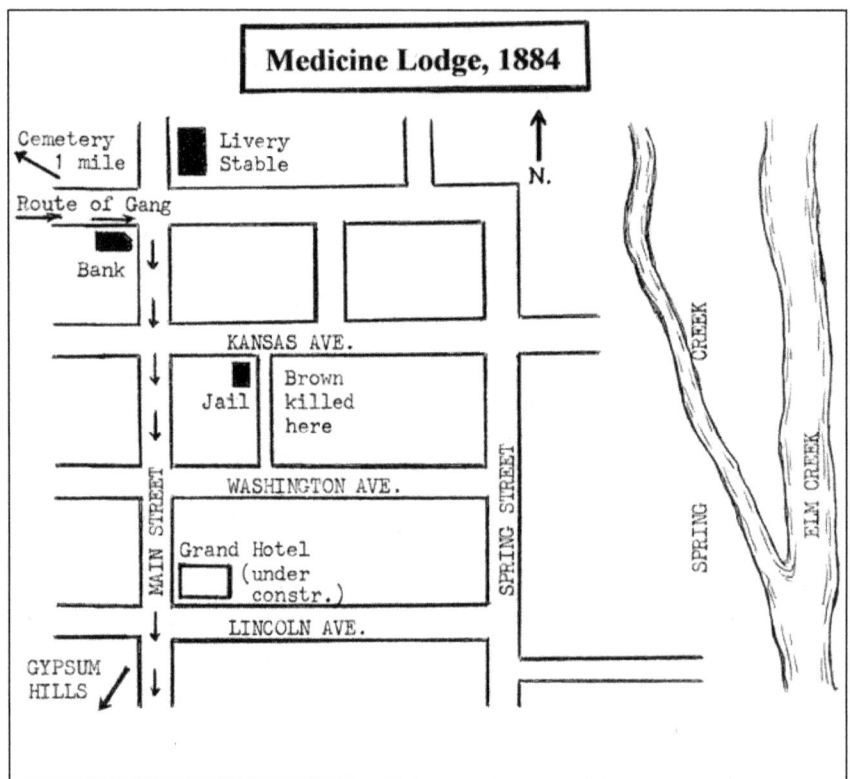

building. Brown ran to the door of the bank and pumped three Winchester shots at Denn.[13]

None of the firing was effective, but it earned a few moments reprieve for the outlaws, who were shouting frantically at each other. With the town aroused, there was no time to force open the safe, so Brown led a break for the horses. Ben Wheeler, who was fast proving to be less than courageous, dropped the towsack and his six-gun, and bolted for the coal shed. The heavy rainfall had drenched the leather reins and the hitch-knots were difficult to untie, but after a panicky moment of furious fumbling the horses were freed. The outlaws swung into their saddles and spurred their mounts down Main Street toward the river crossing.[14]

A dozen of the cowboys in the livery barn vaulted onto their saddled mounts and gave pursuit. Barney O'Connor dashed back to the stable to join the makeshift posse, but found that someone had already appropriated his horse. The only mount left in the stable was a bony crowbait, but O'Connor mounted up anyway, hoping that the nag was a good mudder. Sure enough, he proved to be of better blood than appearances indicated. O'Connor quickly caught up with the other riders, who had just sighted the robbers at the Medicine River crossing, south of town. Once across the river, O'Connor passed his own horse and surged forward on the borrowed mount to lead the pursuit.[15]

Brown and his men paused for a moment to direct a fusillade at their pursuers, but when the posse did not waver, the outlaws stopped shooting and raced ahead. At this point Wheeler's new horse faltered—although speedy over a short distance, it soon tired. Wheeler persuaded one of his partners— perhaps Smith, who was astride a fine black mare—to let him ride double, and he left his exhausted horse behind.[16]

Two miles south of town, homesteader Joe Wiley saw the outlaws gallop past his place and shook his head, thinking they were cowboys already drunk for the day. He was startled a few moments later when the posse raced past and, very shortly, his puzzlement grew when he heard gunfire coming from the Gyp Hills.[17]

The outlaws rode into a canyon opening they thought would lead them through the Gap in the Gyp Hills. Almost immediately they found themselves facing fifty-foot walls of sandstone and clay. Instead of the Gap, they mistakenly had entered

Nine members of the posse which chased down the bank robbers. Barney O'Connor stands second from left at top.

—Courtesy Kansas State Historical Society, Topeka

the only box canyon in the Gyp Hills. They wheeled their mounts, but as they neared the entrance Barney O'Connor galloped into the mouth of what would become known as "Jackass Canyon."[18] O'Connor leaped off his horse and darted to cover as other posse members approached. The outlaws dismounted and sought shelter over the grassy floor of the ravine. Several cowboys reinforced O'Connor at the entrance to the box canyon while the others scrambled up the muddy heights to gain sniper positions. A fierce gun battle erupted, but all parties had concealed themselves so well that no one was wounded. The bottled-up outlaws, however, were trapped; and, to make matters worse, rain was slowly filling the little canyon with run-off water.

Gunfire became spasmodic, but no one in the posse intended to rush their prey. The idea of smoking out the outlaws with kegs of kerosene was considered. The barrelheads could be pierced, and kegs rolled down the steep canyon walls while the kerosene spilled in every direction. Despite the rain, it was hoped that a fire could be ignited, forcing the outlaws from cover. Everyone agreed that reinforcements would be handy, too, and someone was needed to return to town for men and kerosene. Talliaferro and Rev. George Friedley, who had ridden along, volunteered. Ten men remained behind to keep the gang pinned down: O'Connor, Lee Bradley, Roll Clark, Tom Doran, John Fleming, Vernon Lytle, Howard Martin, Alec and Wayne McKinney, and Nate Priest.[19]

Rain continued to pour down and water rose in the box canyon—a foot deep, a foot and a half, finally two feet. The outlaws muttered to each other about the hopelessness of their situation. Wheeler had no heart for a fight, and Brown had too much experience as a posse member to be optimistic. Smith was defiant, realizing that justice would be harsh after the shooting of Payne and Geppert.

Early in the afternoon Henry Brown shouted that he would surrender if the posse would promise protection from lynching. O'Connor and the posse agreed, and Brown waded out to lay down his guns. A moment later Wheeler forlornly followed, with Wesley close behind. Smith had no shred of trust in the promise of protection, and when he finally came out he said reluctantly, "Boys, I came into it with you, and I'll go out and die with you."[20]

The posse members were shocked that their prisoners included lawmen from a neighboring community. O'Connor knew Brown well, and he greatly respected him as a peace officer. But Brown was shackled along with others, and the party headed back toward town.

Immediately after the attempted robbery, as soon as the robbers and posse members rode south, a crowd had swarmed into the bank. Onlookers were horrified to find Geppert lying dead in a pool of blood, and community leader Payne wounded. Payne was taken to his home, where the physicians first expressed "strong hopes of his recovery."[21] Payne related how he and Geppert had been gunned down, and by the time Talliaferro and Friedley had ridden in from the south, the town was in a vicious mood. When the two posse members revealed that the outlaws were trapped in the Gyp Hills and that reinforcements were needed, every man who could find a gun and a horse mounted up. Talliaferro and Friedley described the plan to burn out the outlaws, and Jacob Achenbach, who had witnessed the shooting in the street, agreed to load his spring wagon with coal oil. These preparations proved unnecessary, however, as a rider soon arrived with news that the outlaws—Smith, Wesley, Ben Wheeler, and Marshal Henry Brown—had surrendered.

Most of the men rode to meet the incoming party, which now was nearing town. O'Connor and his men were told that Geppert were dead and Payne badly wounded, but the promise of protection to the outlaws was reasserted. When the wet, muddy outlaws were spotted in Medicine Lodge, however, enraged townspeople surged toward them, screaming, "Hang them! Hang them!"

The posse and local officers managed to hold the crowd at bay, and the outlaws were hustled into a café for food and protection. After eating, the robbers were secured with a single pair of handcuffs and one set of leg irons. One end of the leg irons was fastened to Wesley's left ankle, shackling him to Brown's right leg. Wesley and Brown then had their hands tied behind their backs with rope. The cuffs were manacled to Wheeler's right wrist and Smith's left. The prisoners then were escorted through a hostile crowd toward the jail.

It had stopped raining and a photographer was waiting. The four mustachioed outlaws were aligned in front of the one-story wooden jail. The slumping Ben Wheeler was on the left, and to his right stood John Wesley. Brown was dressed in a dark coat and vest, gray slouch hat, and a light-colored bandana. Ranch foreman Smith, perhaps in an attempt at disguise, wore a railroader's cap. One account states that Brown sank to his knees to beg for mercy,[22] but contemporary newspapers did not record such an act.

As the photographer readied his equipment, the men of

Medicine Lodge crowded into the picture. Smith's cap blocked the face of one citizen, who raised his right hand for the benefit of posterity. A man behind Brown and Smith moved, forever blurring his image. A drummer bobbed up just behind Smith and Wheeler; soon he sent a copy of the photograph and a lurid version of the robbery and lynching to the *New York Times*, and was rewarded with a pair of round-trip tickets to Niagara Falls for himself and his fiancée. Later Barney O'Connor and most of the posse, armed to the teeth, posed for a studio picture, and photographs also were taken of the box canyon and the bank.

County Sheriff C. F. Rigg finally locked the prisoners inside the little jail. Under a heavy guard the drenched outlaws were permitted to change into dry clothing and were provided with writing materials. Henry Brown, preoccupied with the likelihood of a lynch mob, wrote to Maude as dusk began.

Medicine Lodge. April 30, '84

Darling Wife: — I am in jail here. Four of us tried to rob the bank here, and one man shot one of the men in the bank, and he is now in his home. I want you to come see me as soon as you can. I will send you my things, and you can sell them, but keep the Winchester. This is hard for me to write this letter but, it was all for you, my sweet wife, and for the love I have for you. Do not go back on me; if you do it will kill me. Be true

The captured bank robbers stand in front of the jail. Henry Brown is wearing the light hat and bandana, and John Wesley is at his right. William Smith stands between Brown and tall Ben Wheeler.
—Courtesy Kansas State Historical Society, Topeka

to me as long as you live, and come to see me if you think enough of me. My love is just the same as it always was. Oh, how I did hate to leave you on last Sunday eve, but I didn't think this would happen. I thought we could take in the money and not have any trouble with it; but a man's fondest hopes are sometimes broken with trouble. We would not been arrested, but one of our horses gave out, and we could not leave him alone. I want you to send me some clothes. Sell all the things you do not need. Have your picture taken and send it to me. Now, my dear wife, go and see Mr. Witzelben and Mr. Nyce, and get the money. If a mob does not kill us we will come out all right after a while. Maude, I did not shoot any one, and did not want the others to kill any one but they did, and that is all there is about it. Now, good-bye, my darling wife.

H. N. Brown[23]

Early that evening—after the outlaws had been treated to a second meal and after Brown had delivered his letter to Sheriff Rigg—the county attorney was ushered into the little cell. Brown, convinced that a lynching was imminent, said, "We will give you $1000 if you will save our lives till daylight."[24]

The county attorney firmly declined the offer, then was informed by the prisoners that the robbery scheme originated with Geppert. The cashier allegedly had embezzled $10,000 and wanted to cover his crime with a holdup. The robbers claimed that Geppert had assured them that Payne would be on a cattle-selling trip, and considered themselves betrayed when Payne was at his desk. The county attorney regarded the story as preposterous, and he soon left the jail.

Outside, the mood of the town was unmistakably mean. Word of the violent morning had spread like a prairie fire, and people had swarmed into Medicine Lodge from the countryside. Sheriff Rigg, Marshal Denn and their deputies hovered around the jail, but all over town—especially in saloons—men muttered firmly about the necessity of controlling lawbreakers. Westerners were accustomed to dealing with problems directly and quickly, and the citizens of Medicine Lodge were impatient at the prospect of waiting for a legal trial. There was no doubt that the four men imprisoned in the jail had assaulted the bank and killed the unarmed George Geppert. Wylie Payne was suffering great agony and it was feared that he would die. Local businessmen and cowboys alike agreed that retaliation was called for; outlaws should be given a lesson in the dangerous folly of raiding Medicine Lodge. "All afternoon," it was later reported, "little knots of quiet, determined men could be seen, and all over town was that peculiar hush which bodes the coming storm. Little was said, but the impression prevailing was that before many hours the bodies of four murderers would swing in the soft night air."[25]

By nightfall the prisoners feared for their lives. Their cell was solid; it had been constructed in 1878 of two-by-four scantlings and there were no windows. The alert guards nearby made the possibility of escape even more remote. Nevertheless, Wesley found that his shackle had been tightened around his boot, and when the boot was pulled from his foot the chain could be slipped off—and both he and Brown were free to run. Smith had thickly-muscled wrists and small hands, and after a struggle he freed himself of the manacles which chained him to Wheeler.[26]

About nine o'clock, only a couple of hours after dark, three shots were fired. Armed men numbering perhaps three hundred swarmed toward the jail while the officers on duty glanced at each other doubtfully. The lawmen felt not a shred of sympathy for the prisoners, and had no heart whatever for shooting it out with friends and neighbors to protect them. Newspapers later dutifully reported that "notwithstanding their spirited resistance, the sheriff and his posse were overpowered...."[27] But the lawmen did not "resist" to the extent of firing their guns. The mob shouted that the prisoners be turned over to them, and when the officers went through the motions of refusing, the vigilantes swept them aside and forced open the outside door.

Henry Brown coiled just inside the cell door, and when it swung open he plunged into the snarling crowd. Desperately he twisted past the startled mob and emerged into the clear. A flurry of shots followed the frantic escape, but in the dim light Brown was not seriously hit. He sprinted into the alley east of the jail, on the verge of escape into the darkness.

Billy Kelley, a local farmer, was standing at the edge of the crowd, a sawed-off double-barreled shotgun clutched in his hands. As Brown bolted past, Kelley jerked the gun up and triggered both barrels into the fleeing figure.[28]

Cut almost in half by the double blast of buckshot, Brown crumpled into the dirt nearly fifty yards from the jail. Several other shots were fired at his body. Henry Brown died instantly.

A short distance away Ben Wheeler seized his own chance for freedom when the mob turned on Brown. As Wheeler tore through the crowd in the opposite direction, a gun was shoved against him and was discharged. Wheeler staggered at the impact but stayed on his feet. As he fled into the darkness he was illuminated by his flaming vest, ignited by the point-blank explosion. Wheeler broke into the open toward the east, but a fusillade of pistol and rifle fire followed him. A bullet ripped two fingers from his left hand. A Winchester slug shattered his right arm. Still he stumbled forward another 100 yards. The mob surged after him, firing on the run. Slugs chunked into his back and finally he fell, to be pounced upon almost immediately by the pursuers.

Back at the jail Smith and Wesley also tried to escape, but advanced only a few feet before they were seized. Eager hands shoved them toward the creekbed a few hundred yards east of the jail, where a grove of trees flourished in the bottomland. The stunned, bleeding Wheeler was jerked to his feet and pushed alongside Smith and Wesley beneath a particularly large elm.

While stumbling toward the hanging tree, Ben Wheeler whispered a confession, then began begging for mercy. He screamed pitifully as nooses were readied, pleading for reprieve until ten the next morning. "Oh men," blurted Wheeler, "spare my life. There's other fellows mixed up in this and I will tell you everything if only you will spare my life."[29]

Wheeler's cries were ignored. When Wesley was pressed for last words, in a trembling voice he breathed that he had a mother in Texas and asked that she not be told his fate. He added that he had been born in Paris, Texas, requesting that friends in Vernon be informed of his death. Smith disdainfully showed no fear. He requested that his horse, saddle and possessions be sold and the money forwarded to his mother in Vernon. Impressing the onlookers with his courage, he remarked: "What's the use anyway, so pull when you're ready."[30]

At this point the nooses were placed around the necks and the ends of the three-quarter-inch-thick lariat ropes were tossed over a stout limb about fifteen feet high. Wheeler wailed so loudly that he was heard blocks away. Jacob Achenbach stepped forward and coldly asked one of the outlaws how he felt. "My God! My God!" came the terrified reply.[31]

On Thursday morning the bodies were displayed side by side in the lot west of the jail. There the curious came to view the executed felons. Word of the lynching had spread rapidly, and all day settlers came into town from the surrounding countryside. Souvenir hunters stripped limbs from the hanging tree and sliced the three lariat ropes into small pieces. Ben Harbaugh rode into town, and was astonished to see in death two men who had breakfasted at his dugout the previous day.

"Why, those boys had breakfast at my place yesterday

morning," Harbaugh pointed at Wheeler. "I thought that one was too well-dressed and had too good a horse and saddle to be an ordinary cowpoke."[32]

Before noon Wylie Payne died, further hardening public opinion against the dead outlaws. That day the local newspaper stated: "Mob law is to be deplored under almost every circumstance, but in this case the general sentiment of the community will uphold the summary execution of justice by taking of these murderers' lives."[32] That morning the Barber County coroner, J. W. Singer, confidently assembled a jury to conduct an inquiry into the lynching. Singer and the jury members retired to the jail yard and inspected the corpses. Sheriff Rigg had noted that Wheeler, when incarcerated, had on his person forty or fifty dollars, but official examination revealed just eleven cents in his pockets. There also was a lady's gold ring with an amethyst stone, a pocket knife, and a pair of cuff buttons. Someone remembered that he had given a watch to one of his captors, perhaps to be forwarded to his family, but Wheeler's timepiece disappeared as completely as his fifty dollars. In Wesley's pockets was found $5.90, and a search of Smith turned up $2.60. A check of Brown's remains produced "nothing of value." Rigg then testified that he had been "overpowered at the jail by persons so masked that he could not recognize them, and that they spoke in sepulchral tones so that he could not recognize their voices." The jury then delivered their verdict: Brown had died from "gunshot wounds at the hands of unknown parties;" Wheeler had died "either from the effect of gunshot wounds or from hanging or from both causes, at the hands of unknown parties;" Smith and Wesley had died "from hanging at the hands of parties unknown to the jury."[33]

Now that members of the mob as well as jail guards had been exonerated, Sheriff Rigg impounded the personal effects of the outlaws. Later in the day the shrouded bodies were laid into pine coffins which were then loaded into a wagon and hauled to the little graveyard a mile northwest of town. It was not considered proper to bury murdering criminals alongside decent citizens, so a large hole was dug just outside the western boundary of the cemetery. Quickly the four pine boxes were lowered into the common grave and covered with freshly turned dirt.

Payne and Geppert were interred with far more elaborate ceremony. Both men were widely mourned. Everyone ignored the rumors of Geppert's complicity in the robbery. He was warmly regarded in the community, and his dying act of locking the safe brought universal admiration. "It is remarkable," stated one eulogy, "that even while he lived we never heard anyone speak of him in a tone of bitterness, while here was a multitude whom he placed under obligation by acts of accommodation and personal kindness." His funeral was held in the Presbyterian Church on Sunday, April 4, and an overflow crowd stood in the aisles. The local Odd Fellows and Masons assisted in burial services at the cemetery northwest of town. Geppert, who had been born in Germany in 1842, left a wife and son as survivors. Payne's funeral was conducted on Friday, April 2, the day following his death. Local businesses were draped in mourning as people gathered at the Presbyterian Church; and at his gravesite the Masonic Lodge participated in final rites. "We have lost a most excellent man," lamented a local newspaper, "a kind husband and father, and one of our most enterprising citizens." Payne's grieving widow erected a handsome stone with the sentiment: "Loved in life, In death not divided."[34]

CHAPTER TEN

The End of Caldwell's Gunfighter Era

"Madame: It becomes my painful duty to inform you of the death of your husband, H. Newton Brown, at the hands of an infuriated mob."
—Sheriff C. F. Rigg

News of the Medicine Lodge bank robbery reached Caldwell on Thursday morning, about twenty-four hours after the holdup. The participation of Brown and Wheeler was not yet known, but news of a robbery with the shooting of two bank officials excited all of Caldwell. The *Caldwell Journal* had just published its weekly edition, but an extra sheet was hastily printed with the available details. Business came to a standstill as people congregated in the streets to discuss the tragedy. Then, at 6:30 that evening, Ben Miller in Caldwell was startled to receive a telegram from Charles Eldred, a former resident of Caldwell and now the mayor of Medicine Lodge:

Ben S. Miller, Caldwell, Kansas:
　　The bank robbers were Brown and Wheeler, marshal and deputy of Caldwell, and Smith and Wesley. All arrested. Tried to escape. Brown killed. Balance hung. Geppert dead. Payne will die.
　　　　　　　　　　　　　　　　　　Chares H. Eldred[1]

Within an hour this incredible news had spread throughout Caldwell. At first the citizens were unable to believe that their respected law officers had committed robbery and murder. Several community leaders made plans to travel to Medicine Lodge and investigate. Maude Brown was informed. Not until late at night were the streets clear of little knots of people buzzing, gossiping, and digesting this startling information.

The next morning, Ben Miller, John A. Blair, Harvey Horner, and Lee Weller left by train for Medicine Lodge. Miller and Blair intended to visit the bereaved families to extend their personal regrets and the sympathy of Caldwell. Horner and Weller went "to look after the property that belonged to them."[2] They arrived in Medicine Lodge at ten o'clock that evening, and they were met at the depot by Mayor Eldred and another former resident, Dr. Moore, who put their friends on good terms with the understandably touchy men of Medicine Lodge. (Moore formerly had been in business with Weller, and in May 1883 Brown and Wheeler had recovered a saddle from John Caypless that had been stolen from "Moores & Weller.") The quartet from Caldwell learned that Payne had died that morning and that there were rumors that the robbery had been carefully planned. These rumors were fueled when either Horner or Weller inquired about the "property" that he had loaned Wheeler just before the lawmen had departed Caldwell. Wheeler apparently had been loaned $300 in cash, a diamond stickpin valued at $50 or $60, a gold watch claimed to be worth $625. It seemed that someone had provided a stake for Wheeler, presumably in return for a share of the loot. There was little sorrow in Medicine Lodge that the money, jewelry, and watch had vanished. The *Cressett* denounced this as "a dishonorable piece of business," and proclaimed "we have no sympathy to waste on a man who was foolish enough to lend a man of Ben Wheeler's character, a $625 watch and $300 in money."[3]

Before leaving town, the delegation from Caldwell asked to see the robbers' bodies—no doubt in the hope that there had been a mistake in identifying and Wheeler. They were taken to the cemetery and the grave was opened. When the lids were pried off the coffins the men from Caldwell realized that there had been no error, and observed "that the features of the dead men were as natural as if they were asleep."[4]

Once back in Caldwell, Miller and the others confirmed the participation and death of the town's police force, and added a number of details. The town was electrified anew, adding to Maude Brown's depression. By now Brown's widow had received a few minor personal effects from her husband's pockets, along with Brown's last letter and an accompanying message from Sheriff Rigg:

Medicine Lodge, May 1st

Mrs. H. N. Brown, Caldwell, Ks.

Madame: — It becomes my painful duty to inform you of the death of your husband, H. Newton Brown, at the hands of an infuriated mob. Your husband and three others attempted to rob the Medicine Valley Bank, and in so doing killed Mr. Geo. Geppert, the cashier, also wounding the president, Mr. Payne, from which wounds he will surely die. I wish to say that in my capacity as sheriff of this county I did my best to protect my prisoners; but by being overpowered I was forced to submit. Perhaps it will be some satisfaction to you to know that his death was instantaneous and quite painless, being shot two or three times, dying instantly, while his comrades in crime were taken some distance from town and hung. There are some effects in this town the property of your husband, and as soon as I can get them together I will forward them to you. I also send to you a letter written by your husband and handed to me to send to you. He wrote it a little before dark last evening.

C.F. Rigg
Sheriff.[5]

Maude Brown allowed the editor of the *Journal* to read and copy both letters, and they were published as part of a detailed account on the following Thursday. Charles Siringo also talked to the *Journal*, filling them in on Brown's background and adding considerably to the biographical information which had been provided to reporters by Barney O'Connor.

People regretted losing "the best officer the city has ever had," agreeing that the town had been "exceptionally quiet" during Brown's tenure because he was the only marshal the cowboys genuinely feared.[6] No sympathy was possible, however, for men whose annual salaries totaled $1,500 and $1,200, far higher incomes that that of the average wage earner. Because the act seemed to reflect dishonor upon Caldwell, the city council appointed a committee to draft a resolution of apology and regret to Medicine Lodge.

The resolution expressed "the unutterable amazement and mortification of our citizens" and denounced Brown and Wheeler as "murderers, robbers, cowards and villains of the worst type." Sympathy was extended to the bereaved families and to the citizens of the neighboring town, and hearty approval "of the summary manner" of execution of "the depraved creatures" was duly recorded.[7]

The *Police Gazette* lost no time in sensationalizing the robbery and lynching. John Wesley supposedly had concealed a pistol in his boot and opened fire when the mob approached. But the crowd shot back, riddling Wesley with nineteen bullets. An accompanying illustration depicts Wesley shooting at the advancing mob, while one citizen returns his fire and another waves a noose in the air. When this edition reached Medicine Lodge there was a rush on the post office, "but an expression of profound disgust spread over the buyers" as they read the exaggerated account and as they recognized themselves represented in the drawing as "long-haired, villainous looking men,"[8] instead of as righteous, clean-cut upholders of justice.

According to another story, on the day after the lynching Maude Brown arrived in Medicine Lodge in a lumber wagon. She had her husband's body exhumed and placed in the seat beside her; then headed back to Caldwell for final burial. There is no mention in contemporary newspapers of this bizarre and unlikely occurrence, and no one has ever found a gravesite for Brown in a Caldwell cemetery. However, T.A. McNeal states that the outlaws' remains were eventually disinterred and their skeletons displayed in various area doctors' offices.[9]

A couple of weeks after the holdup and lynching, a public sale was conducted in Medicine Lodge, offering for auction the

Theorizing that Henry Brown's remains were moved from Medicine Lodge to Caldwell's City Cemetery, historian Rod Cook (right of center, peering into open grave) and a team of biological anthropologists conducted a search. On October 31, 2003, two likely graves were opened — and found to be empty.

—Courtesy Rod Cook

horses and saddles of the dead outlaws. Smith's worn saddle brought a mere $10.00, Wheeler's sold for $22.00, Wesley's for $24.50, and Brown's for $25.00. Wesley's grey was auctioned off for $120.00, and Smith's mare went for $123.50.[10]

Wheeler's new horse, abandoned during the chase, had been recovered, but neither this unreliable animal nor Brown's mount was available at the auction. Mrs. Burton, Ben Wheeler's most recent wife, employed an attorney who claimed the horses of Wheeler and Brown. Mrs. Burton-Wheeler had received little financial support from her husband during his lifetime, and when he died she traveled to Caldwell from Nebraska to salvage whatever assets might be available. The *Journal* mentioned that she was responsible for her eighteen-month-old baby, as well as her mother and sister, "and in her brave resolution she will no doubt meet with ready help from the kindhearted ladies of this city."[11]

Hopefully the women of Caldwell lived up to the editor's expectations, because Wheeler left little behind except his horse. The cash and jewelry he carried disappeared not long after his arrest and his guns also vanished. The single-action Colt .44-40 Army revolver he bought in Caldwell in 1883 somehow wound up in the hands of English gun collector Harry Leah. It had a 5½ inch barrel and on the backstrap was imprinted: "Ben Wheeler, Caldwell, Kansas, 1883." Wheeler's other six-gun, a similar model to the weapon obtained by Leah, eventually emerged in Medicine Lodge as the property of Orville Post. Post was given the gun by his uncle, a blacksmith in Byron, Oklahoma, who received it in payment for a debt from an oldtimer who got it from a bank robber. Four notches were cut in each rubber grip, and on one grip is Wheeler's trademark: a wheel carved around a screw, which serves as the hub. To the right of the wheel are written the letters "ER" and the date "1882."[12]

Henry Brown's widow had a somewhat more substantial estate than that available to Alice Burton. Presumably she was allowed by Mrs. Burton's lawyer to dispose of Brown's horse. Brown's guns disappeared, although the famous gold-plated Winchester eventually surfaced. Reputedly the weapon was given to Barney O'Connor or Sheriff Rigg, but Maude Brown somehow regained it. Maude had become friends with P.J. and Mollie Foster, who recently had moved to the Caldwell area from Cripple Creek, and Maude relied heavily on the Fosters after Henry's death. Maude had no use for a pistol or rifle, and gave the guns to the Fosters, who migrated to Taylor, Texas. The revolver vanished but the engraved Winchester was quietly purchased by a collector in Waco. After many years in this superb private collection, the coveted Winchester was purchased by representatives of the Kansas State Historical society, and today it is on display in the State Museum in Topeka.

Maude Brown realized that she must rid herself of the debt she owed for the two lots and house which had been purchased for $900. There was a mortgage of $735 on the property, and Brown owed another note for $300. Levi Thrailkill and William Morris had co-signed the $300 note. Soon after Brown's death they approached the widow with a business proposition designed to release her from Brown's financial obligations. They would assume the $300 note, thus relieving her of the responsibility, and they would purchase her house and lots, allowing her to keep the furniture, household items, and milk cow. E.T. Battin, Dan Jones and J. R. Swartzel were appointed to appraise the estate. The items retained by Mrs. Brown were inventoried at $181, while the lots and house were listed at $800, "being more than three-fourths of the appraised value of said real property." Thrailkill and Morris, assuming the mortgage and $32 probate cost, paid $855.36 for the property. Maude Brown thus kept her household belongings, was freed from financial obligations, and received nearly $70 in cash."[14]

On this meager stake Maude prepared to move far from the scene of her humiliation. She offered her furniture for sale, advertising that she would "be at her residence" from nine until eleven in the mornings and from three until five in the afternoons, beginning Saturday, May 24. That Saturday night "Henry Brown's fine silver-bitted bridle was put up at a raffle at Horner's drug store." Later that summer, having raised as much money as possible, Maude left for Devil's Lake, Dakota Territory (her adoptive parents had moved to Dakota Territory in November 1882). She arrived there in August 1884, but found a fresh start difficult. Late in 1887 she was notified of the costs of the final settlement of the Brown estate. On Christmas Eve, 1887, she replied by letter that she was "wholly destitute" and requested that she be discharged as administratrix of the estate. Maude left Devil's Lake and attended a normal school in Indiana. In 1891 she moved to Frankfort, Indiana, serving for many years as a hospital superintendent. She had been a widow for half a century when she died in 1935.[15]

The death of Henry Brown signaled a halt to Caldwell's period of Wild West violence. Since the first year of its existence, Caldwell had been the site of shootouts and lynchings. During a period of a decade and a half, 1871 through 1885, nearly three dozen men died violently in and around Caldwell. Shootings or lynchings did not occur every week, or every month or, in the case of 1873, 1876 and 1878, even every year. But gunplay or extralegal hangings occurred often enough to brand Caldwell as "one of the worst towns in the country," according to cowboy Charles Colcord; "a fast and dangerous town" in the judgment of George Freeman; and Kansas newspaperman T.A. McNeal wrote that "Caldwell was the wildest town on the Kansas border."[16] Indeed, there was enough sustained frontier violence in Caldwell to rank it alongside bullet-riddled Dodge City or Abilene or any other Kansas cattle town, as well as with Tombstone in the early 1880s, Lincoln in the late 1870s, Tascosa during the 1880s, or El Paso during the 1890s.

Before his shameful end, Henry Brown provided a resolute style of law enforcement—spiced with a lethal hint of danger—that stopped saloon and street shootouts in Caldwell. Brown was a deadly, experienced shootist, skilled with revolvers and rifles, and prompt to pull a trigger. During the two years before Brown pinned on a badge, four former or current officers were shot dead in Caldwell. But no one shot Henry Brown in Caldwell. The only two men killed in Caldwell during Marshal Brown's tenure were shot by the marshal himself. Brown served a useful apprenticeship as assistant marshal under rugged Bat Carr, then he imposed his will and the city ordinances on Caldwell for more than sixteen months. No Caldwell city marshal had ever served longer than a few months, and Brown's lengthy term provided an unprecedented consistency that was instrumental in his success as a lawman.

After Marshal Brown shot Spotted Horse and Newt Boyce in 1883, there was virtually no more fatal gunplay in Caldwell. Late in 1884 a drunken cowboy was killed by Caldwell officers, a powerful statement that Brown's successors would brook no resumption of street violence. There would be one more lynching and, several years later, a fatal stabbing over a card game, but they proved to be isolated incidents—the final gasps of frontier violence in the Border Queen. Other factors were at work, including a successful temperance and anti-saloon movement, as well as the virtual disappearance of roistering cowboys. But it was the protracted, no-nonsense tenure of Caldwell's deadly outlaw marshal that ended gunfighting in one of the West's most violent towns.

Rest in Peace

1871 **George Peay**, shot by O'Bannon

1872 **William Manning**, shot by George Epps
Eugene Fielder, shot by Michael McCarty
Doc Anderson, shot by Michael McCarty
Michael McCarty, shot by Caldwell vigilante
John D. Lynch, hanged in Wellington by Caldwell vigilantes
Frank Moore and **James Harris**—cowboys shot each other just outside Caldwell
Cowboy, killed by another cowboy north of Caldwell
Tom Smith, lynched north of town

1874 **Bully Brooks**, **L. B. Hasbrouck**, and **Charley Smith**—lynched in Wellington, following mass arrests in and around Caldwell
Frederick Ricer, shot by L. L. Oliver
L. L. Oliver, lynched by Caldwell vigilantes

1875 **Henry Hopkins**, shot by Henry Colbert

1877 **Hiram Jones**, shot by Charles Lyons

1879 **Geo. Wood** and **Jake Adams**, shot by George Flatt and John Wilson

1880 **George Flatt**, assassinated
Frank Hunt, assassinated (in Red Light)

1881 **George Wood**, shot by Charlie Davis (in Red Light)
Mike Meagher, shot by Jim Talbot
George Spears, shot by W. N. Hubbell

1882 **Marshal George Brown** shot (in Red Light)

1883 **Spotted Horse**, shot by Henry Brown
Newt Boyce, shot by Henry Brown

1884 **Marshal Henry Brown**, lynched in Medicine Lodge
Deputy Ben Wheeler, lynched in Medicine Lodge
Deputy Sheriff Cash Hollister, slain near Hunnewell
Oscar Thomas, shot by Caldwell lawmen

1885 **Frank Noyes**, lynched by prohibitionists

1888 **Robert Sharp**, stabbed by Douglas Riggs

1891 **J. L. Tracey**, shot by W. O. Brooks

CHAPTER ELEVEN

The Cherokee Strip Live Stock Association

"The principal office and place of business of the corporation shall be at the city of Caldwell."
— Cherokee Strip Live Stock Association Charter and By-laws

Livestock associations provided a significant feature of the cattle frontier. Stockmen recognized the need to organize themselves against cattle thieves and to coordinate roundups and other ranching practices. Many of these associations were only county-wide or regional, but others were far larger and exercised great influence. By the 1880s the Wyoming Stock Growers Association, which traced its roots to 1871, had become the most powerful stockmen's association in the West. Also organized in the 1870s, the Texas and Southwestern Cattle Raisers Association steadily grew in membership and influence. The Colorado Stock Growers Association was founded in 1867, while the Montana Stock Growers Association was established in 1884. One of its members was Dakota rancher Theodore Roosevelt, whose cattle regularly crossed into Montana to graze. Roosevelt founded and served as president of the Little Missouri Stockmen's Association. During the 1890s Idaho cattlemen, irked with the encroachment of sheep, boldly organized the Izee Sheep Shooters, which unapologetically lived up to its name.

The Cherokee Strip Live Stock Association was unique among stockmen's organizations, and despite its brief existence was one of the most famous. William W. Savage, Jr., historian of the Association, concluded that even though short-lived, "the Cherokee Strip Live Stock Association achieved historical significance unsurpassed by surviving regional cattlemen's associations."[1]

This notable stockmen's organization was closely tied to Caldwell. The Cherokee Strip Live Stock Association headquartered in the Border Queen, with offices in the front suite on the second floor of the Stock Exchange Bank building. The Association's first president was prominent Caldwell cattleman Ben S. Miller. A majority of board members, as well as numerous other ranchers who belonged to the Association, also made their homes in Caldwell. Annual and semi-annual conventions of the Association, as well as board meetings, were held at the Border Queen. Cattlemen who attended these events were welcome guests at Caldwell's hotels, restaurants, and saloons. So were the railroad officials, cattle buyers, barbed wire salesmen, and out-of-work cowboys who also attended the meetings. The free-spending cattlemen—and their wives—who lived in Caldwell exerted an impact on the economy, as well as the social life, of the Border Queen. The Cherokee Strip Live Stock Association added measurably to the aura of Caldwell as a boss cattle town.

The term "Cherokee Strip" had a double use, and one of those uses came to be interchangeable with "Cherokee Outlet." The original Cherokee Strip resulted from an error in an early survey of the lands allotted to the Cherokee Nation. When the southern boundary of Kansas Territory later was surveyed, it was discovered that the Kansas line extended about two-and-a-half miles south of the earlier line. The original Cherokee Strip, therefore, was a long, narrow sliver of land extending from the Missouri boundary westward to the 100th meridian. The Cherokee Strip was 276 miles long and 2.46 miles wide, containing about 435,000 acres of Kansas land. The Cherokee Nation was compelled to cede the Strip by treaty in 1866, but in 1872 an act of Congress provided for sale of the land at $1.50 or $2.00 per acre. Money from these sales would be invested in five percent government bonds for the benefit of the Cherokee Nation.[2]

The Cherokee Outlet originated early in the nineteenth century, when Cherokee tribes were forced to move from their Southern homelands to the northeast corner of Indian Territory. The Cherokee Nation requested an outlet to hunting grounds in the West. The Cherokee Outlet extended to the 100th meridian and was sixty miles wide, north to south. But the Cherokee people settled into an agricultural existence as farmers and stockraisers, seldom venturing into the Outlet. In 1866 the federal government purchased from the Cherokee Nation large segments of the eastern Outlet as reservations for Osages, Pawnees, and several other tribes. (These transactions were made at the same time the Cherokee Strip cession was arranged).

After 1866, therefore, the Cherokee Outlet was reduced to a length of approximately 226 miles and a width slightly less than fifty-eight miles. The Cherokee Outlet encompassed more than six million acres of grassy plains and rolling hills. Four rivers, angling in a southeasterly direction, along with tributaries, provided water for Outlet livestock. From west to east, these major waterways were the North Fork of the Canadian, the Cimarron, the Salt Fork, and the Arkansas. Adequate rainfall nurtured an assortment of grasses across the Outlet.

Texas cattlemen discovered this excellent pasturage in 1867, when the Chisholm Trail was opened along the eastern third of the Outlet. A few years later Texas longhorns began to be herded toward Dodge City, across the west end of the Outlet along the Western Trail. When driven slowly across these grasslands, lanky longhorns usually gained weight before being delivered to market. The Cherokee Nation levied a tax of ten cents per head on cattle and horses through the Outlet. Later, this levy was increased, but collection from cattlemen always would be a problem.

During this period ranchers and cowboys began to refer to the Outlet as the Cherokee Strip. After the original Cherokee Strip was eliminated by treaty in 1866, the term "Cherokee Strip" came to be used interchangeably with "Cherokee Outlet."

"The Texas Trail Drivers had not failed to observe the fine quality of grass in the Indian Territory as they slowly grazed their herds from southern Texas to northern markets," reflected Cherokee Strip cowboy George Rainey. "When delayed by swollen streams or other causes, these cattlemen permitted their herds to scatter and fatten ... on the grass which cost them nothing." At shipping points such as Caldwell or Hunnewell, if further delays were caused by lack of stock cars or market conditions, "cattle were simply turned back into the Strip and pastured throughout the grazing season."[3]

The next development was inevitable. "From this it was but a step to grazing the herds in the Strip throughout the grazing season," explained Rainey. "For why, the cattlemen reasoned, should they make these long and toilsome drives when good or better range than that in Texas might be had free or nearly so? It was therefore not long until ranches began to be located in the Cherokee Strip and ere long the Strip began to take on the appearance of the ranges of Texas."[4]

By the late 1870s numerous herds grazed in the Outlet, and in 1878 the Cherokee Nation received permission from the federal government to assess and collect grazing fees. The next year L. B. Bell was appointed Special Tax Collector for the Cherokee Outlet. Bell and his assistants managed to collect $1,100 from about two dozen stockmen who declared 20,000 head of cattle. Thirty other ranchers avoided paying. These fifty-odd cattlemen employed a total of nearly 200 cowboys, and they erected corrals and headquarters buildings—mostly dugouts—on "their" Outlet grazing areas.[5]

With the number of cattlemen in the Outlet increasing rapidly, the Cherokee Nation recognized that their western lands could become a source of significant revenue. The capital of the Cherokee Nation was located at Tahlequah. There was a Principal Chief, a bicameral Cherokee Council, and a system of courts. Two diverse parties, the Union and the National, represented the politically sophisticated Cherokee people. For 1880 the Cherokee Nation intended to impose a grazing fee of fifty cents per head, in return issuing a receipt in the form of a grazier's license. The Treasurer of the Cherokee Nation, Major D.W. Lipe, personally visited the Outlet and collected a total of $7,620 in fees. While this amount was disappointing to Lipe and to Principal Chief Daniel W. Bushyhead, to cattlemen it was increasingly clear the question of grazing rights in the Strip must be confronted.[6]

George Rainey recalled that Outlet cattlemen "had for years maintained a loose sort of organization; rules had been laid down governing roundups, recognition of brands, and the extent of lands assigned to each of the several ranches.... A number of ranch owners met in Caldwell in March, 1881." There was a "Stock Convention" attended by more than a dozen cattlemen the following August in Anthony, twenty-five miles west and north of Caldwell. In October 1881 there was another meeting in Caldwell, along with a "Pool Meeting" of ranchers who intended to organize "a winter pool."[7]

Several adjoining ranches would form a pool of herds and cowboys. Dugout line camps were utilized throughout the win-

A ranch cabin in the Cherokee Strip.
—Courtesy Caldwell Historical Society

ter, and during the subsequent spring roundup participating herds were separated. But on September 1, 1881, a cattleman calling himself "Cow-puncher" published a letter to the editor of the *Post*, expressing in detail the growing sentiment of Outlet ranchers for a long-term lease with the Cherokee Nation. "With a ten-year lease holders could afford to fence their ranges and obviate the very serious evil of overstocking the range, a matter which so few seem to fully comprehend."

Even the one-year leases now being issued by the Cherokee Nation encouraged some ranchers to fence in their Outlet ranges. Fencing eliminated the need for line riders and allowed ranchers to cut their crews, which produced drastic reductions in wage expenses. Enclosed cattle would not scatter onto adjoining ranges, and herds would not become mixed. A number of ranchers took the precaution of placing their enclosed leases under the name of a Cherokee citizen, who provided his signature in return for a fee. But Cherokee Treasurer Lipe approved of fencing, feeling that enclosed herds made it easier for his tax collectors to accurately assess grazing fees.

Treasurer Lipe attended the stockmen's meeting in March 1881, and he opened a branch office in Caldwell, where he installed two Cherokee collection agents. Joseph G. McCoy was employed by the Cherokee Nation to assess the situation in the Strip, reporting to Principal Chief Bushyhead that it would be difficult to collect grazing fees from individual cattlemen, and recommending that a ten-year lease would greatly increase revenue to the Nation. George Rainey observed that "the cattlemen paid the head tax, but this according to their own reports as to the number of cattle grazed. No doubt these reports, or any of them, did not include the whole number of cattle owned." Although Lipe's efforts garnered more than $41,000 in grazing fees during 1882, it seemed clear that far more cattle were scattered across the vast expanse of the Outlet, and that an annual fee for the entire Outlet would place considerably more money in the Cherokee Treasury, with far less collection effort.[8]

In the first week of March 1882, Outlet cattlemen gathered in Caldwell for another Stockmen's Convention. The 1882 convention was a larger and more organized meeting than of the previous spring. Several newspapermen were in attendance, including Tell Walton of the *Caldwell Post* and W. H. Hutchison of the *Caldwell Commercial*, along with journalists from Hunnewell, Medicine Lodge, Kansas City, and other communities. Major Andrew Drumm, one of the earliest and most prominent of the Cherokee Strip ranchers, nominated Ben Miller of Caldwell "as

Whittlin' and Tradin'

In 1881 Ben Miller left his Circle Bar ranch in the care of a foreman and moved "to cattle headquarters at Caldwell," where he could "watch the market." He found Caldwell teeming with cattlemen and buyers who "were there with money and nothing would stop them. They paid the prices asked, in many instances accepting the count of the number of cattle from that of last fall's books."

Miller described Caldwell as "indeed a beehive," and Main Street featured a small but useful item of

(cont. next page)

President of the Association for the entire year" (even though "the Association" had not been formally organized). W. E. "Shorthorn" Campbell of Caldwell nominated John A. Blair of Caldwell as secretary. Campbell himself agreed to serve as one of the two vice-presidents.[9]

A year earlier each rancher or cattle company with herds in the Strip agreed to pay fifty cents each to publish a brand book, but for 1882 the assemblage voted to increase dues to one dollar. Detailed plans were made about the coming roundup. A resolution was passed establishing a "line of separation and quarantine between through cattle and wintered cattle." Quarantine pastures would keep trail herds from mixing with Outlet cattle, which lowered the chance of spreading "Texas fever." And although not recorded in newspaper accounts, there must have

Ben "Circle Bar" Miller, rancher, community leader, and president of the Cherokee Strip Live Stock Association.

—From the frontispiece of Miller's 1896 memoir, *Ranch Life in Southern Kansas and the Indian Territory*

been considerable discussion among the cattlemen in Caldwell about formalizing their organization and negotiating a long-term grazing lease for the Cherokee Strip. Indeed, by December 1882 the *Caldwell Post* speculated that an agreement would be negotiated by the next spring, and warned Outlet ranchers to stop arranging fencing contracts "with the citizens of the Cherokee Nation," which might complicate a larger ontract.[10]

Cherokee Strip cattlemen scheduled their next convention for March 6 and 7, 1883, in Caldwell's Danford Hall. Ben Miller chaired smaller, early meetings in January and February, when ranchers already were using the name "Cherokee Strip Live Stock Association." By 1883 about one hundred herds were being kept on Outlet ranges, and Caldwell was expecting at least a couple of hundred visitors for the convention. The *Post* anxiously conducted "an investigating tour" around town to determine "the number of stockmen and herders [who] could be comfortably grazed, rounded up and bedded down during next week at our hotels and restaurant." The Leland might squeeze in 135 guests "by a little hydraulic pressure," but the Southwestern was not yet open, and the town's other hostelries were small. Businessmen were planning to offer "a soft-sided plank and a blanket" if necessary.[11]

"The grand ball given annually by the citizens of Caldwell to the stockmen of the Cherokee Strip is billed for March 7," reported the *Kansas City Daily Journal*. "This is the annual social roundup sensation of Southern Kansas, and is always looked forward to with delight. The city reservoir is filled with champagne, and dry goods boxes filled with 25-cent cigars [are] placed at intervals of ten feet. It is a great occasion."[12]

Ben Miller called the open session to order on Tuesday, March 6. Minutes and the treasurer's report were read, and nearly sixty new members were introduced. For two days there were morning and afternoon sessions, capped off with the banquet and dance on Wednesday night.[13]

The most important business of the convention was approving the incorporation of the Cherokee Strip Live Stock Association. "The principal office and place of business of the corporation shall be at the city of Caldwell." Each member would pay the treasurer ten dollars per year. A three-man board of arbitration would be appointed "to settle old questions in dispute between members of this Association." Nine stockholders agreed to serve as directors, including five men "whose residence is Caldwell, Kansas": Ben S. Miller, Andrew Drumm, M. H. Bennett, A. J. Day, and Sol Tuttle. The other four directors

---

cattle town infrastructure. "The hotels, restaurants, outfitting stores and saloons provided benches outside, and there dozens and dozens of men sat and whittled and talked trade all day long and away into the night. . . . Very shortly the men would cut the softwood benches out from under them, and the citizens then put in hardwood seats and furnished a supply of pine expressly for the cattle dealers to cut into shavings."

From Miller, *Ranch Life*, 154-155.

★★★

were E. M. Hewins, E. W. Payne, Charles H. Eldred, and J. W. Hamilton. Curiously, the by-laws, which were published in the *Post*, did not provide for officers. But the board of directors elected Ben S. Miller president, "and at the same time appointed John A. Blair as secretary and M. H. Bennett as treasurer." All three of these officers made their home in Caldwell. The offices of secretary and treasurer would become salaried positions.[14]

"The stockmen were now in shape to effect a lease of the Cherokee Strip from the Cherokee Nation," explained the *Post* while reporting on the convention. Later in the spring of 1883 Chief Bushyhead called the Cherokee National Council into special session. Association directors Andrew Drumm and Charles Eldred journeyed to Tahlequah to represent their new organization in negotiations. In May 1883 a lease bill was hammered out, then passed by the National Council. As lessee, the Cherokee Strip Live Stock Association would rent the Outlet for five years at $100,000 annually (a little more than two cents per acre). The Association would deliver $50,000 to Tahlequah on April 1 and October 1 of each year.[15]

The Association's board of directors called a meeting for May 29, 1883, in Caldwell. Details had to be worked out by the ranching community, while Chief Bushyhead and Association lawyers developed a detailed lease. Bushyhead and Charles Eldred, who held power of attorney for the other directors, signed the lease on July 5, 1883. By that time there were between

Men of Caldwell enjoyed hunting in the Cherokee Strip. M. H. Bennett, treasurer of the Cherokee Strip Live Stock Association, reclines in the foreground. Sadly, Bennett died at 42 in 1890, about six years after this hunting trip.
—Courtesy Border Queen Museum, Caldwell

200,000 and 300,000 cattle grazing in the Strip, including strays from ranches in southern Kansas. More than 950 miles of fencing had been completed, and the other Outlet ranchers were hurrying to fence in their allotted ranges. A large quarantine grounds was established at the head of the Chisholm Trail south of Caldwell. Wide pathways were allotted for the Chisholm Trail and the Western Trail. Less wide pathways were established for the cutoff to Hunnewell, as well as for the army roads and a few other lesser trails. The military reservation at Camp Supply, in the western quarter of the Strip, was as large as the quarantine grounds. All of these allotments reduced the land available for leasing to a little more than five million acres. But every parcel was surveyed and assigned to one of just over one hundred members—individual ranchers or companies or pools—of the Cherokee Strip Live Stock Association.[16]

C. F. Hulbert and other Caldwell hardware merchants sold enormous amounts of barbed wire. "All wire set out by the manufacturers is of the best quality of steel, put up in snug, compact spools and well painted and Galvanized," advertised Hulbert. In May Tell Walton, consumed by the excitement generated throughout Caldwell by the flurry of recent events involving the new Association, sold his newspaper to become a "Live Stock Broker," dealing in cattle, horses, and "Ranch properties." The *Post* and *Commercial* soon merged to form the *Caldwell Journal*. With most of its advertising from the Association, especially pages and pages of cattle brands, or from ranch-related sources such as barbed wire, the *Journal* was a pro-cattleman newspaper. In January 1884, however, Tell Walton returned to his true profession as editor of the *Journal*, announcing that the publication would be enlarged and would be "a livestock journal."[17]

THE JOURNAL.

THURSDAY,   February 19, 1885

OFFICIAL PAPER OF THE CHEROKEE STRIP

LIVE STOCK ASSOCIATION.

TELL W. WALTON,   Editor.

The Caldwell Journal proclaimed itself the "Official Paper of the Cherokee Strip Live Stock Association."

The Protection of the City Marshal

The Caldwell Post of March 1, 1883, was full of news about the upcoming meeting of the Cherokee Strip Live Stock Association. One item contained a bitter irony that would not be revealed for a year.

"Hon. E. W. Payne, secretary Comanche County Pool, president of Medicine Valley Bank, editor and businessman of Barbour County Index, president Barbour County Stockmen's Association, etc. etc., of Medicine Lodge ... has engaged rooms at the Leland Hotel for the

(cont. next page)

next week." The popular T. A. McNeal of the Medicine Lodge Cressett also was expected. "We tender these two illustrious individuals the freedom of the city and the protection of the city marshal."

The city marshal was Henry Brown. Wylie Payne and T. A. McNeal were perfectly safe during their visit to Caldwell. But one year later Marshal Brown led a robbery attempt on the Medicine Valley Bank and murdered Payne, thereby costing Medicine Lodge its most prominent citizen and the Cherokee Strip Live Stock Association a key member.

★★★

The mayor of Caldwell when the Cherokee Strip Live Stock Association was organized was rancher A. M. Colson. A pioneer settler of the Caldwell area, Colson began raising livestock north of town, then became one of the first ranchers to graze a herd in the Cherokee Strip. He brought his bride to his Outlet ranch, about twenty-five miles southwest of Caldwell, where she gave birth to a daughter on March 3, 1874. Colson's cowboys called her "Fawnie" for a young fawn that wandered in and out of ranch headquarters. Fawnie Colson was regarded as "the first white child born in the Cherokee Strip," according to George Freeman and George Rainey and many other early settlers. Sadly, Mary Goldy Colson died in 1879. But the next year Colson was remarried to Mary Garretson, a widow who also had a daughter, Katie. Serving as mayor of Caldwell from 1882-1884, Colson boosted the formation of the Cherokee Strip Live Stock Association, and was an important committee member in the Association.[18]

Former cowboy Charlie Siringo prospered on Caldwell's Main Street during the boom stimulated by Association activities. He quit the range in order to stay at home with his teenaged bride, as well as with his mother. Siringo opened a tobacco and cigar stand in the fall of 1883, just a few months after the incorporation of the Cherokee Strip Live Stock Association. He enjoyed the patronage of ranchers and cowboys, including drovers with Texas trail herds and ranchmen from the Strip. Taking advantage of "unlimited" credit, "I rented an adjoining store room, and cut an archway between the two. In this I opened up an ice-cream and oyster parlor. Soon I had five clerks and attendants in my employ."[19]

From a tobacco factory Siringo ordered 10,000 nickel cigars with the label "Oklahoma Boomer Cigars," a reference to the homesteaders who were trying to settle on Oklahoma lands. He commissioned a large oil painting of a mounted cowboy who had roped a longhorn steer, with the sign " 'Oklahoma Boomer' Cigars at Charlie Siringo's." Siringo had the colorful painting "locked with iron chains to the overhead framework of the iron bridge" that now spanned Bluff Creek. Passing cowboys enjoyed taking potshots at the overhead sign. "The last time I saw it, about twenty years later, it was riddled with bullet holes." Siringo said that eventually he sold 100,000 Oklahoma Boomer Cigars.[20]

Siringo spent $150 for a wooden "Indian squaw" to place in front of the store, and he advertised freely in the *Journal*. He installed a soda fountain and he sold hot peanuts and apple cider, while his lunch stand featured "oysters in any style, ham and eggs, porter-house steak and red hot coffee." Encountering Shanghai Pierce, Siringo invited his old ranch boss to dinner. At the dinner table Shanghai "expressed surprise at my wearing suspenders instead of a silk sash. Here Mamie, my girl wife, confessed that she had burnt my silk sash."[21]

Brands of members of the Cherokee Strip Live Stock Association were published regularly during the 1880s.
—Courtesy Caldwell *Post*, May 10, 1883

The Cherokee Strip Live Stock Association   159

While Siringo had lost his cowboy sash, Caldwell had lost its Chisholm Trail traffic. After 1882 cattle prices fell steadily at the Chicago stockyards as overproduction across the West drove beef prices downward. Railroads were built into West Texas, rendering the long drives obsolete. In 1884 the Kansas legislature further tightened quarantine laws, ruling that no Texas cattle could be driven into the state except in December, January, and February, when it was too cold for the ticks that spread Tick

Fever, or Texas Fever. The last year of the Chisholm Trail was 1884, but for a few more years Caldwell remained a cattle railhead because of the Cherokee Strip Live Stock Association. For as long as they were permitted to remain in the Cherokee Strip, ranchers could ship their cattle out of Caldwell. Although the Chisholm Trail had closed, the Border Queen was still in the cattle business.

The "SECOND ANNUAL MEETING" of the Cherokee Strip Live Stock Association was held on Wednesday and Thursday, March 12 and 13, 1884. (Although there were meetings in 1881 and 1882, the Association, of course, was not incorporated until 1883). In Danford Hall at 10:30 on Wednesday morning, President Miller opened the convention with an address that was frequently interrupted by applause. Miller "congratulated the members of the Association and the cattlemen of the West in general upon the successful year just closed in their business," and he outlined the satisfactory and cordial "relation of the Association to the government of the Cherokee Nation and the United States."[22]

The two-day agenda was primarily devoted to the regular business of roundup organization, brand books, and committee reports (A. M. Colson, as usual, was appointed to two key committees). The nine directors were re-elected as a board by acclamation, and Secretary John A. Blair and Treasurer M. H. Bennett were returned to office. Ben Miller was re-elected to the presidency by the board. In addition to the customary banquet, Caldwell staged a stock show for the cattlemen. W. E. "Shorthorn" Campbell showed a dozen of his finest Herefords, as well as two thoroughbred race horses. Dr. W. A. Noble entered a pair of trotting horses, and two Clydesdales were shown, along with numerous other quality animals.

By the end of the meeting there was a general conviction that 1884 would be a banner year. "The Cherokee Strip will send something near 200,000 beeves to market this year," predicted Tell Walton with his customary optimism. The Santa Fe Railroad tore down their old stockyards in March and began erecting a larger and more efficient set of pens. Completed by May, the new "yards proper" measured 225 x 240 feet, with four loading chutes and an unloading platform. Four hundred yards to the southwest, and connected by a twelve-foot fenced alley, a set of holding pens extending 60 x 200 feet was built. The *Journal* proclaimed that "Caldwell can boast of having the best shipping yards in the state."[23]

The Santa Fe announced a shipping rate of $40 per car to

ship cattle—about two dozen per car—from Caldwell to Kansas City. By the end of November 2,885 cars of cattle and horses, totaling 54,855 head of stock, had been shipped out of Caldwell's stockyards from the Cherokee Strip ranges. About the same total had been sent out of Hunnewell and other shipping points. Prices were weak throughout the shipping season, and ranchers left many cattle on the range. Nevertheless, more than 100,000 cattle were shipped in 1884, producing over $3,000,000 in revenue.[24]

In September the Association conducted a semi-annual meeting, with only about forty members in attendance. There was merely a single session, on Monday afternoon, September 15. The principal issue was collecting the assessments for the October 1 payment of $50,000, but it also was necessary to select a board member to replace E. W. Payne, murdered a few months earlier at the hands of Henry Brown.[25]

Caldwell's dangerous reputation weighed on the mind of a

A. M. Colson, pioneer rancher, two-time mayor of Caldwell (1882-1884, 1901-1903), and prominent member of the Cherokee Strip Live Stock Association.
—From Freeman's *Midnight and Noonday*, facing p. 248

trail boss who led one of the last herds up the Chisholm Trail. Arriving in Caldwell in October 1884, he sold the herd for more than $14,000, which he was paid in currency. Worried about thieves and killers in notorious Caldwell, he stayed awake in his hotel room throughout a long night, "close herding" the cash. The next morning the exhausted trail driver "declared that he would rather herd a thousand cattle over night in a rain storm than their value in greenbacks in a Caldwell hotel."[26]

It was somehow fitting that in Caldwell the closing of the Chisholm Trail was punctuated by a fatal gunfight involving a drunken cowboy. Oscar Thomas, who worked for one of the big cattle companies in the Strip, came to Caldwell for a spree in November 1884. He spent a week in town, drinking and—in defiance of city ordinances—openly carrying a Colt .45 and a sheath knife. When his friends tried to persuade him to turn in his weapons, Thomas growled "that he would carry them if he wanted to, and that no man or officer could take them from him."[27]

Thomas was furious when he was refused credit at Witzelben & Key, a store at the corner of Sixth and Main. He returned several times to berate clerk Mack Killibrew. Thomas belligerently re-entered the store and stalked Killibrew at the rear of the building. Determined to take no more abuse, the clerk picked up an axe, but Mr. Witzelben seized it from him. When Thomas pulled his .45, Mack grappled for control of the revolver.

At that moment City Marshal John Phillips barged onto the scene. Tipped off about the trouble, Marshal Phillips approached Thomas with a drawn six-gun and ordered, "Throw up your hands!"

Thomas ignored the lawman, who repeated his order. The drunken cowboy instead tried to pull his gun. Phillips fired his Colt. The .45 slug struck Thomas on the left side of his breast and tore out near his spine. The wounded man dropped behind a counter and once more refused to raise his hands on the marshal's order.

Association headquarters were located in the front office suite on the second floor of the Stock Exchange Bank building. These rooms are unoccupied today. —Author photo

Assistant Marshal Bedford Wood entered the back door of the store and triggered a round from his Colt. The bullet ripped through the cowboy's head, "lacerating the brain in its course," according to Dr. Noble.

Carried to the jail, Thomas died the next morning. Justice of the Peace T.H.B. Ross conducted an inquest which exonerated the peace officers. The dead cowboy was buried in Caldwell's City Cemetery.

The winter of 1884-1885 was severe, but losses among the enclosed cattle of the Cherokee Strip were not serious. At the Association convention in Caldwell in March 1885, President Miller congratulated members of the organization "upon their good fortune in not having lost all their cattle during the past winter."[28]

In June a trailing firm, Wooten & Miller, brought 2,000 contracted steers from Texas up the Chisholm Trail. Wooten & Miller had delivered the first herd up the trail the previous year, but they were twenty days later in 1885, and few other Texas herds tried to go north during the 1885 season. In September more than a dozen Texas stockmen were indicted by a federal grand jury in Wichita "for bringing cattle from Texas in the northern part of Indian Territory," a law passed the previous winter by Congress.[29]

Western cattlemen were devastated by the ferocious winter of 1885-1886, but once again President Miller was able to inform the convention of March 1886 "that the reports concerning the cattle were all encouraging; that the cattle had fared much better than any one had expected them to."[30]

In 1887 the Rock Island Railroad built into Caldwell, connecting area ranchers with Chicago, the world's largest meat processing and market center. The first shipment to Chicago, shortly after completion of the Rock Island line into the Border Queen, was a "mammoth stock train composed of sixty-one cars, carrying 1,200 of the finest beeves ever shipped by the Cherokee Strip Live Stock Association, [which] fitly inaugurates the completion of the great Rock Island system to this point." It was a gala occasion in Caldwell, and most of the town came to the depot and stockyards to watch and cheer.[31]

At four in the morning on September 15, 1887, a train whistle split the night air to summon shippers and cowboys to the depot. Within less than half an hour everyone was aboard, and the train steamed south to the stockyards. "On arriving there," reported the *Journal*, "horses were saddled, and the bunches of cattle reposing on the prairie around were driven into the pens."

The cattle were loaded twenty-two to the car. The cars were thirty-four feet long, and the "floors were well littered with hay and sand to absorb all the refuse." Sol Tuttle of Caldwell had "the honor of penning the first car load of cattle." Tuttle had eight carloads consigned to Chicago, and another consignment to a Chicago firm was loaded by Colson & McAtee (A. M. Colson had partnered with Judge J. L. McAtee, attorney for the Association).

The first division of twenty cars was loaded by nine o'clock and returned to the depot, where "immense crowds" had gathered. "Each car was decorated with muslin, running its full length on both sides" and painted with mottos and "appropriate designs," such as "a cowboy on a firey [sic] mustang, throwing a lasso." One motto read: "From Caldwell, Kas., the gateway to Oklahoma and the Indian Territory, where grass is king." Another motto invited: "Come to Caldwell and take a hand, a jack pot awaits you." Yet another inscription was hopeful: "Wanted—a car load of grass widows and fair damsels."

Within half an hour the first train rolled north out of the station and was followed into the depot by the second section, which also was decorated. There were twenty stock cars, as well

Beginning in 1885, Association meetings were held in Caldwell's Grand Opera House. —Caldwell *Journal,* March 3, 1887

as the Pullman "San Francisco" for excursionists to Chicago, and a caboose for employees. Nearly a score of cattlemen boarded the Pullman, including A. M. Colson, J. L. McAtee, and Sol Tuttle. Caldwell newspapermen were on board, and so were the Rock Island division superintendent, the train master, and the stock agent. The third section of the train also carried twenty stock cars.

The decorations attracted attention at every village and town en route. One morning the train pulled into Davenport, Iowa. The three divisions arrived at nine o'clock, 10:45, and 11:20. Caldwell journalists left their Pullman car to distribute copies of the *Journal* and the *News* to members of the growing crowd. A *Davenport Times* reporter was impressed by the cattlemen and their colorfully decorated train, especially the sign on the Pullman car: "We are the cowboys you have heard so much about. We ship our beeves by the great Rock Island route." A *Times* article was headlined, "THE DECORATED TRAIN," and the ranchers were praised as "a jolly but courteous set of men [who] appeared very proud of their efforts."[32]

After reaching Chicago, the Kansas delegation visited the enormous Union Stock Yards, often called "the eighth wonder of the world." They were given a guided tour of Chicago, taken to a play starring the famous Lotta Crabtree, and treated to a champagne banquet at the Hotel Florence. The bill of fare was reproduced in a *Caldwell Journal* article entitled, "HIGH JINKS IN CHICAGO."[33]

As the 1887 shipping season neared its end, Caldwell had sent out thirty-three stock trains to Chicago or Kansas City. Some 528 stock cars had left the Caldwell yards, carrying a total of nearly 12,000 head, or nearly $300,000 in sales. All of these figures represented about one-third of the totals from the Cherokee Strip Live Stock Association Other shipping points, including Hunnewell, handled about two-thirds of Association cattle and horses. But even multiplied by three—36,000 cattle, $900,000 in sales—the 1887 totals were considerably lower than in earlier years of the Association.[34]

In 1888 Ben Miller finally stepped aside as Association president and was replaced by Ed Hewins. John A. Blair and M. H. Bennett remained in office as secretary and treasurer, although Bennett left the board. The most pressing issue facing the Association was the scheduled expiration of the five-year lease on October 1, 1888. Hewins reported to the spring convention, held in Caldwell during the first week of April, that a committee had worked through the winter at Tahlequah to obtain a

166 *Border Queen Caldwell*

new lease. Nothing had yet developed, but Hewins hoped that a special meeting of the Cherokee National Council might produce a contract.[35]

Indeed, Association representatives had been lobbying for a new lease for two years. The Association cause was staggered in December 1887, when Principal Chief Bushyhead was defeated in an acrimonious election by Joel B. Mayes. Bushyhead was an

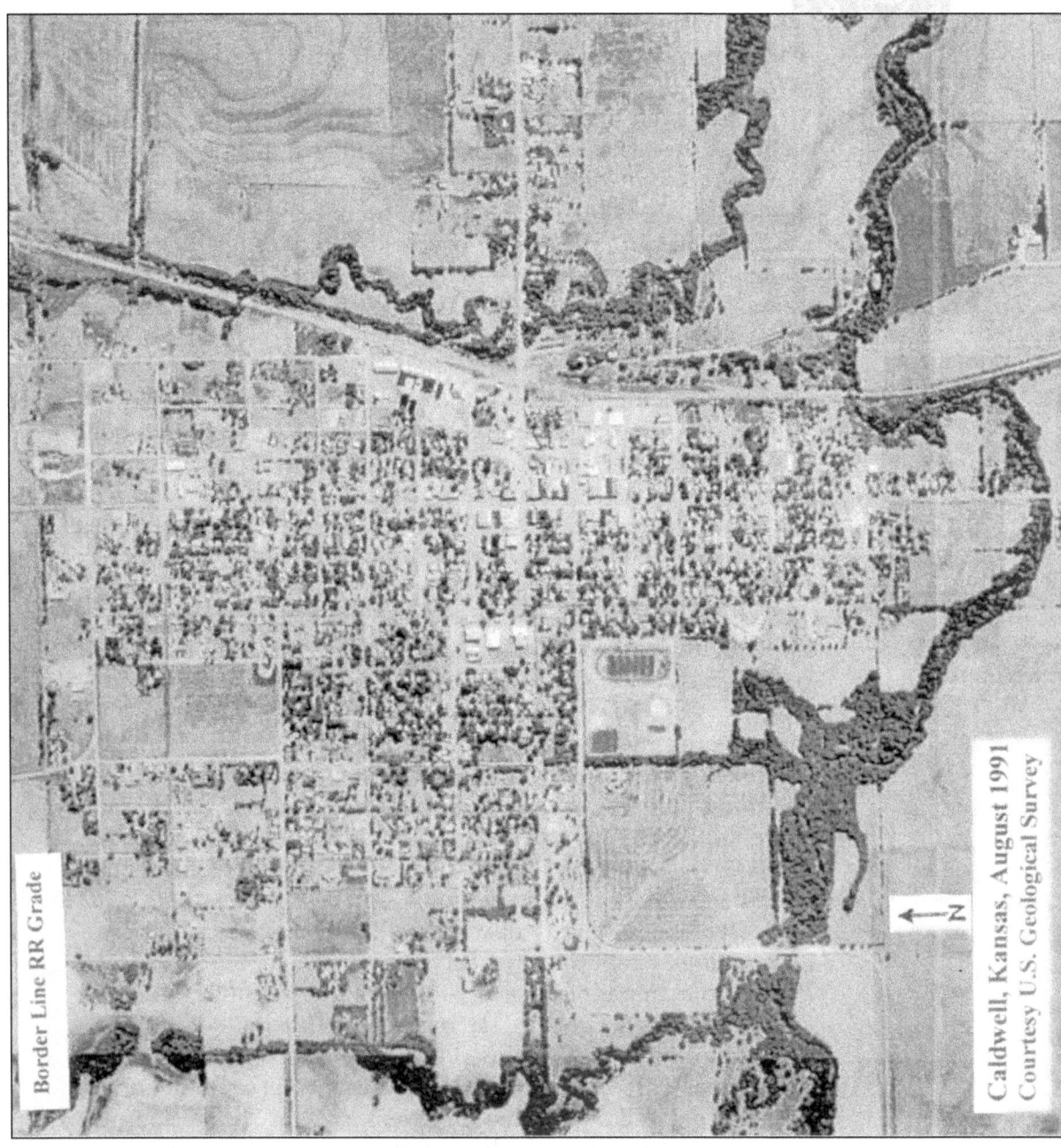

Caldwell, Kansas, August 1991
Courtesy U.S. Geological Survey

Border Line RR Grade

advocate of the Association, while Mayes—quite appropriately—sought to produce as much revenue as he could from the Outlet, and he became increasingly exasperated with the Association. The Association's representatives offered $125,000 annually for a five-year extension of the lease, but the new Principal Chief vetoed a bill to that effect. In July 1888 the Association raised its offer to $150,000 per year, but Chief Mayes

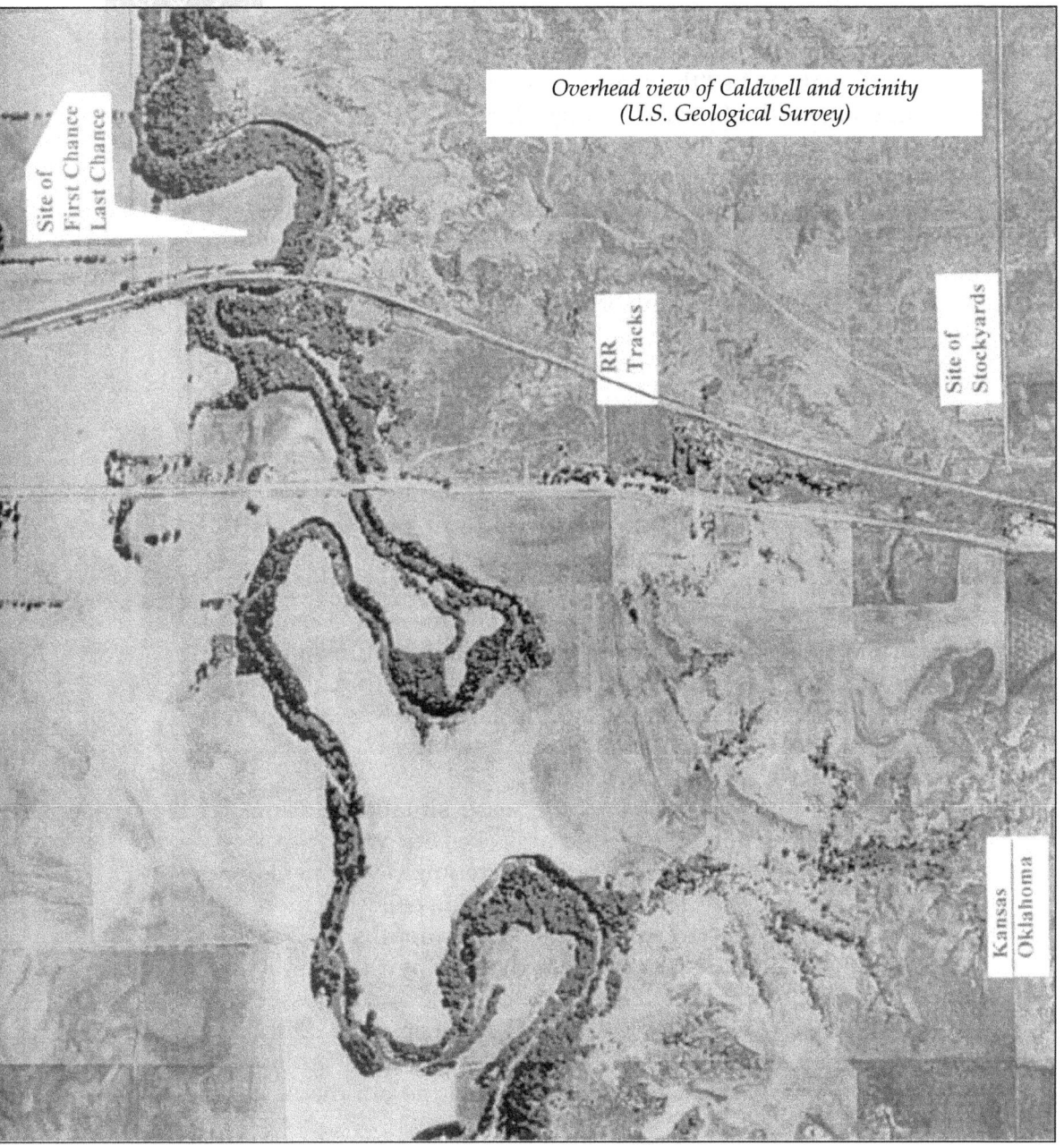

Overhead view of Caldwell and vicinity (U.S. Geological Survey)

revealed that two Texas firms recently had offered $160,000 and $175,000. When the Cherokee Strip Live Stock Association matched the $175,000 offer, the leading Texas company increased their bid to $185,000. And in September, on the eve of expiration of the original lease, Secretary of the Interior William Vilas informed Chief Mayes by letter that the federal government no longer would recognize lease agreements for the Outlet.[36]

In Caldwell on Tuesday, September 18, the Association held what was thought to be "their last semi-annual meeting" in the office suite above the Stock Exchange Bank. Although apparently attended only by the directors, officers, and a few other members, an Associated Press reporter was present. The chief question regarded the necessity of surrendering ranch improvements to the Cherokee Nation. "All this country is under fence. Every pasture has smaller pastures fenced in for horses, beeves, etc., making the total amount of improvements hard to estimate." But when the lease expired on October 1, no force moved into the Cherokee Strip to remove the cattlemen. So the herds stayed on their Outlet ranges, and the ranchers began to hope for a lease renewal when the Cherokee National Council met in November.[37]

On the next to the last day of October a number of prominent members of the Association met in Caldwell. Believing that the dislike by Chief Mayes for the Cherokee Strip Live Stock Association was a major barrier to the new lease, it was decided to disband and form a new organization. The meeting was adjourned, and all of the cattlemen boarded the evening train for Kansas City. The next day the South Western Grazers Association was chartered and Andrew Drumm was elected president. The new Association submitted an offer of $200,000 annually for a five-year lease.[38]

The National Council debated the lease situation during November, recalling how reliable the Cherokee Strip Live Stock Association had been at delivering their required payments. Meanwhile, the Cherokee Treasurer successfully collected more than $43,000 in grazing fees for the last three months of 1888. Reminded of their satisfactory relationship with the old Association, on December 3, 1888, the National Council passed a bill leasing the Outlet to the Cherokee Strip Live Stock Association at an annual fee of $200,000 for five years. Perhaps ready to settle the matter, Chief Mayes signed the bill the next day.[39]

With new life, the Association met in Caldwell on Monday

and Tuesday, December 17 and 18, 1888. "Mostly every member of the association was present, all of whom took an active interest in the proceedings." Shanghai Pierce came to town to be around his friends, and he was "the center of attraction." Sensing divine opportunity, Rev. O. E. Shank of Tahlequah made an appeal on behalf of his church and collected $150 from the cattlemen.[40]

Another large and enthusiastic crowd came to Caldwell for the spring meeting, on Monday and Tuesday, March 18 and 19, 1889. Cattlemen began to arrive on Saturday, and by Monday the Leland and Southwestern hotels were jammed. With a keen instinct for mending political fences, Principal Chief Mayes came to Caldwell. The convention assembled in the Grand Opera House, and after the minutes of the last meeting were read and approved, President Hewins introduced Chief Mayes. The Principal Chief assured the cattlemen "that they need have no fear about being removed" and that "he spoke for every Cherokee in the Nation."[41]

Following his address, Chief Mayes accepted questions which reflected the primary concerns of the cattlemen. The first question was about a government commission appointed by President Benjamin Harrison to negotiate the purchase of the Cherokee Outlet at a price of $1.25 per acre. "We will not sell for $1.25 per acre," emphatically declared the Chief. Another question was what would happen if soldiers arrived to remove the herds. "That will be an easy matter," replied Mayes, "serve an injunction on them." A third cattleman was worried about the "boomers" who hovered around the border trying to slip into the Outlet. The Chief intended to eject any boomers: "We will send Cherokee police to patrol the country and keep them out." With this resounding statement, Texas cattle baron A. J. Snider loudly moved that Chief Mayes be made an honorary member of the Association, and the motion carried unanimously. Chief Mayes offered heartfelt thanks and stated that "you can count on me as one of you."[42]

But Chief Mayes overestimated his power and influence. Half a century earlier the federal government forced the Cherokees to leave their Georgia homeland and move to Indian Territory. In 1866 the government compelled the cession of the original Cherokee Strip and the sale of considerable Outlet lands for reservations for other tribes. Now homesteaders clamored that the Cherokee Outlet be opened for settlement. On April 22, 1889, by proclamation of President Harrison, nearly two million acres south of the Outlet was opened to settlers, triggering a spectacular land rush. Also in 1889 the federal commission traveled to Tahlequah to "negotiate" the sale of the Outlet. It soon became clear that the Cherokee Nation had no choice but to sell the Outlet to the federal government for $1.25 per acre, despite the objection of Chief Mayes.

"As to the Outlet the Cherokee tenure is very feeble ...," admitted former Principal Chief Bushyhead in a lengthy explanation printed by the *Caldwell Journal* on October 10, 1889. "Unquestionably the outlet will be opened for settlement. Congress will see to that."

Later in the month Attorney General John W. Noble decreed that all cattle in the Outlet must be removed by June 1, 1890. The Cherokee Strip Live Stock Association protested to government officials and to Chief Mayes. There were 250,000 head of cattle in the Outlet. Such a number could not be relocated onto the overcrowded ranges of the West, and dumping a quarter of a million beeves onto the market would have ruinous consequences. Furthermore, the ranchers would be forced to forfeit fencing and other improvements worth an estimated $250,000.

Chief Mayes could do nothing. There would be no injunctions against the federal government, no bargaining over the sale price, no use of Cherokee police. He realized that "the Cherokees have not the warriors to withstand the United States soldiers, that day is gone." President Harrison pushed back the removal date to October 1, 1890, and later the cattlemen obtained another sixty-day extension, to December 1. By that time the cattle were being sold off—with the predicted depressing effect on the market—or, in the case of a few resourceful ranchers, driven to other ranges.[43]

The Caldwell stockyards enjoyed flurries of activity, handling many of the herds that were shipped to market. During a busy week in November 1890, the *Journal* nostalgically reported that Caldwell "looked like the old days ... The town was full of cow-boys." In the Strip, as cattlemen abandoned their lease ranges, Oklahoma settlers "swooped down upon the wire fences ... and hauled away all the material they could get on their wagons." A gang of rustlers stole cattle—as many as one thousand head through the summer of 1890—to supply meat markets in booming Guthrie, Oklahoma Territory, settled in the Land Rush of 1889.[44]

Some Outlet ranchers ignored the December 1 deadline and kept herds in the Strip during 1891. Principal Chief Mayes demanded the $200,000 fee from the Cherokee Strip Live Stock Association, but most members no longer supported the organization. On Saturday, July 11, 1891, Treasurer John Nyce was in the Association offices in the Stock Exchange Bank building. The county sheriff and another man from Wellington, Charles Gambril, entered the office. Sheriff Morse served papers that Gambril had been appointed receiver of the Association, upon petition of Chief Mayes. Association records were collected, and the Cherokee Nation filed a lawsuit in the District Court at Wellington. On the same day that Sheriff Morse marched upstairs at the Stock Exchange Bank, four companies of U.S. Cavalry swept into the Outlet and began rounding up cattle; "several thousand head were found and a number of cow boys were arrested."[45]

In December 1891 the Cherokee Nation consented to sell the Outlet for $8,595,736.12. "The Outlet no longer existed," explained Association historian William W. Savage, "nor did the Cherokee Strip Live Stock Association." The lawsuit dragged on until March 24, 1893, when the court ruled that the original lease was in violation of federal law and was not binding on either party. The suit was dismissed, although attorney John L. McAtee attempted through the courts to obtain his legal fees from a cattlemen's association that no longer had members or offices or funds.[46]

With the demise of the Cherokee Strip Live Stock Association, Caldwell ceased to be a cattle town. The Chisholm Trail had put Caldwell on the map of the cattle frontier, first as a wild trail town, then as a railhead—successor to Abilene and Newton and Wichita. But by the time the famous trail closed, the Cherokee Strip Live Stock Association was in its prime. For several more years cattlemen and cowboys continued to be a familiar part of the Caldwell scene, while the stockyards handled one herd after another. And even though the ranchers and cowboys finally were replaced in Caldwell by wheat farmers, even though the stockyards were torn down and the saloons closed, the Border Queen soon would experience one more spectacular Wild West adventure.

CHAPTER TWELVE

Life in the Border Queen

"The bevy of soiled doves formerly inhabiting the second story of one of the Main Street business blocks were invited to leave the city. They went. There are a few more that could be spared."
—Caldwell *Journal*, April 23, 1885

They were the pride of Caldwell, and nearly half the community jammed the Grand Opera House to honor them. Two "young gentlemen" dressed in dark suits and ties and six "young ladies" attired in "fleecy white dresses" were the subjects of an unprecedented event that brought a sense of urban accomplishment to the Border Queen. The *Journal* reported that "every seat in the opera house was occupied last night, the first annual commencement of the Caldwell high school."[1]

This memorable event commanded Caldwell's attention on Tuesday evening, May 25, 1887. The big stage at the Grand Opera House was decorated with "a cheery display" of blossoming plants, hanging baskets, statuary, "and a large flag with vivid stars and stripes." Seated onstage were Professor C. M. Kingsley, Caldwell's school superintendent, Mayor George Snelling, the county school superintendent, two preachers, other prominent citizens, and the eight graduates: Clara Bates, Walter Donaldson, Lucy Elsfelder, Lizzie Kelpatrick, Belle Lovell, Bertha Meloy, James Rhodes, and Ada Rowen. There was musical entertainment, as well as the valedictory and salutatory addresses, and other graduates delivered an oration or an essay. Throughout the program "the applause was frequent and prolonged, and the floral offerings were generously bestowed upon the class, individually and collectively."

In 1887 there were fewer than 2,500 high schools in the entire United States, and the Census of 1890 revealed that less than seven percent of young Americans between the ages of fourteen and seventeen remained in school. Late in the nineteenth century most boys and girls left school after a few elementary years. A high school diploma was a rare achievement, and commencement exercises indicated that a town "is a commonwealth of refined, educated and industrious people," according to the *Journal*. "One of the most characteristic signs of a high state of civilization is the interest or disinterest manifested in education," stated the *Journal* on the occasion of Caldwell's second commencement, in May 1888.[2]

Advancing toward "a high state of civilization" in 1885, Caldwell's school board erected a fence around the school grounds in order to keep out cattle that often wandered loose around town. The outhouses were improved, and the school well was cleaned out, "Several old hats, handkerchiefs, etc., were taken out in a rather advanced state of decomposition," reported the *Journal*. "The water was very foul, and would in time have been the cause of much sickness."[3]

In the fall of 1885, 465 students enrolled in grades one through six and in the high school department. The largest enrollments were in the first and second grades, with eighty-five and eighty-three pupils respectively. An average of seventy students crowded into the first-grade classroom each day, and the second-grade teacher also had to deal with an average of seventy pupils daily. Forty-three students were enrolled in the high school department, where Miss May Vasey taught alongside whoever the male superintendent was from year to year. Caldwell's busy mothers sometimes sent pre-school children off to class with older sisters and brothers, a babysitting practice that was publicly discouraged.[4] Elementary teachers today would shudder at the prospect of a classroom crammed with seventy pupils, plus a few toddlers.

As Caldwell grew, overcrowding continued to be a major

The children filling this yard also filled the eight rooms of Caldwell's brick school.
—Courtesy Caldwell Historical Society

school problem. In 1887 a school census of the Caldwell district revealed 330 boys and 330 girls. With the brick school at capacity, it was necessary to rent extra space in the commercial district. C. M. Kingsley was employed as superintendent in 1887, and he guided the first four graduating classes. Prof. Kingsley was paid $1,000 per year, while Miss Vasey received $50 monthly. During the second commencement in 1888, the Class of '87 sat onstage, and early graduates soon formed an alumni association. When Sam P. Ridings (Class of '90) returned to Caldwell as an attorney in 1893, he became president of the alumni association.[5]

The Grand Opera House, where the annual high school commencement was held, was Caldwell's most imposing building. Caldwell's first opera house was the long, second-floor hall above commercial space in the Danford Building. But the stage and stageworks at Danford Hall were not up to professional standards. With Caldwell in its heyday as a cattle town, cattlemen and progressive businessmen saw the need for a "Grand Opera House" to serve not only as an expanded center for entertainment, but as a civic auditorium worthy of a city on the grow.

Men who envisioned this project called for a meeting to be held at the offices of the Cherokee Strip Live Stock Association on Friday afternoon, February 1, 1884, a meeting which was carried over to Saturday. A "joint stock company for the erection and maintenance of an opera house in this city" was organized.

Caldwell High School graduated its first class of seniors in 1887.
—Courtesy Border Queen Museum

Cattleman W. E. Malaley agreed to serve as president, and fellow Strip rancher Ben Miller would be vice-president of the Caldwell Opera House Company. A building committee was appointed, along with another three-man committee "to solicit subscriptions to the capital stock." Capital stock was authorized for $16,000, divided into 640 shares of $25 each. Thirty-three men promptly pledged four to forty shares apiece, for a total of $9,400. Subscribers included local businessmen (H. C. Unsell and Carey Lumber Co., twenty shares apiece) and ranchers (Malaley, forty shares; Miller, ten shares; Sol Tuttle, ten shares; John Blair, four shares). Treasurer John Dobson (forty shares — $1,000) was assigned to visit opera houses at Wichita, Newton, Emporia and Leavenworth, then bring back the information to the building committee, of which he was a member. A site was desired on the west side of Main Street "at the extreme southern portion" of the commercial district.[6]

Astoundingly, a rival faction of "north-enders" promptly proposed to build an opera house for the north end of the business district, across Main Street from the Southwestern Hotel. Cattle town historian Robert Dykstra discussed a Main Street competition between north-enders and south-enders, even though Caldwell's commercial section was barely three blocks in length. By 1884 there was a three-story brick hotel and a bank in each end of the commercial district, and there was jockeying for city political positions between the two factions. When an opera house was announced for the south end of town, "A few of the more volatile north-enders immediately announced plans to build a rival opera house," explained Dykstra. "Economic sanity prevailed over factional rivalry, however, and only the first project actually came to fruition."[7]

The officers and committee members of the Caldwell Opera House Company were men of action who were accustomed to getting things done. The proposed site was acquired, and John Dobson took charge of construction, lining up a foreman, carpenters, masons, mechanics, plasterers, and building materials. The walls were up by July, the iron furnace was set in place, and in August the roof was completed.

The big auditorium included a full balcony, with total seating for 1,200. Beginning in November 1885 the basement was opened as a skating rink, and also would be used for dances, church fairs, and other community events. The auditorium was not yet finished. Gas lighting was ready in December, and stage scenery and equipment arrived in January 1885. Shortly thereafter the Templeton Opera Company opened the Grand Opera

House, providing Caldwell an occasion that "will ever be remembered as a red letter day." The new facility was "the finest opera House in the West," according to a visiting journalist.

The Grand Opera House opened in 1885. This imposing structure could seat 1,200 in the auditorium and balcony, and the basement boasted a skating rink.
—Courtesy Caldwell Historical Society

Stage and apron of the Grand Opera House.
—Courtesy Caldwell Historical Society

"The audience was as well and fashionably dressed as any place in Kansas could present."[8]

After the new wore off, however, crowds at the Grand Opera House dropped drastically. With a population of no more than 2,000, Caldwell would seldom produce audiences of profitable size. "We were sorry to see so poor a house at the Grand Tuesday evening to greet the Chicago Comedy Co.," lamented the *Journal* in December 1886. In October 1887 the New York Opera Company played to a house that barely exceeded 100 patrons, and they left town rather than complete their engagement before "empty chairs" the next night. In August 1889 a married couple, singer Frank May and his wife, a pianist, put on an excellent musical performance, but "the audience was exceedingly thin." First-class troupes seldom came to Caldwell.[9]

Beginning in 1887, the Grand Opera House would enjoy a rare packed crowd each May with high school commencement exercises. Local talent became the only way to attract a large audience. On Saturday, March 16, 1889, the school secured the Grand Opera House to exhibit the efforts of the music program taught by Prof. Holmes. More than 600 schoolchildren were maneuvered on and off the stage, and predictably mothers and fathers turned out in large numbers. "The opera house was jammed full of people." On the night after Christmas in 1891, A. M. Colson starred in the title role of *The Vagabond* and "kept the audience in one continual round of merriment." Caldwell's amateur thespians enjoyed "a good sized audience." The next year Mr. and Mrs. E. W. House, private music teachers in Caldwell, brought their pupils to the Grand Opera House. The performance was "well advertised and a splendid audience greeted them ..., which testified eloquently for the interest which our people take in home talent entertainments."[10]

Caldwell responded in greater numbers to less sophisticated entertainments than opera companies and theatrical troupes. A Wild West show arrived in June 1886 and played "to a packed tent, both in the afternoon and evening. In the first performance there was scarcely standing room, while in the evening nearly every seat was taken." The next year another Wild West show came to Caldwell, parading down Main Street before enthralling an enthusiastic audience that afternoon with "31 elegant Arabian horses," a re-enactment of the Custer Massacre, and "California Frank riding Texas steers and wild and wooly horses." These and other acts "drew forth loud applause from the audience."[11]

The Fourth of July continued to attract enormous crowds to Caldwell. In 1883 "a grand barbecue" was staged for cowboys who attended the festivities. Rancher Ben Miller and rancher-mayor A. M. Colson were appointed, respectively, "President of the Day" and "Marshal of the Day." It was estimated that 5,000 visitors came to Caldwell on the Fourth. In 1884 Caldwell's new Driving Park—soon converted to a fair grounds—was officially opened on the Fourth, and activities from races to fireworks to cowboy events were moved to the grandstand and grounds outside town. Charlie Siringo opened a booth in 1884 and 1885, while competing in cowboy events both years. (The retired cowboy did not compete successfully in 1884, but the next year he won a gold ring for his young wife.) On the Fourth of July in 1885, the Caldwell Journal Association beat the Wellington Clippers, 7-4, at a diamond laid out at the Fair Grounds, while there was a ball that night at the skating rink in the Grand Opera House. The Independence Day celebration of 1886 began early in the morning, with a brass band playing "from the hurricane deck of the Grand Opera House." The reputation of Caldwell's Fourth festivities had spread, and more than 8,000 people crowded the streets of the Border Queen.[12]

In March 1885 Charlie and Mamie Siringo became the parents of a baby girl, Viola. By this time Charlie was writing about his experiences as a cowboy. The manuscript was completed by the fall, and in September he sold his flourishing business to

A local production on the stage of the Grand Opera House.
—Courtesy Caldwell Historical Society

W.A. Sturm. Siringo now could finance his book, engaging a Chicago publishing company. A limited edition was published in December: *A Texas Cow Boy, or, Fifteen Years on the Hurricane Deck of a Spanish Pony.* The *Journal* alerted prospective readers that the book would cost one dollar "and will be sold only by subscription." The first autobiography of a cowboy, the book was lively and filled with fascinating incidents, as well as with Siringo's encounters with such famous Westerners as Shanghai Pierce and Billy the Kid.[13]

Early in 1886 Siringo moved his family to Chicago to supervise a reprint of *A Texas Cow Boy.* Soon he became a Pinkerton detective, and through the years other autobiographical books were written about his two fascinating careers. Not only did Siringo launch his remarkable efforts as an author in Caldwell—

Outdoor entertainments — an occasional circus or Wild West Show–were popular in Caldwell. —Caldwell *Journal*, August 4, 1892

Caldwell in the mid-1880s, looking northwest. The large brick building at right center was the new Opera House at the south end of the business district. The new school is visible in the background at left.
—Courtesy Kansas State Historical Society, Topeka

during his Caldwell years he became acquainted with another Texas trail driver who would develop into a noted cowboy writer. Andy Adams was in and out of Caldwell during the 1880s and sometimes was mentioned in the newspapers. ("Andy Adams shipped two car loads of horses to Nebraska Tuesday morning.") Influenced by his friend Siringo, Adams eventually began writing. Many of his early short stories featured Caldwell or the Cherokee Strip Live Stock Association, subjects to which he would periodically return.[14]

Emulating Charles Siringo, Caldwell pioneer George Freeman decided to write the exciting story of the Border Queen and sell his book by subscription. Freeman entitled his book *Midnight and Noonday*, explaining in the preface: "I give the reader deeds of crime and dark deeds of horror as 'Midnight' and the beautiful country of the plains and the grand 'Queen of the Border' as they are seen today, as 'Noonday.'" The title page is filled with subtitles, ending with "Incidents Happening in and Around Caldwell, Kansas, From 1871 Until 1890." Like Siringo, Freeman journeyed to Chicago to find a publisher, and the first edition was released in 1890. Two years later Freeman produced an improved edition and went door to door, then town to town selling copies. *Midnight and Noonday* is an invaluable memoir of early Caldwell.[15]

Ben Miller soon added his own autobiographical impressions. A native of New York State, Miller was attracted to the range cattle business in 1878. Miller and a couple of partners began stocking a range adjacent to the Kansas line in the Cherokee Strip. The Circle Bar ranch was forty-five miles west of Caldwell, where the partners went for supplies. The Caldwell newspapers sometimes referred to him as Ben "Circle Bar" Miller. By 1881 Miller had sole control of the Circle Bar and, like other Strip ranchers, moved to Caldwell. Also in 1881 Miller was elected president of the fledgling Cherokee Strip Live Stock Association, and in November he went back East to marry Josephine Bowen. Miller prospered and the family traveled, spending the winter of 1885-86 in sunny California. When ranching ended in the Strip the Millers moved to Oklahoma City, but Ben enjoyed visiting "his host of friends" in Caldwell. He wrote *Ranch Life in Southern Kansas and the Indian Territory, As told by a Novice, How a Fortune was Made in Cattle*. Covering his adventures from 1878 through 1881, *Ranch Life* contains numerous references to Caldwell. Miller published his book in 1896.[16]

Another community leader also found a bride in the East. In 1882 Asa Overall imported from Pennsylvania the twenty-two-

MIDNIGHT AND NOONDAY

OR

THE INCIDENTAL HISTORY OF
SOUTHERN KANSAS AND THE
INDIAN TERRITORY,

GIVING TWENTY YEARS EXPERIENCE ON THE FRONTIER; ALSO
THE MURDER OF PAT. HENNESEY, AND THE HANGING
OF TOM. SMITH, AT RYLAND'S FORD, AND
FACTS CONCERNING THE

TALBOT RAID ON CALDWELL.

ALSO THE

DEATH DEALING CAREER OF McCARTY

AND

INCIDENTS HAPPENING IN AND AROUND CALDWELL, KANSAS,
FROM 1871 UNTIL 1890.

BY
G. D. FREEMAN, CALDWELL, KANSAS,
1892.

The title page to G. D. Freeman's 1892 book about Caldwell.

year-old sister of cattleman John Nyce. The couple wed in Caldwell, and three years later welcomed a son, Monroe. But the new mother soon began suffering from consumption, and although Asa sought medical help in a number of cities, she died in 1887. Her husband and brother took her back to Pennsylvania for burial, then Asa placed his two-year-old son with his mother in Cameron Junction, Missouri. The next year, although only forty, Asa was stricken with a sudden illness while visiting Cameron Springs, and he died there the next month. Overall had arrived in Caldwell as an ambitious young man of twenty-three, and he had been a key member of the community for seventeen years. "He came here a poor boy," eulogized the *Journal*, "but through his untiring energy he had amassed quite a neat fortune."[17]

Caldwell already had lost another early settler who played a prominent role in civic affairs. T.H.B. "Bent" Ross came to Caldwell in 1873. He engaged in numerous business enterprises and immersed himself in community activities. He served as school board secretary for nearly a decade, was a justice of the peace and police judge, and belonged to the Odd Fellows and the G.A.R. Ross rented the basement of the new Grand Opera House as a skating rink. He brought in "the famous light-weight skater, Master Willie Sidney," and he staged dances on the rink floor. But early in 1885 Ross developed an abscess over his jugular vein, and he died within a couple of weeks. The *Journal* understood the impact of his loss: "Caldwell, in the death of Judge Ross, loses one of her most enterprising and valuable citizens and one that will be hard to replace."[18]

Moving into the vacuum of community leadership was S. H. "Harve" Horner. Horner came to Caldwell in 1879, opened the City Drug Store, and became involved in civic activities. Considered "one of our most enterprising citizens," Horner built a handsome new commercial structure in 1887. The *Journal* sent a reporter: "to say that the interior is gorgeous would be but faintly expressing it." Later Horner set up a phonograph with "a huge funnel," and gave "daily free concerts to all who go into his drug store."[19]

Soon after moving into his new store, Horner and his wife had a baby daughter. Also in 1887 Horner was asked to take over the city's troubled water works system. Constructed in 1886, Caldwell's water works suffered problems from the beginning, and went into receivership in 1887. Horner was "the unanimous choice of all parties" to become receiver and, assuming the superintendency, he worked for years to put the system on a functioning and profitable basis. In 1889 Horner took over another unsuccessful Caldwell enterprise, leasing the Grand Opera House and attempting to attract quality acts to the Border Queen. "Fireworks and considerable shouting" celebrated Horner's election as mayor in 1891. The popular and progressive Caldwell leader was re-elected mayor, and later was sent to the state legislature.[20]

Longtime community leader A. M. Colson, although a busy and successful rancher, continued to serve Caldwell. Not long after leaving the mayor's office he leased and, for a time, managed the Southwestern Hotel. Colson also served as president of a new financial institution, the Citizens Bank of Caldwell. His daughter, Fawnie, went through Caldwell schools, and, with "a host of friends, both young and old," was a favorite around town. Like many other Caldwell females, Fawnie enjoyed horseback riding, but she "met with a very painful accident" early in 1888. She was thrown to the ground when her mount stumbled, then further injured when her horse fell on her. "Her right limb was severely fractured close to the ankle, and two teeth were knocked out, besides bruising her severely all over."[21]

Horse wrecks were part of life in Caldwell.

Caldwell druggist S. H. Horner served as mayor and was elected to the Kansas Legislature. His ads in the Journal mixed business and politics.

Like Westerners everywhere, many Caldwell men rode horseback, along with more than a few ladies and children. In addition to saddle horses, horse-drawn vehicles plied the unpaved—and dung-strewn—streets of Caldwell, and there were oxen and mules as well. There were freight wagons, chuck wagons, buggies, carriages, and other light private vehicles. Even horses with placid temperaments can be startled in a stampede, while other equines with an ornery streak are constantly on the lookout for an excuse to bolt. The legions of dogs that prowled the town and often howled through the night sometimes yapped at the heels of the larger beasts, while gusts of wind could send scraps of paper whipping in front of the horses. Runaways often erupted in the streets of Caldwell, with bruises and broken bones and wrecked vehicles the inevitable result. Horse travelers—like Fawnie Colson—were in constant peril.

Caldwell newspapers reported numerous runaways. In October 1880, for example, the horse of a local milkman bolted, creating "a first-class run-away..., which deposited his spring wagon in front of Dimke's blacksmith shop, sadly in need of repairs." The next month, in early November, there was a one-horse runaway. Before November ended a "little horse and mule matinee" amused Main Street spectators. "The horse and mule performed on a lumber wagon, and succeeded in breaking the tongue, tangling harnesses, and giving the owner's pocketbook the sweany [sic—"sweeny" was a slang term for atrophy]."[22]

In October 1882 "little Lem Manning was riding down

Caldwell's Great Western Band in 1892
—Courtesy Caldwell Historical Society

> **Side by Side**
>
> On Wednesday, January 25, 1888, four-year-old Walter Spiker died at the home of his grandparents on Second Street. Bereavement in the house was intensified because Walter's grandmother, Mrs. Susan Spiker, lay dying in anther room. Susan was fifty-seven, the wife of Jefferson Spiker and the mother of eleven children.
>
> The Spiker family came to Caldwell during the boom of 1879. "She was a kind and indulgent mother, her whole pleasure being centered on the care and welfare of her family,"
>
> *(cont. next page)*

Market Street" when he was thrown. "His foot catching in the stirrup, he was drug some eight or ten rods, the horse going at full speed." Miraculously, the boy suffered only bruises. In September 1884 a young man named Mitchell, whose team recently had stampeded, was driving away from the depot when the horses again spooked. "A bit broke and then the fun began. They slid across the open block east of the Star stable and ran up Sixth street to big George's stable, where they telescoped Major Drumm's ranch buggy. In less than three seconds there was one heap of ruins, made up of two buggies, two ponies, one man and several pieces of harness piled up in reckless profusion. Mitchell sustained a sprained ankle, the ponies several bruises, the harness a total wreck, Major Drumm's buggy three wheels with never a spoke left in, the top looking like the skeleton of last year's hoop skirt."[23]

The next year, in May 1885, Frank Hood rented a team and buggy from a livery stable and was driving with a female companion when the wagon tongue broke. "The team skipped out at a forty-mile gait up Main street with the buggy bouncing around from one sidewalk to the other. The buggy turned bottom side up at the Southwestern Hotel corner." The occupants were spilled onto the ground, while the horses "took a turn around town," then returned to the livery stable, hungry from their exercise.[24]

"A lively run away" exploded on Caldwell's streets in November 1889. "A buggy was made into kindling wood in a very few moments." On a September night in 1891, "A team belonging to the Bartholomew boys got frightened at something ... and started down Main street at break-neck speed." At Fifth Street the horses wheeled to the west, while the Bartholomew brothers leaped desperately from the careening vehicle.[25]

The following year, on a Saturday morning in April 1892, "a grey team, hitched to a wagon," caused "quite a sensation." The town teemed with the usual Saturday crowd of farmers when the runaways barreled up Fifth Street toward Main. "They upset the wagon opposite Hoffman's bakery, left the hind wheels at the corner by Dill & Keeling's office, then dashed towards the west side of Main, striking a buggy and twisting the hind wheels, then dashed down Main Street strewing the remains of the wreck all about till finally they freed themselves of the entire wagon."[26]

There are a great many other variations on these vehicle accidents in newspapers of the era. And in the fall of 1893, with thousands of Oklahoma Boomers in and around Caldwell, there was a predictable jump in the number of runaways. But while there were many bruises and occasional broken bones, there were no fatalities. Although from time to time there were fatalities from gun and rail yard accidents, somehow no one died in the dozens of Caldwell horse wrecks.

While no one was killed in scores of runaways, a heart-breaking element of life in Caldwell was the frequent death of babies and children. Infant and child mortality during the nineteenth century was commonplace everywhere, and Caldwell was no exception. After Caldwell became large enough to support a weekly newspaper, all too many issues reported the sad news of the death of at least one child in the community. Rev. and Mrs. J. B. Rideout lost two children while ministering to the souls of Caldwell during the 1870s. Nearly two decades later Superintendent of Schools J. F. Clark and his wife lost a daughter, Jennie. Their youngest son, twelve-year-old Johnnie, "said he did not see how he could live without Jennie," according to the *Caldwell News*. "He had been in feeble health for several weeks and he gave up completely on the death of his sister." On Friday, March 18, 1892, two days after Jennie was buried in the City Cemetery, Johnnie Clark died at the family home. In between the devastating losses of the Rideouts and the Clarks, one set of Caldwell parents after another suffered the heartbreaking loss of a child.[27]

A handful of other fatalities suggested the years "when Hell was in session in Caldwell." On Saturday morning, October 18, 1884, veteran lawman Cash Hollister was shot dead while part of a posse attempting to make an arrest near Hunnewell. The thirty-nine-year-old Hollister was a brave officer who had served as Caldwell's city marshal and who resided in the Border Queen. His funeral was the next day, and "almost the entire population of the city" attended his burial. "The moans of his widow at the last parting at the grave were enough to chill the heart of a stone."[28]

Of course, Hollister's death did not occur in Caldwell. But the next year, on December 8, 1885, gambler and bootlegger Frank Noyes was taken from his house and lynched. About an hour after midnight on Tuesday morning, several men came to his house on Fifth Street behind Danford Hall. Awakening Noyes and his wife, the men announced that they had a warrant for his arrest and needed to take him to Wellington. Noyes went with the "posse" — and the next morning he was found hanging from the crossbeam of a gate near the depot. A note pinned to his body was signed "Vigilante Committee," and other men around town received vigilante letters of warning.[29]

eulogized the Journal on February 2, 1888. She was "a prominent member of the Ladies Relief Corps," and on her deathbed she asked to be buried with her "badge upon her breast." Several months earlier she was badly injured in a fall while descending into her cellar. Susan never fully recovered, and in January 1888 she was ravaged by pneumonia.

She had lost three of her children, and now her grandson had died. Aware that she was slipping away, Susan asked to be buried in the same grave with little Walter. She died on Thursday

(cont. next page)

morning. A double funeral service was conducted on Friday afternoon at the Presbyterian Church, attended by a "vast assemblage." Grandmother and grandson were interred together, side by side, in the City Cemetery.

★★★

Caldwell had not witnessed a lynching in more than a decade, and city fathers had no intention of permitting any more extralegal executions. Additional policemen were placed on the streets for a week. "Mob law is a poor law and one that should be condemned," lectured the *Journal*. The identity of the vigilantes could not be determined, and since the forty-three-year-old Noyes had not killed anyone, the motive for the lynching was a mystery. Some suggested that there was vengeance for "a young lady he had ruined," while another rumor accused prohibitionists.[30]

By 1885 Kansas saloons were closed through state prohibition laws, but bootleg liquor continued to be sold in drugstores and billiard parlors and "tigers" — establishments "where whiskey was sold by an unseen hand." Noyes and another bootlegger had been arrested in July 1885, fined, and sentenced to thirty days in the county jail.[31] The Caldwell chapter of the Women's Christian Temperance Union had been railing for years against liquor and saloons in the Border Queen, but no one seriously suspected that the ladies of the WCTU were behind a lynch posse.

The previous year the city had spent $2,000 to erect a stone jail with steel cells, an institutional warning that the wild old days would no longer be tolerated. A week and a half after the lynching, cowboys on a Saturday night spree decided to "run blazers" through Caldwell—gallop up and down Main Street firing their revolvers. This traditional revelry was abruptly halted by a host of citizens brandishing shotguns. "It don't pay to 'run blazers' on Caldwell just at present," warned the *Journal*. Four years later an old-timer called Kip came into Caldwell on a Saturday and "proceeded to fill up on Kansas prohibition." In the afternoon Kip mounted up and began to ride through the streets, drunkenly firing a gun—until Mayor John W. Nyce dragged him off his saddle and hauled him before the police judge.[32]

When Deputy Marshal Cash Hollister was killed in 1884 at Hunnewell, he was buried in Caldwell's City Cemetery. —Author photo

Caldwell citizens responded to

the Noyes lynching by halting "run blazers" and by publicly organizing a "Law and Order League." There were no more lynchings, and misbehavior of every sort declined. "Rowdyism, lawlessness, debauchery and immorality have long since passed away...," exulted the *Journal*. "The faro tables have been turned into the desk of the real estate dealer and the writing desk of the editor. Morality holds the city in her unrelenting but soft embrace, and crime and its evil effects have decreased in two years from 602 cases to 47 trivial offenses."[33]

A few months earlier in May 1887, a "trivial offense" occurred when Elmer Davidson found Dave Sharp "paying rather marked attention to Davidson's wife." Davidson hit Sharp in the face, then fired a wild shot at his fleeing figure. Davidson swore out a warrant, and Sharp was duly arrested. There was a certain amount of public opinion "that it was to be regretted that the bullet went wide of its mark."[34]

Despite Caldwell's veneer of morality it remained easy to find beer and liquor around town. The WCTU and other prohibitionists continued to oppose bootlegging and tigers, but community-wide contention over the issue eventually demanded accommodation. "Our citizens are tired of the continual strife that has been always waged on this question and have at last arrived at the sensible conclusion that the city might as well receive some benefit from the traffic and to have the trade in the hands of known men than to have the town overrun with bootleggers." It was so easy to buy liquor in Caldwell that periodically the county sheriff and a few deputies would come to Caldwell and arrest "parties who have been complained of for selling liquor."[35]

The absence of open saloons certainly was a contributing factor in the absence of gunfights. But early in 1891 J. L. Tracey, a Rock Island employee, left his train during the middle of the night to seek out Mrs. W. O. Brooks at her home, where she frequently entertained male guests when her husband was absent. Her husband, another railroad man stationed at a water stop ten miles south of Caldwell, often was absent, but not on this particular night. Brooks ordered Tracey to leave. "Come out doors you son of a bitch and I will show you who will get hurt," growled Tracey, who kicked the door twice. Brooks replied with a Bulldog revolver, and a .38 slug coursed through Tracey's liver and into his left kidney. He walked away from the house, stood still for a moment, then collapsed and died.[36]

While her husband was standing trial, Mrs. Brooks—"A woman of unsavory reputation"—was arrested and fined. A few months earlier "two colored prostitutes" were run out of town by authorities, who now cast Mrs. Brooks away from Caldwell on a Rock Island train.[37]

If Caldwell's gunplay now was limited once every few years to an occasional shot at the lover of a man's wife, at least the Border Queen had a connection to one of the most notorious Western shootouts of 1891. Ed Short, a deputy U.S. Marshal who also served as city marshal of Hennessey, Oklahoma, was well known in Caldwell and often mentioned in the newspapers when his duties brought him to town. In August 1891 Black-Faced Charley Bryant, a member of the Dalton Gang, fell ill and was taken by his comrades to Hennessey for care. Bryant, who was nicknamed because of powder burns from a point-blank pistol shot which creased his cheek, once had crowed, "Me, I want to get killed in one hell-firin' minute of action."[38]

Ed Short located Bryant in Hennessey, then slipped into his sickroom to arrest him. The next day, Sunday, August 23, 1891, Short placed his handcuffed prisoner in their baggage car of a northbound train to Wichita. Concerned about a rescue attempt by the gang, Short stood guard on the platform. Short was armed with a revolver and Bryant's rifle, and he handed Bryant's six-gun to the express messenger. The messenger carelessly shoved his gun into a pigeonhole on his desk and returned to his work. Bryant suddenly seized his revolver and shot Short in the chest. Short began working the Winchester, sending bullet after bullet into Bryant. The outlaw emptied his pistol, then fell dead. Short was helped to a cot, where he expired within moments. John Dobson, a former Caldwell merchant, was struck in the arm by a stray bullet, but he was patched up by John Schaeffer, head of the Schaeffer Undertaking Parlors in Caldwell.

The shooting happened only a few miles outside Hennessey. When the train reached Enid, railroad authorities directed that the bodies be taken to Caldwell, fifty miles to the north. By the time the train pulled into the Caldwell depot, several hundred onlookers gathered. John Schaeffer took charge of the bodies. After preparing the corpses for burial, he sent Bryant's remains to relatives in Decatur, Texas, while Short's body was shipped to his family home in Osgood, Indiana.

Although the tranquility of Caldwell was almost never broken by gunplay after 1884, fire continued to threaten the Border Queen. During its growth years, Caldwell miraculously escaped the conflagrations that often leveled the commercial districts of other boomtowns. For years the *Journal* "howled" for the organization of a fire company and construction of a water works system. An hour past midnight on Tuesday, July 7, 1885, fire erupted at "the mammoth agricultural implement warehouse of Kelpatrick & Yorke," located on Market Street between Fourth and Fifth. Repeated gunshots roused the slumbering community, "and in less than ten minutes more than four hundred men" rushed to the site of the blaze, bringing buckets and tubs of water, as well as lengths of rope. But the fire soon was out of control, and volunteers rushed inside to wheel out various types of farm machinery. John Blair and another man rolled the safe onto the sidewalk, then "five strong men" wrestled it onto the street. A nearby boarding house also went up in flames. Winds happened to the favorable, and the preventive efforts of hundreds of men halted the fire short of the Southwestern Hotel and the northern part of the business district.[39]

The next month another fire consumed a livery stable, and a few days late the city council appointed a twenty-five-man fire brigade, with A. M. Colson as fire chief. But there was little done to develop the brigade until an arsonist burned a residence on the last night of August. The brigade drafted a constitution and by-laws and met with the city council. "The matter of water-supply, paraphernalia, etc., for use at fires, was discussed at length, Chief Colson being instructed to determine what was needed by the brigade, to procure the same, and report to the council." Soon the fire brigade boasted two companies: "Kansas Hose Co. No. 1" and "Queen of the Border Hose Co. No. 2."[40]

Simultaneously with the organization of the fire brigade were efforts to build a water system, to provide water to homes

Caldwell Fire Department during the early 1890s.
—Courtesy Caldwell Historical Society

and businesses, but foremost to supply water to fire fighters. A proposed system was worked out in detail by early 1886, and a public meeting was called for Friday evening, February 5, at the Grand Opera House. The meeting indicated strong public support, and on Saturday the city council met to approve a water works ordinance. Construction soon began on a $50,000 system of wells, pumps, fire hydrants, and more than 21,000 feet of water mains. The city council accepted the system in September, and although there were system malfunctions, problems with administering the company, and two years of litigation, Caldwell had taken a major step toward modern infrastructure.[41]

In 1887 the Caldwell Electric Light Company was formed to build a light plant and provide incandescent lighting for streets, businesses and homes. "There is not another town of our size or importance in the state but what has electric lights of some kind," importuned the *Journal*. During the 1880s and into the 1890s the telephone system expanded impressively across the Border Queen. "Caldwell's telephone and telegraph lines make the town seem more metropolitan every day."[42]

The most significant improvement to the city of Caldwell was the introduction of *two* new railroad lines. In January 1886 Caldwell Township voters approved overwhelmingly, 469 to 10, a bond proposal for an east-west "Border Line" Railroad.

This commercial block was erected late in 1886 and 1887 on the east side of Main at Sixth, cater-corner to the Leland Hotel. There were four storerooms on the lower floor, offices on the second floor, and a Masonic Hall on the third floor.
—Caldwell *Journal*, November 18, 1886

The Border Line would be part of the Frisco system, which would offer Caldwell a direct rail route to St. Louis. The city council offered the Border Line its choice of right-of-ways through Caldwell, and north-enders and south-enders competed for the depot site. The Border Line chose to build across the northern outskirts of Caldwell, erecting a frame depot three-quarters of a mile northwest of the commercial district. A three-mile branch line would connect the route with "the State line for cattle shipping." In June a Border Line grading crew with about eighty teams established a camp in the northeast part of Caldwell, and tracks reached Caldwell by August. For the first time Caldwell would enjoy competitive freight rates.[43]

Rate competition soon escalated further in Caldwell. Caldwell's railroad committee did not stop working when the Border Line agreed to build into town. During 1886 there were negotiations with the Chicago and Rock Island Railroad. In February 1887 the Rock Island awarded a grading contract to extend their line south of Caldwell, and in June the railroad announced that the Border Queen would become a division point. There would be a roundhouse and numerous other structures—and a $20,000 monthly payroll. By July the railroad buildings were going up and grading crews had reached town. Track layers reached the new Rock Island depot late in August, and by the next month passenger and freight trains were running and a switch engine was working the Caldwell rail yards.[44]

By 1887 Caldwell had three railroad lines, which greatly expanded transportation possibilities for both passengers and freight.

—Caldwell *Journal*, July 28, 1887

Predictably there was a real estate boom in Caldwell. On November 11, 1886, *Journal* headlines proclaimed: REAL ESTATE BOOM ... Our Real Estate Men Doubling Their Forces." One week later the newspaper ran a related story: "Our hotels are crowded to their utmost capacity every night. Cots are placed in the halls, blankets are placed on the floor and room to lay down on is considered a luxury.... The restaurants are having all they can attend to.... Many new houses are going up but not half enough to supply the demand."

The boom exploded early in 1887, and through the spring there was wild speculation in real estate. On February 17 the *Journal* announced that "Four Hundred and Eighty Thousand Dollars Worth and City and Suburban Property Changes Hands in Four Days." On March 24 another front-page headline proclaimed: "$39,900.00 Worth of Property Sold by One Firm Before 10 o'clock A.M. Saturday Morning." One week later a similar headline exulted: "OVER $150,000 WORTH OF CALDWELL DIRT Disposed of Yesterday." A certain amount of construction was stimulated by this orgy of real estate dealing, but the boom fizzled out by mid-1887.

Although Caldwell's growth leveled off, there was a permanent population of more than two thousand and well over one hundred businesses, including large mercantile establishments, a wide variety of specialty shops, four drugstores, five grocery stores, fifteen freighting firms, one steam laundry, six livery stables, five blacksmith shops, three lumber yards, three barber

The Rock Island round house, built in 1889 in southeast Caldwell.
—Courtesy Caldwell Historical Society

shops, three agricultural implement dealers, and three well diggers. There were eight doctors, two dentists, one auctioneer, seven civic societies, and six churches—Methodist, Presbyterian, Christian, Catholic, Baptist, and a "Colored Baptist" congregation. The town boasted electric lights, a water works system, a telephone exchange, "two of the best hotels in Kansas," and "the finest and best opera house in the state." It also was the opinion of the *Journal* that "Caldwell has the prettiest and comeliest blue-eyed damsels in the world."[45]

After the boom of 1886-1887 receded, it soon became obvious that the introduction of the two new railroads to Caldwell would not generate the kind of excitement as the first line had just seven years earlier. The Chisholm Trail and Caldwell's saloons had been closed for a couple of years, and the Cherokee Strip Live Stock Association soon would disband. There were no more Texas drovers in town looking for a spree, no more professional gamblers or prostitutes. Gunplay was limited to sleepy men getting up in the middle of the night to take potshots at the packs of dogs that continued to roam the town.

Excitement in Caldwell now became less raucous and violent, more subdued and refined. The churches often staged emotional revivals that produced numerous baptisms. Each winter brought enthusiastic sleigh riding, and every spring and summer the male population eagerly played baseball. "The common west of the opera house is filled every evening by men and boys playing ball," reported the *Journal* in 1890. An occasional horse

Caldwell's brick Methodist Church, with the congregation dressed in their Sunday best. —Courtesy Caldwell Historical Society

race at the fair grounds would attract one hundred or so spectators, whose excitement level rose with the amount of their bets. Betting also was rampant in 1888 when a prize fight took place before an audience of three hundred at the Grand Opera House. A more genteel and widespread activity was bicycle riding. Caldwell's leading "wheelman" was community leader Harvey Horner, who rode to Hunnewell and South Haven and even to Wellington.[46]

By the late 1880s Caldwell was noticeably tamer than in the early years of the decade. Cattle town Caldwell was becoming a community of wheat farmers. But it was farmers who, surprisingly, would bring a final, sensational Wild West adventure to the Border Queen.

Caldwell's Christian Church (left) was built in 1892, while the Catholic Church was erected in 1888.

—Courtesy Caldwell Historical Society

CHAPTER THIRTEEN

Boomers and Land Rushes

"At high noon on the 16th of September at the crack of the soldier's gun, the whole earth seemed to move forward."
—John F. Ryland

Buffalo hunters. Bullwhackers. U.S. Cavalrymen. Gamblers. Sporting ladies. Deadly gunmen. A host of cowboys and ranchers. For more than a decade and a half Caldwell witnessed a parade of these colorful frontier characters, and the Border Queen became the scene of almost countless episodes, large and small, that characterized the legendary last West. When these flamboyant Westerners finally were gone from Caldwell, the town became a quiet center of the least colorful pioneers. Farmers were scorned by cowboys as "plow chasers," "fodder forkers," "fool hoe men," "stubble jumpers," "churn twisters," "sodbusters," and "hay shakers." But it was the lackluster, clodhoppered sodbusters that provided the Border Queen with its final and most spectacular Western adventure.

During the three decades following the Civil War, more than one million farms were established in the West. More land was settled than in all of American history before that time. Between 1870 and 1900, 430,000,000 acres were populated and 225,000,000 acres were placed under cultivation. During the 1870s—Caldwell's first decade—Kansas gained 347,000 new settlers. Most were farmers or farm families, hoping to claim a 160-acre homestead and grow wheat. The price of wheat often reached one dollar a bushel during these years, a price which meant prosperity for the farmer. England, the wealthiest country in the world, imported vast amounts of American wheat during the 1870s. The peak year was 1880, when 153,000,000 bushels were sold in England for $191,000,000. Even more wheat was sold and consumed domestically. Between 1870 and 1900, the population of the United States nearly doubled, from 38,500,000 to 76,000,000, including more than 12,000,000 immigrants. At the same time more and more Americans became non-food producers, living in urban areas and working for industry—and thereby providing an expanding market for wheat, as well as for other Western products such as beef and corn.¹

Few regions of the West were better suited to wheat farming than the countryside adjacent to Caldwell. "Caldwell has the most fertile agricultural vicinity in the world," boasted the *Journal* in 1887. "Our agricultural and commercial territory on the north, east and west is located in the far famed Arkansas Valley, which is supposed to be the most productive area of land in the western hemisphere." With similar modesty the *Journal* declared the climate to be "absolutely perfect, and without an equal."²

During the 1870s, while a few dozen urban pioneers tried to develop trail town Caldwell into a community, homesteaders moved onto the nearby prairies, building dugouts and breaking the virgin sod. After the railroad reached Caldwell in 1880, area farmers now had ready access to markets. The Border Queen was the railhead of the Chisholm Trail and the headquarters of the Cherokee Strip Live Stock Association. Caldwell's saloons and stores catered to cowboys and cattlemen and ranchers. But a growing number of homesteaders were customers, buying provisions and clothing, seed and farm implements. Farm families were a major presence in town on Saturdays, parking their wagons for a day of shopping and visiting. Farmers unloaded stacks of hay on Main Street for sale, "making the street look like a barn yard," complained the *Journal*.³

Although Caldwell newspapers were dominated by livestock news and Cherokee Live Stock Association advertising, there were more and more items about farmers and wheat prices. "Ask the old settlers if they ever knew a finer wheat harvest," observed the *Post* in 1882. The next summer a *Journal* reporter was invited to see "the first wheat cutting of the season" at the farm of the Barnard family. "The machine used was a Deering Twine Binder," and a description of the harvest followed.⁴

In the same way that Caldwell businessmen had staged entertainments and celebrations for cowboys and ranchers, a Harvest Fair and Festival was planned to take place in August 1883. "All the farmers, merchants, mechanics and ladies of the county are respectfully invited to bring the products of the soil, and labor of their hands and samples of their goods." Caldwell merchants offered various prizes: "a dozen cans of assorted California fruit for the best bushel of wheat"; "a parlor lamp for a package of the best butter exhibited"; "a cashmere dress pattern for the best half bushel of potatoes"; "One year's subscription [to the *Journal*] for the best collection of melons"; etc. Nearby townships helped with planning, and "farmers and their wives took an interest in the project from the start." Response exceeded all original expectations. Hundreds of exhibits and a horde of Fair visitors symbolized the rising impact of farmers on Caldwell and its economy.[5]

Grain elevators and flour mills were built along the railroad tracks. "The first load of wheat of the season" was reported each summer, and there was a banner harvest in 1886: "The wheat is the finest yet seen in this county, not excepting 1874." By the late 1880s steam threshing machines were being brought into the area at harvest time. "There are thousands of acres in this vicinity to be harvested," stated the *Journal* in 1891. "Threshing machines are coming in from various parts of the state to assist in preparing our immense wheat crop for market."[6]

"About the happiest looking men in this city nowadays are the grain men," observed the *Journal* in 1889. By 1889 the Chisholm Trail had been closed for four years and the Cherokee Strip Live Stock Association was on its last legs, and it was "grain men," not ranchers, who now were "the happiest looking men" in Caldwell. "The wheat market was booming Saturday in this city," announced the *Journal* in 1891. A few years earlier it was the cattle market that boomed in Caldwell. The cattle trade had been king of the Border Queen, but in 1891 the *Journal* proclaimed a new monarch: "Wheat is King."[7]

While farmers were on the ascendancy in and around Caldwell, other pioneer farmers took aim at the uncultivated lands of Indian Territory. As early as 1879 small bands of home seekers slipped across the Cherokee Outlet into the "Oklahoma District," nearly two million acres of lands unassigned to any tribe. This invasion was halted by federal troops, which established six army camps along the Kansas border, including one outside Caldwell. But land-hungry farmers would not be deterred, and in 1880 "Boomers" found their leader.

David L. Payne was forty-three in 1880. Raised on an Indiana farm, he and his brother came to Kansas in 1858. A tall, impressive man, David Payne often supported himself as a buffalo hunter, a guide for wagon trains, and a guide and scout for the army. During the Civil War he saw action with Kansas volunteer units. Mustered out in 1864, Payne was elected to the Kansas Legislature, but early in 1865 he again answered a call for volunteers. Two tears later he volunteered for service against Indian warriors, commanding a company in the Fifteenth Kansas Volunteers. Again elected to the Kansas Legislature in

1871, he later was appointed Sergeant-at-Arms of the Kansas Senate, and he served as assistant to the Doorkeeper of the U.S. House of Representatives in 1875 and 1879.[8]

Payne's work as a hunter and guide had taken him into Indian Territory, and in 1880 this restless adventurer led a small party of Boomers into Oklahoma District and tried to establish a settlement near the future site of Oklahoma City. Discovered by the army, Payne and his followers were escorted back to Kansas. Soon returning with another small party, Payne again was found and forced out of Indian country. This time he and his followers were fined $1,000 apiece—a meaningless penalty since none of the offenders had money or property. Payne began actively to recruit Boomers, publishing the *Oklahoma War Chief* and organizing colonists. Between 1880 and 1884 Payne launched fourteen Boomer intrusions, usually from Kansas but sometimes from Texas.[9]

Payne was in and out of Caldwell during the early 1880s. "Oklahoma Payne paid our city a visit the latter part of last week," reported the *Post* in November 1880. The next month the *Post* related that "D. L. Payne, 'President of the Oklahoma Colony,' as he styles himself, has just published in Kansas newspapers a call to his followers for another raid into Indian Territory." This long article disapproved of Payne's "lawbreaking" activities. The *Post* was a cattleman's newspaper, but other Caldwell citizens were receptive to Payne's movement.[10]

In mid-December 1880 Payne brought his third group of colonists to Caldwell from Arkansas City. A "meeting of the Oklahoma Boomers at the school house" was chaired by Mayor Mike Meagher. The rally "was well attended" and featured a speech by Capt. Payne, as well as remarks by some of his lieutenants. On Tuesday afternoon, December 14, a delegation of Caldwell sympathizers went out to meet the approaching expedition. A local band marched at the head of the procession as it entered Caldwell from the east on Fifth Street. Capt. Payne rode in a buggy with two prominent citizens, and his lead wagon flew a United States flag. The wagons turned south on Main Street, and at the outskirts of town angled east to a campground about a mile away on Fall Creek. There were perhaps thirty-five wagons and 150 men. But troops were present to block the border, and two blizzards soon struck Caldwell and the camp. Suffering colonists began to drift away, and on January 21, 1881, Payne and his remaining followers broke camp and departed for Wichita.[11]

Caldwell newspapers continued to report Payne's coloniza-

Boomer Ballad

As Boomers enthusiastically rallied to David Payne, a ballad was composed. It was published in the Caldwell Journal on December 23, 1880, under the title, "Oklahoma Boom."

O! for a thousand tongues
  to sing
Our Oklahoma's fame;
Let the emigrant wagons ring
Along with Captain Payne.

Who cares for President Hayes
Or any other civil name?
We have some better ways,
Devised by Captain Payne.

General Pope has got the power,

(cont. next page)

tion attempts and his legal misadventures. But journalistic criticism of Payne persisted and he did not again use Caldwell as a base. The forty-seven-year-old Payne died of a heart attack in Wellington on November 28, 1884. "If Capt. Payne had died in Caldwell as suddenly as he did in Wellington," suggested the *Journal*, "our citizens would have been accused of poisoning him."[12]

For well over a decade soldiers were in and out of Caldwell while on border duty to halt Boomer intrusions. Soldiers were camped just outside Caldwell during the mid-1870s as a deterrent to hostile Indians. They returned throughout the 1880s to try to control the legions of Boomers who incessantly attempted to penetrate the "B.I.T." (Newspapers constantly used the abbreviation B.I.T. — Beautiful Indian Territory.)

Early in 1881 a cavalry detachment erected a stable on Fall Creek about three-quarters of a mile southeast of the depot. Later in the year two companies of the Ninth Cavalry encamped near the stables. The Ninth and Tenth cavalry regiments were "buffalo soldiers," and the African-American troopers were eager customers at Caldwell's saloons, sporting houses, and lunch stands. The commander of the Ninth Cavalry was Colonel Edward Hatch, who often was in Caldwell during the next few years. A brevet major general in command of a Union division at the end of the Civil War, he usually was referred to as "Gen. Hatch" in Caldwell newspapers.[13]

In October 1884 Col. Hatch established his winter headquarters in Caldwell, leasing the fairgrounds until the following June. The buildings were converted to barracks, and farmers and merchants would enjoy solid sales to soldiers and quartermasters throughout the winter. The *Journal*, painfully aware of the recent closing of the Chisholm Trail, proclaimed: "Caldwell is not dead yet, by any means."[14]

In June 1885 three companies of the Eighteenth Infantry took over Camp Caldwell. The next month Gen. Phil Sheridan and his staff arrived by train in the Border Queen. Sheridan was preparing to depart by horse-drawn conveyance for Fort Reno, I.T., when A. M. Colson approached, representing the G.A.R. About forty Union veterans hastily gathered, and Sheridan told Colson that "it would give him great pleasure to again meet them." Sheridan shook hands and spoke to the veterans, several of whom had served under the General during the Civil War. "A photographer was on the ground," reported the *Journal*, "and the General good naturedly stood among his old friends while the camera did its work."[15]

But the law is on our side;
We can march at any hour,
For Captain Payne's our guide.

Don't desert your noble chieftain;
Stand by this man of fame;
And we'll march to Oklahoma
Along with Captain Payne.

It's a place for making money—
A rich and fertile plain;
It always flows with milk and honey—
So says our Captain Payne.

On to Oklahoma, boys!
"We know the land is ours,"
we claim.
Dodge the soldiers if you can,
And follow Captain Payne.

★★★

Soldiers stationed in Caldwell and elsewhere along the border were constantly on the move trying to head off the Boomers. After the death of David Payne late in 1884, leadership was assumed by his lieutenant, W. L. Couch. A thirty-four-year-old businessman from Wichita, Couch promptly organized a large-scale invasion. A number of Boomer groups crossed the border at various points. While soldiers intercepted several of these groups, four hundred men eluded capture and camped under "Captain" Couch on Stillwater Creek. The Boomers were discovered by cavalrymen in January, but Couch threatened to fight. Col. Hatch instead surrounded the camp, cutting off supplies. Couch soon surrendered, and he and his followers were escorted back to Kansas. "Couch Colony Hoofing It Out of the B.I.T.," announced the *Journal*. "Bloodless Battle Breaks the Boomers."[16]

Early in 1885 a movement began to organize an Oklahoma colony in Caldwell. Fifteen men held an initial meeting in January, and by late February circulars announced a public gathering at Danford Hall. About 250 citizens attended, and after another couple of meetings thirty or forty men formed "a 'sure enough' colony." Overtures were extended to W. L. Couch, and in May 1885 he transferred his most recent band of Boomer colonists from Arkansas City to Caldwell.[17]

"Boomerville" was established beside Bluff Creek near Caldwell's stockyards. There were about two dozen tents and the same number of wagons "laid out along main street about sixty feet wide." A U.S. flag flew above Couch's tent, and about 200 Boomers were in camp. A Saturday night reception for

When Gen. Phil Sheridan stepped off a train in Caldwell in 1885, A. M. Colson immediately gathered local veterans of the Union Army for an impromptu reunion. Sheridan is the portly gentleman in front and left of center, with his left hand on his hat brim and right hand on a cane. Colson stands beside the General, also with his hand on his hat. —Courtesy Caldwell Historical Society

Couch and his followers was held at Danford Hall on May 9. Caldwell citizens enjoyed visiting Boomerville, and when Sunday services were held in a grove near camp on May 24, attendance was estimated at 500.[18]

But when a ferocious windstorm blew away several tents in Boomerville, the *Journal* decided that: "The Lord is certainly not on their side." The *Oklahoma War Chief* began publishing from the Caldwell camp. In July 1885 a deputy U.S. marshal served warrants on everyone in Boomerville, and arrested the editor of the vituperative *War Chief*, who proclaimed he would go to jail before providing bail. "He is not like the editor of the *Journal*," wrote the editor of the *Journal*, "who would give a whole armful of bail, if he could get it, before he would go to jail."[19]

The Boomers had almost no money, so there was little benefit to Caldwell's economy from their presence. Desperate for work, some of the Boomers hired out for a pittance, driving wages down for local workmen. A band of Boomers crossed the border, but soon were escorted back by a cavalry detachment. Thwarted from entering the Outlet, some Boomers threatened to burn the pastures used by Cherokee Strip ranchers, who in turn were reluctant to purchase winter grain from Caldwell farmers. "WHAT THE BOOMERS HAVE COST US" announced the headline of a long editorial by the *Journal* on November 19, 1885. The financial ramifications of each of these problems was discussed in detail. "Caldwell has made a fool of herself on this boomer business," declared the *Journal*. "She has never gained a dollar by it, and what is more, she never will." The *Journal* concluded "that Caldwell did a very foolish and unwise thing when she gave succor and aid to the poor little outfit that came over here last summer." With growing disenchantment in Caldwell, Couch was entertaining offers to move his colony to another town. The *Journal* was emphatic: "Let them go."

During this period the Ninth Cavalry was replaced along the border by the Fifth Cavalry. The colonel of the Fifth, Civil War general Wesley Merritt, succeeded Hatch as commander of military affairs in the District of Oklahoma. Unfortunately, a member of the Fifth—perhaps inebriated—was fatally injured when he tumbled to the bottom of a Caldwell stairway, and a few months later another enlisted man drowned while bathing in Bluff Creek. In 1890 yet another Fifth Cavalryman died in Caldwell under suspicious circumstances following a drinking bout.[20]

Couch moved out of Caldwell in 1886, but Caldwell citizens, from their townsite overlooking the border, remained interested in the accelerating campaign to open Indian lands to settlement. "Since the opening of the decade western congressmen, railroad lobbyists, and 'Boomer' spokesmen had bombarded Congress with petitions, bills, and resolutions demanding the Indian Territory be opened," described historian Ray Allen Billington. From 1885 through 1888 "Couch led party after party into Oklahoma whenever the border patrols turned their backs."[21]

Under intense pressure, the federal government began taking steps to admit settlers. Late in 1888 a large colonization effort was organized under Major Gordon W. Lillie, popularly known as "Pawnee Bill." (Born in Illinois in 1860, Lillie moved with his family to Sumner County in 1874, and the youngster

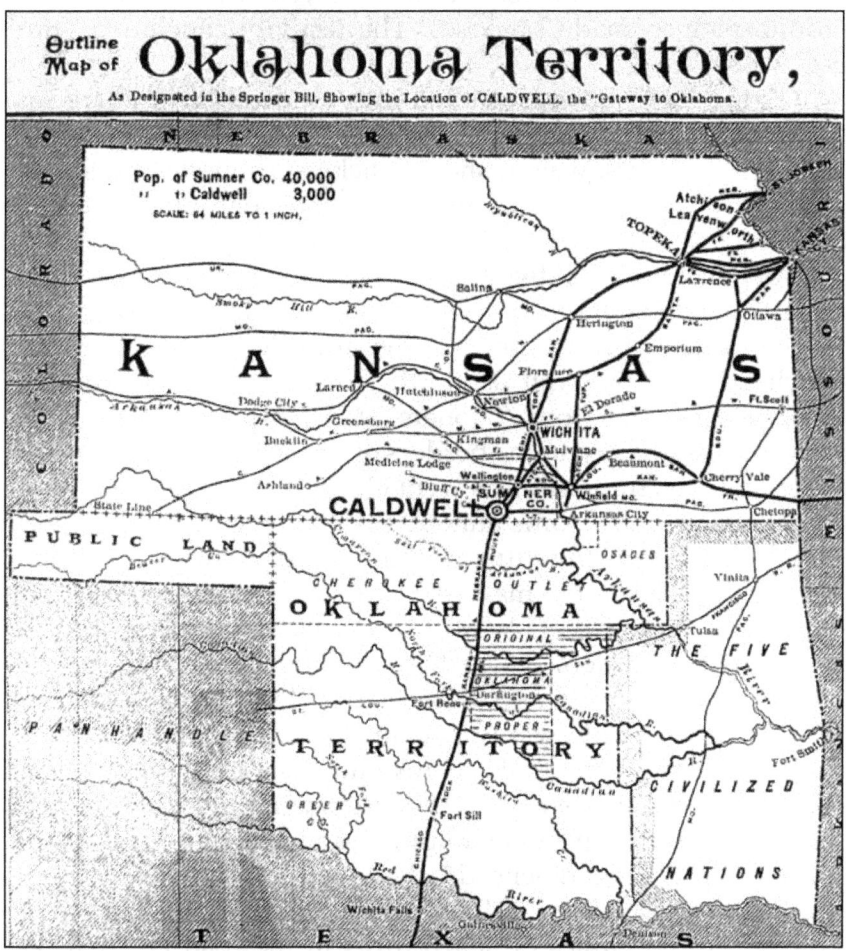

The Oklahoma District (horizontal lines, labeled "ORIGINAL OKLAHOMA PROPER") was opened to settlement on April 22, 1889. The Cherokee Outlet, three times as large (six million acres), was opened on September 16, 1893.
—From the Caldwell *Journal*, April 26, 1888

worked for a time in a Caldwell café.) At least 2,000 colonists awaited directions in Wichita and Arkansas City, along with "several hundred ready for the command at Caldwell." On February 5, 1889, Pawnee Bill and his lieutenant, "Oklahoma Harry" Hill, arrive in Caldwell to inspect the old Couch campsite and to make preparations to establish headquarters at the Border Queen.[22]

Before Pawnee Bill could organize his colony, President Benjamin Harrison announced in March that the Oklahoma District would be opened to settlers at noon on April 22, 1889. Caldwell responded with an enthusiastic open air celebration on Tuesday night, March 5. A bonfire blazed at the intersection of Main and Fifth. Exuberant citizens "were sure that at last the promised land was theirs." A band played, and half a dozen prominent men made speeches. The festivity concluded with fireworks.[23]

During April Boomers rolled into Caldwell to prepare for the run to the Oklahoma District. "Attention Oklahoma Boomers, For tents, wagon sheets, slickers, rubber coats, shoes, hats and all kinds of clothing get to the Lone Star Clothing House big stock low prices." The Lone Star Clothing House was only one of many Caldwell businesses that advertised for the trade of the Boomers.[24]

A few days before the run, the army left the border and marched south (as well as north from Texas) to guard the Oklahoma District from "Sooners." On April 19 settlers were permitted to advance to the borders of the District. Caught up in the excitement, some citizens went along "to witness the scramble for claims." Dr. Hume announced that he would take a few days off "to see the fun at the 'grand opening.'" Other Caldwellites decided to make the run.[25]

On the morning of April 22, 100,000 settlers impatiently waited at the borders of the District. Men—and women—on horseback and in wagons, carriages, bicycles, and almost every other type of vehicle were lined up for miles, while troopers were stationed at intervals to restrain the horses until noon. Officers peered anxiously at synchronized watches. "At precisely 12 o'clock the bugle sounded and the free for all race across the prairie commenced," described the *Journal*. "It was a mad scramble, horses fell, wagons broke down or were stranded in the gullies or sharp turns in the road and wrecks were to be seen in every direction." By nightfall Oklahoma City was a tent city with a population of 10,000, while 15,000 had staked out lots in Guthrie.[26]

W. N. Hubbell secured a main street lot at the new community of Lisbon, "and is selling hardware in wholesale quantities." A. M. Colson staked a 160-acre claim near Lisbon. Both Colson and Hubbell soon would return to Caldwell. The widow of Cash Hollister and a "Mrs. McKeegan were among the successful ones to secure good claims in Oklahoma." W. L. Couch filed a claim adjacent to Oklahoma City and was elected mayor. His claim was disputed by a frustrated Boomer, and in April 1890 the two men exchanged rifle shots at long range. Couch was struck in the leg, and when doctors delayed amputation he suffered blood poisoning. Couch died fifteen days after the shooting, leaving a wife and five children.[27]

In 1890 the director of the U.S. Census concluded that in the West "the unsettled area has been so broken into by isolated bodies of settlement that there can hardly be said to be a frontier line." On the heels of one of the West's most phenomenal spectacles, the frontier was declared officially ended. For nearly three centuries there had been frontier lands available beyond the western edge of American settlement, but now there remained no other great expanses of open land.

Except for the Cherokee Strip. With six million acres the Cherokee Strip was triple the size of the recently opened Oklahoma District. In 1889 a federal commission traveled to Tahlequah to force upon the Cherokee Nation a cession agreement and sale price for the Strip. "Unquestionably the outlet will be opened to settlement," predicted Chief Bushyhead in the *Journal* on October 10, 1889. "Congress will see to that." Cattlemen were ordered to vacate the Strip in 1890, giving rise to the hope that President Harrison "will declare the country open to homesteaders." This hope was expressed in November 1890, by which time "hundreds of men are preparing to go into the Strip on the first of December and take up claims."[28]

A repeat of the Oklahoma District pattern began to occur, with Caldwell—as a long-established gateway to the Cherokee Strip—a focal point of events. On March 20, 1890, the *Journal* headlined a front-page article: "OPEN THE STRIP!" The article began: "the people are clamoring for the opening of the Strip to settlement ...," while the final sentence insisted, "The people want this land, and the necessary legislation preliminary to giving it to them should be hurried through as fast as possible." On the same front page an article entitled "TROOPS ORDERED HERE" reported that two companies of the Fifth Cavalry were heading to Caldwell "To Keep Boomers Out of the Forbidden Land." The next year two more Fifth Cavalry companies camped on Bluff Creek and began "scouring the Strip in search of invaders."[29]

Articles in the *Journal* reflected a growing consensus about the Strip, a consensus typical of the Manifest Destiny approach that for decades had justified American expansion across a series of frontiers. "Every day we are in receipt of letters of inquiry regarding the Cherokee Strip. From now on the question will be agitated all over the country." A lengthy article opened with the assumption that "the Cherokee Strip is an all-absorbing question at present."[30]

A band of boomers began "Cherokee City" six miles south of Caldwell late in 1889 before being removed by the military. A year later "between four and five hundred families" were camping on the Kansas side of the border "within a few miles of Caldwell." In January 1891, with the army preoccupied by tragic problems with the Sioux at Wounded Knee, Boomers crossed into the Strip in large numbers. Later in the year Pawnee Bill, disregarding the successful run of his Wild West Show in Atlantic City, New Jersey, again tried to promote a colony with Caldwell as his headquarters.[31]

Friday, March 3, 1893, was the last day of the Fifty-first Congress. Saturday was Inauguration Day for Democrat Grover Cleveland, and marked the end of the Republican administration of President Benjamin Harrison. Among unfinished business was a bill to open the Cherokee Strip to homesteaders. The bill had gone through the legislative process, and "the most objectionable features" had been removed. For Westerners the most objectionable feature was limiting homestead claims to eighty acres, but an amendment had restored the 160-acre dimension that had been in effect since 1862. No community was more absorbed in the passage of the bill than Caldwell, and by early Friday evening "anxious throngs were on the streets, gathered in

President Benjamin Harrison finally secured passage of the Cherokee Strip bill on the last day of his term, March 3, 1893. —Courtesy National Archives

groups on every corner," while checking constantly with the telegraph and telephone offices.³²

A little before eight o'clock "a wild, hysterical yell" came from a man in front of the telephone exchange. News that the bill passed raced through the crowd, "and then the shout was taken up by dozens, by scores, by hundreds, till the very air rang with hurrahs." Someone began beating a drum, someone else blew a horn. "Everybody smiled and shook hands" as the crowd marched through the streets.³³

President Harrison promptly signed the bill. Provisions were included to reimburse the federal government for the $8.6 million purchase price of the Strip that had been paid to the Cherokee Nation. The Strip would be divided into three sections: East, Middle, and West. The choicest lands were in the East, where settlers would pay $2.50 per acre; Middle lands would cost $1.50 per acre; and the arid West claims would cost $1.00 per acre.

Almost immediately prospective homesteaders began arriving in Caldwell, parking their covered wagons or pitching tents on vacant lots or on the outskirts of town. "Every house in town is full," stated the *Caldwell News*, and renters also filled available housing in Arkansas City, another departure point for the anticipated land rush.³⁴

Secretary of the Interior Hoke Smith made preparations for the massive event. The Strip would be divided into seven counties, and four land office buildings would be erected. Nine land office booths—to be housed in army tents—would be placed along "the regular lines of travel," five on the northern boundary and four on the southern line of the Strip. Everyone intending to make the run would have to register at one of the booths, then would receive a certificate. This system was

---

THE OPENING
---OF THE---
Cherokee Strip
Is Now Certain.

The report of the Committe is Now Favorable.

The bill is the second one on the Calendar.

And the new country will soon be opened for the home seekers of the nation. Therefore, believing that it is my duty that you should prepare yourself for the occasion, and as we are always

To the Front
we now propose

To Offer You the Greatest Inducements

in the following lines of goods that was ever offered to the people of Sumner County.

For the Next 30 Days

we will slaughter goods at prices that will make the earth resound with our thunderous BARGAINS, the PEERLESS BARGAINs of the

BOSTON STORE.
READ ON, DON'T BELIEVE IT, BUT CALL AND SEE OUR PRICES.

Boys' Clothing

At one half what Clothing Houses ask. One lot embracing all of fine Knee Pants Suits, double and single breasted, made from imported cheviots, cashmeres and worsteds. No goods in this lot worth less than $5.50, at $3.75. Boys' cape and ulster overcoats in different styles, in plaids, fancy checks and plaids made in the best styles by union tailors. Goods none worth less than $4, at $2.58. One lot of boys' suits and overcoats, worth $3, at $1.50.

Odds and Ends.

65 mens' suits from 1 to 3 of our style. We will close them out at 65c ON THE DOLLAR.

Shoe Department.

Mens' Velvet Embroidered Slippers, regular $1.50 slipper, now 85c. 350 pairs of mens' and ladies' shoes, prices ranging from $1.50 to $3. We will close them out at $1.20.

Just as Caldwell merchants long had catered to ranchers and cowboys, in 1893 the theme of advertising became the Cherokee Strip land rush and homeseekers.

devised to keep out Sooners, and the army was charged with sweeping the Strip for Sooners beforehand.³⁵

The Strip bill required the president to announce the opening date within six months of passage—by September 3, 1893. President Cleveland issued his proclamation on August 22, listing the details that had been formulated by Secretary Hoke and announcing that the Strip would be opened on Saturday, September 16, at noon.³⁶

Caldwell, already crowded, now was descended upon by thousands of hopeful settlers. "Almost every 'stripper's' wagon has a cart or a buggy behind it," noted the *News*. "Many of them have an extra horse, doubtless for running purposes." The town was filled with fine horses, and impromptu races were frequent occurrences. Caldwell had three tonsorial parlors, but enterprising barbers came from other towns and set up tents. Lunch counters also were opened, and so were shooting galleries. Blind men came to Caldwell to beg on street corners, standing beside gamblers who operated shell games. Minstrels sang their way through the crowds. "The air is full of excitement and nothing but Strip talk goes."³⁷

Extra trains followed regularly-scheduled passenger trains into Caldwell, "one after the other, pouring multitudes in, to wander around in vain for shelter and lodging." Hotels and

For weeks before the Cherokee Strip Land Rush, Caldwell's Main Street teemed with wagons and homeseekers. The three-story building (today reduced to two stories) housed the Citizens Bank. The two-story structure across Fifth Street is the Danford Building, with the old opera house on the second floor.
—Courtesy Caldwell Historical Society

boarding houses were jammed, "and every available space is crowded with cots." Many men spread their blankets on vacant lots and even on boardwalks. The post office was besieged by men who waited in line for hours to check for a letter from home. On Thursday night, September 14, the New York Ideal Concert Co. capitalized on the immense crowd and provided an evening of entertainment at the Grand Opera House.[38]

"From morning till night and from sunset till sunrise, in one continuous stream, the people intending to locate on the Strip have been pouring in," reported the *News* two days before the run. "There seems to be no cessation to the roll and rumble of

Looking north on Main Street, the photographer probably was standing on the second-floor balcony of the Leland Hotel. —Courtesy Caldwell Historical Society

Covered wagons outside Caldwell's stockyards.
—Courtesy Caldwell Historical Society

wagons, the clatter of horse's feet, the din and roar of the human and animal tide rolling this way." An estimated 15,000 home seekers, out of a total of 100,000, clustered in and around the Border Queen.[39]

On Monday morning, September 11, the registration booths opened. Men began gathering at the tent south of Caldwell on Sunday night, and at dawn on Monday 1,300 home seekers were in line. By Tuesday evening 5,000 men were in line to register. Gamblers brought small tables to start games among the waiting men. Peddlers worked the line with water canteens, beer, whiskey, sandwiches, candy, and blankets for overnighters. George Rainey described the "dusty and thirsty men and women as they patiently stood in line," and "the many jibes" against Secretary Smith's booth system as a means of controlling Sooners. "It did not work," scoffed George Rainey, "and the whole booth system was a big joke." The *News* railed against the "needless torture" inflicted on thousands who had to stand in line under a blistering sun. "The whole business of opening the Strip from beginning to end was a bungled failure, a roaring farce and demonstrated the supreme ignorance of the Interior department as to western people and western methods. Hoke Smith is execrated from one end of the Strip to the other."[40]

Throughout Friday night, September 15, wagons were moved into position. George Rainey was one of the many home seekers who placed his wagon on the starting line early, "then a few minutes before twelve o'clock" on Saturday brought up his

The Leland Hotel at left commands the corner of Main and Sixth, while the three-story Southwestern Hotel may be seen at the far end of the street.
— Courtesy Caldwell Historical Society

team, fresh for the run. In addition to wagons, there were buckboards, buggies, surreys, and two-wheeled carts drawn by a single horse. "Some were foolish enough to attempt the race on bicycles," recalled Rainey. "Those were left behind in the dirt."[41]

Saturday dawned with a bright sun and a wind from the northeast. The horse riders jockeying into position included a number of women. "The sight along the line ... was one that ever will be forgotten by all who saw it," reported Robert T. Simons, editor of the *News*. "It was like an army massed for battle. In the front were the horsemen. The steeds were fine looking animals, and they stamped and fretted under restraint, The noble animals seemed to realize that something extraordinary was expected of them and they wanted to be up and going." Spectators were in the rear, standing on high ground or atop buggies and wagons.[42]

Seventeen-year-old John Ryland had helped herd cattle in the Strip below Caldwell, and he was asked by a homesteader from Missouri to ride along as a guide. Ryland eagerly agreed. The young cowboy, born in Caldwell in 1875, wanted to experience the excitement. He was not disappointed. "At high noon on the 16th of September at the crack of the soldier's gun, the whole earth seemed to move forward, and it was several minutes before this sensation seemed to subside." After a hard ride of seventeen miles, the Missouri home seeker filed a claim. Although Ryland was not legally old enough, he also staked a claim, "then traded it off for a shot gun" to an unsuspecting homesteader.[43]

Rails had been extended through Oklahoma, a Territory of the United States since 1890, and two trains were poised to transport thousands of home seekers. The front train was made up of thirty-five stock cars, while the train in the rear had fifteen passenger cars. "The cars were jammed with people — in the cars, on top of the cars, hanging on the sides and even riding the coal tenders," related George Rainey. "Both trains were pulled by two engines each," described Robert T. Simons. "The stock cars were crowded like sardine boxes." Simons estimated "that 150 men were on each car and that 7,000 men were on both trains."[44]

At the sound of the noon gun "the line broke and fled," wrote Simons. "It seemed as if the horses made a leap into the air, neath the stroke of the whip. On! on they rushed, leaping ditch and ravine, climbing bank and ridge, stretching out into a mighty run across the level prairie. Some of the fleetest were soon out of sight." Several saddle girths gave way and a number of horses were seen "running around riderless," but some men managed to continue the race bareback.[45]

The heavily loaded trains labored up a steep grade as the horsemen raced out of sight toward the townsites and choicest homesteads. "The passengers were almost frantic at the delay.... They cursed the railway company [and] cursed their luck...." Many passengers jumped from the slow-moving trains to find a homestead on foot. "Lou Jackson, the colored cook at the Leland, got a fine claim." After leaving the train Jackson ran for three miles to stake out a homestead.[46]

Many other Caldwell citizens made the run. Merchant H.A. Ross raced to the first quarter section below the line, but had to split the 160 acres with another horseman who arrived at the same moment. Dr. Scribner filed on "a splendid claim," and

The front train at the Caldwell line was made up of 35 stock cars, with perhaps 150 men jammed inside and atop each car. The train behind had 15 passenger cars, and it was estimated that the two trains carried 7,000 men.
—Courtesy Border Queen Museum

As noon approached on September 16, 1893, thousands of homeseekers were poised south of Caldwell to rush into the Cherokee Strip.
—Courtesy Caldwell Historical Society

A. M. Colson took a quarter section near Enid. Lone Star Clothing proprietor H. C. Unsell filed a claim on Pond Creek, but like others he did not intend to leave his home in Caldwell. A couple of weeks later the *News* commented upon the merchant and his homestead: "Farmer ... Unsell is wondering what he is going to do with it anyway."[47]

Unsell was only one of numerous Caldwell merchants who ran sales on homesteader items. "Tents! Tents! Tents! Of all sizes and weights will be closed out at very low prices for the next 30 days, at the Lone Star Clothing House." Freight trains busily made runs to the new towns. But a great many unsuccessful home seekers could only return to their homes. "One continuous stream of boomers are going north," reported the *News*. "They are wondering what they came for."[48]

Even those who failed to secure claims had participated in an event of unforgettable drama and magnitude and pandemonium. "It was a time of wonderful excitement," summed up Robert T. Simons immediately after the run. "The opening of the strip was a sight to behold and one never to be forgotten," recalled John Ryland to a *Caldwell Commercial* reporter in 1961. Ryland was eighty-five and nearly six decades had passed. But he described the day in detail, then reflected upon fictional attempts to depict the Land Rush in Western movies and novels. "Several vivid descriptions of that race have been given in story and screen..., but none gives so great a thrill as that of having seen it."[49]

There was a blur of motion after the signal gun sounded. Teenager John Ryland said that "the whole earth seemed to move forward, and it was several minutes before the sensation seemed to subside." —Courtesy Caldwell Historical Society

CHAPTER FOURTEEN

Celebration of the Border Queen

"Boys — it's the last of the West."
—William S. Hart in Tumbleweeds

There was so much traffic in and out of Caldwell during the aftermath of the Strip run that special policemen continued on duty, and business, for a time, remained unusually brisk. A lunch counter was operated in a tent on Main Street by a couple from Colorado, G. F. and Ella Boyd. Ella recently had engaged in a romantic tryst with a first cousin, Ed Hawley. Boyd broke up the two and brought his wife to Caldwell. But Hawley soon turned up, and quarrels at the tent became a "frequent occurrence."[1]

This ill-matched trio rented rooms at the Diamond Front, located on the south end of Main Street. Late on Tuesday afternoon, September 26, five gunshots were heard from the second floor of the Diamond Front. "A large crowd gathered at the place almost before the report of the last shot had died away." Ella ran downstairs crying, "He has killed my Eddie!"

Hawley was found lying between two beds, clad only in a shirt and shot twice in the torso. Lifted onto a bed, he died within moments. Mayor S. H. Horner was one of the first to arrive on the scene. Boyd had followed his wife downstairs, claiming that he had not shot Hawley and that Ed "was as wide-awake as he was." But Hawley was dead, and Mayor Horner ordered a special policeman to take Boyd to the city jail. Boyd soon admitted that "he caught Hawley in bed with his wife and shot him."

On Wednesday a coroner's jury ruled that the "shooting was done feloniously," and Boyd was transferred to the county jail at Wellington. That afternoon Ed Hawley was buried in Caldwell's City Cemetery, an interment arranged by his brother.

The shooting of Hawley by a husband incensed over a tawdry affair between first cousins did not rank with the gunfights of cattle town Caldwell. It certainly did not compare with

George Flatt, a revolver in each fist, outdueling two cowboys in a saloon melee. Nor did it match up with Marshal Henry Brown trading shots across Main Street with gambler Newt Boyce. Nor with the wild shootout between citizens and the Jim Talbot "Gang." The killing of Ed Hawley may well have been justified, but he was unarmed. This fatal shooting immediately in the wake of the Cherokee Strip Land Rush did not signify a return to the Border Queen's wild old days.

Indeed, soon after the Cherokee Strip Land Rush there were steady rains in the vicinity of Caldwell. This timely precipitation put the ground in prime condition for planting, and area farmers immediately went to work sowing wheat.[2] Caldwell settled into a long and quiet existence as the commercial center of a wheat farming region. For a town with such a turbulent and colorful beginning, the Border Queen now became a model of rural serenity.

For decades farm town Caldwell stayed about the same size—between 1,600 and 1,800—as it was during its years as a railhead of the Chisholm Trail. The business section remained three blocks long. Although the Grand Opera House burned in 1918, the two three-story hotels stood until the 1970s. (The Southwestern was painted white and was converted to a hospital, while the Leland long remained Caldwell's best hostelry

Dr. W. A. Noble spent most of his professional life serving the people of Caldwell. He rests beside his prominent family stone in the City Cemetery. — Author photo

and featured the town's best restaurant.) But even though the three most prominent buildings of the Border Queen are gone, the Stock Exchange Bank still stands, along with many other commercial buildings and a scattering of residences from the late 1800s.

Wichita is a city of more than 350,000; Dodge City's population exceeds 25,000; Newton is a growing town of 18,000; and even Abilene, at 6,500, is four times as large as when it was the Chisholm Trail's first railhead. When the Interstate System was built, I-35 came up from South Texas through Oklahoma and to Wichita — passing seventeen miles to the east of Caldwell. Like many other agricultural centers, Caldwell's population has dwindled in recent years, holding at 1,200 as of this writing. But with the expansion of urban Wichita, almost all of the architectural heritage of the cattle town era was replaced by more modern structures. On a smaller scale the same pattern has removed most of the nineteenth century buildings from the other cattle towns. But in Caldwell, more than in any other of the old Kansas cattle towns, it remains possible to walk the streets and study the buildings and — especially in the half-light of dusk or dawn — recapture some of the feel of a trail's end, perhaps sense a few ghosts of cowboys and ranchers and urban pioneers.

The cowboy ballad *The Old Chisholm Trail* contains a verse about Caldwell:

Pioneer settler A. M. Colson (1843-1924) lost his first wife, Mary, who died at 19 after giving birth to daughter Fawnie. Colson's second wife also was named Mary. He is buried in City Cemetery between Mary A. (1860-1879) and Mary J. (1853-1934). — Author photo

We hit Caldwell and we hit her on the fly,
We bedded down the cattle on the hill close by.

If the old-time cowboys understood Caldwell's place in the lore of cattle towns, the Border Queen went largely unrecognized by the Western novelists and filmmakers who popularized America's last frontier during the twentieth century. Andy Adams, who knew the Border Queen as a cattle town, often used Caldwell as a setting for his Western stories. But later writers turned to other towns, or to purely fictional communities, as their Western backdrops.

Western movies did even more than novels to familiarize the public with Wild West lore. In 1939 *Dodge City*, starring Errol Flynn, offered a rousing version of the most famous of all cattle towns to moviegoers. Six years later *Abilene Town* used the first Kansas railhead as a backdrop for Randolph Scott. In 1955 Joel McCrea starred as Wyatt Earp in *Wichita*.[3] Most of the many films about Wyatt Earp have included Wichita and Dodge City as backdrops, just as many motion pictures about Wild Bill Hickok have included Abilene. Dodge City was a popular setting for a great many other Western movies, and for twenty seasons Dodge was the television home of *Gunsmoke*. During the 1959-1960 season Joel McCrea starred on TV in *Wichita Town*.

Caldwell never received title billing for a Western movie or TV series, and the Border Queen almost never was used as a backdrop. There was one notable cinematic exception.

William S. Hart was a popular star of Western films from 1914 until his retirement from the screen in 1925. During the 1870s Hart spent a few boyhood years in Dakota Territory, before his family moved back East. Captivated by the West of his youth, Hart always tried to achieve authenticity in his movies. In 1925 Hart lensed his final motion picture, *Tumbleweeds*, the story of the 1889 [sic] Cherokee Strip Land Rush.

William S. Hart in *Tumbleweeds,* with the set used as Caldwell in the background.
— Author's collection

Although the script confused the date of the Strip opening with the 1889 rush to the Oklahoma District, many elements involving Caldwell are portrayed onscreen. Cattle are cleared out of the Strip and driven to Caldwell, while homesteaders guide their wagons into the Border Queen, depicted onscreen as a ramshackle village of 200—until "almost overnight the little town ... mushrooms into a seething, rawboned metropolis." The re-enactment of the run is a magnificent, sweeping scene. And early in the film Hart and his cowboys shove a vast cattle herd off their government lease toward Caldwell, along with herds from other leases. The drovers gaze upon this final drive with sadness, and Hart pulls off his hat. "Boys—it's the last of the West."

Hart's mournful line could serve as a suitable valedictory for the Border Queen. The Cherokee Strip Land Rush was not precisely the last of the West: Butch Cassidy's Wild Bunch flourished for several more years; cattlemen and sheepherders continued to clash into the twentieth century; a few gunfights erupted here and there across the West; and during the opening years of the twentieth century the Arizona Rangers battled outlaws in the last sustained violence of the Old West. But such events were sporadic signals of the end of the Wild West. And for the Border Queen the 1893 Land Rush indeed was "the last of the West."

Fortunately a strong sense of the rich heritage of the Border

The refurbished Danford Building now serves as meeting place and museum for the local historical society. Danford Hall, the old opera house, was upstairs. Jim Talbot stood behind this building when he shot Mike Meagher. Frank Noyes was taken from his house behind the Danford Building, then lynched. —Author photo

Queen continues to motivate local citizens. Handsome historical markers have been placed throughout town describing important events or buildings. The active and resourceful local history organization has acquired the Danford Building, refurbishing the old opera house for use as their meeting place and museum. The City Cemetery is beautifully maintained as a walkway through Caldwell's past. In September 2007 a herd of Texas Longhorns was driven up the route of the Chisholm Trail, and upon reaching Caldwell early in October there was a community-wide celebration reminiscent of the Border Queen festivals staged during the 1880s for cowboys and cattlemen. The Old West of the nineteenth-century Border Queen may be past, but today it can be revisited, remnants can be savored in Caldwell.

In 1939 *Tumbleweeds* was re-released, with a musical soundtrack and an eight-minute prologue by William S. Hart. The old Western star described the cattle frontier, the Cherokee Strip, and "the mad dash for destiny" of the homesteaders. Then he spoke with deep emotion about making Western films, at one point exclaiming, "O, the thrill of it all!"

If a cinematic history of the Border Queen were rewound, like a William S. Hart movie, back through a projector, it would begin with "the mad dash" for the Cherokee Strip. Then back through the prosperous years as headquarters for cattlemen of the Cherokee Strip Live Stock Association, before winding back past the rip-roaring half decade as railhead of the fabled Chisholm Trail. Then through the boom when the first railroad

Chuckwagons, cowboys, and cattle moving north up Caldwell's Main Street, in front of an enthusiastic crowd of spectators. —Courtesy Karen Sturm

came to Caldwell, and the wild years as a lawless little trail town. Homesteader hordes—cattlemen—cowboys—gunfighters—dance hall girls—urban pioneers—buffalo hunters. The Grand Opera House—the Leland Hotel—the Red Light—the First Chance-Last Chance.

O, the thrill of it all!

Entertainment for the 2007 cattle drive resembles the Border Queen celebrations of the 1880s. —Courtesy Karen Sturm

Endnotes

Chapter 1: First Chance on the Chisholm Trail
1. Frantz, *Texas*, 126.
2. Clay, *My Life on the Range*, 107-108.
3. *Caldwell Messenger*, Centennial Edition, May 8, 1961. "History of Sumner County Was One of Color, Turmoil, Fear, Sorrow and Joy" was an article written by local historian Chester C. Heizer and published in the Centennial Edition. Current studies of Coronado's journey contend that his route was north of Sumner County.
4. McCoy, *Historic Sketches of the Cattle Trade*, 116.
5. Halsell, *Cowboys and Cattleland*, 214.
6. Fehrenbach, *Lone Star*, 554.
7. Haley, *Charles Goodnight*, 466.
8. Dobie, *The Longhorns*, 110.
9. Halsell, *Cowboys and Cattleland*, 112.
10. Freeman, *Midnight and Noonday*, 79-80; *Caldwell Messenger*, Centennial Edition, May 8, 1961. "E. A. Detrick Kept 'Thumbnail' History of Early Events in Caldwell." Detrick moved to Caldwell in 1885 and carefully chronicled the past of the Border Queen.
11. The best description of the town company and its founding activities is in "Caldwell Founded in 1870-71; Named for U.S. Sen. Caldwell," *Caldwell Messenger*, Centennial Edition, May 8, 1961. Also see "E. A. Detrick" article in same edition.
12. "Caldwell Mail Service Dates to May 29, 1871, Used Stone's Store," *Caldwell Messenger*, Centennial Edition, May 8, 1961; Freeman, *Midnight and Noonday*, 31.
13. "Caldwell Founded in 1870-71 . . . ," *Caldwell Messenger*, Centennial Edition, May 8, 1961.
14. Freeman, *Midnight and Noonday*, 32; "E. A. Detrick," *Caldwell Messenger*, Centennial Edition, May 8, 1961.
15. Hunter, *Trail Drivers of Texas*, 87, 866-869.
16. Freeman, *Midnight and Noonday*, 24.
17. Ibid.
18. Ibid., 24, 28-31.
19. Ibid., 282-285.
20. Ibid., 36-39.
21. Ibid., 39-40.
22. Billington, *Westward Expansion*, 6-7.
23. Lake, *Frontier Marshal*, 44.
24. Ibid., 54-55, 68.
25. Freeman, *Midnight and Noonday*, 44.
26. G. D. Freeman provided the only detailed account of the shooting and participants, in Freeman, *Midnight and Noonday*, 45-48.

27. Freeman, *Midnight and Noonday*, 49-55. For Sullivan's arrival see "Caldwell Founded in 1870-71 ...," *Caldwell Messenger*, Centennial Edition, May 8, 1961.
28. Freeman, *Midnight and Noonday*, 179-180.

Chapter 2: Shootouts and Vigilantes

1. Freeman, *Midnight and Noonday*, 56-59, is the primary source for the shooting of William Manning by George Epps.
2. Metz, *Dallas Stoudenmire*, 93-95.
3. Freeman, *Midnight and Noonday*, 238.
4. Ibid., 75.
5. Freeman describes McCarty and his first shooting in *Midnight and Noonday*, 72-74. Mrs. J. B. Rideout also offers a first-hand description of McCarty and his gunplay in *Six Years on the Border*, 58-63.
6. McCarty's second shooting is described by Freeman in *Midnight and Noonday*, 76-79. Publishing a second-hand account on May 8, 1872, the *Topeka Daily Commonwealth* stated that McCarty "bet the whiskey that he could shoot through the 'plug' hat of a certain gentleman in the bar-room without hitting his head. The whiskey was set and McCarty fired, but the ball, unfortunately, went into the fellow's skull between the eyes killing him instantly." Also see *Wichita Eagle*, April 26, 1872.
7. An extensive history of the vigilante movement was presented by Richard Maxwell Brown in *Strain of Violence: Historical Studies of American Violence and Vigilantism*. Also see Frank Richard Prassel, *The Great American Outlaw: A Legacy of Fact and Fiction*; Wayne Gard, *Frontier Violence*.
8. Freeman, *Midnight and Noonday*, 79-80.
9. Freeman provides the only primary account of the raid on the First Chance–Last Chance and the vigilante pursuit of Michael McCarty in *Midnight and Noonday*, 81-85, 89.
10. Freeman, *Midnight and Noonday*, 96; *Wichita Eagle*, May 31, 1872.
11. Freeman, *Midnight and Noonday*, 96.
12. Ibid., 86-88; *Wichita Eagle*, June 14, 1872.
13. These names were related in the *Wellington Banner*, October 16, 1872, as cited in White, *The Border Queen*, 40.
14. Freeman fully described this incident in *Midnight and Noonday*, 93-95.
15. The killing of Oliver's (or Olive's) herder is related in Freeman, *Midnight and Noonday*, 96-99.
16. Freeman, *Midnight and Noonday*, 101. Freeman's first-person account of the grueling pursuit is on pages 100-116.
17. Freeman described the lynching of Tom Smith in *Midnight and Noonday*, 117-123.

Chapter 3: Trail Town on the Grow

1. Gard, *The Chisholm Trail*, 190.
2. Freeman, *Midnight and Noonday*, 183n.
3. "Early Day School Record Books Show Dist. 20 Formed on September 5, 1872," *Caldwell Messenger*, Centennial Edition, May 8, 1961.
4. "E. A. Detrick...," *Caldwell Messenger*, Centennial Edition, May 8, 1961; *Sumner County Press*, May 7, 1874; Coke, *Caldwell*, 42.
5. For the story of Caldwell's first church, as well as the Rideout family's often difficult years of the Kansas mission field, see Mrs. Rideout's 1883 memoir, *Six Years on the Border*.
6. White, *The Border Queen*, 38. In 1872, before the line was extended into Indian Territory, Caldwell was the southern terminus of the Southwestern Stagecoach Company. Northbound coaches from Caldwell departed for Wellington and Wichita each Tuesday, Thursday, and Saturday, while coaches arrived from Wellington each Monday, Wednesday, and Friday, *Wichita Eagle*, December 5, 1872. For daily runs, see *Sumner County Press*, November 27, 1873.
7. *Wichita Eagle*, December 5, 1872.
8. White, *The Border Queen*, 39.
9. Ibid., 38-39.

10. *Wichita Eagle*, September 13, 1872.
11. *Sumner County Press*, October 23, 1873; March 5 and May 21, 1874.
12. Ibid., April 23 and May 7, 1874.
13. Ibid., May 21, 1874.
14. Ibid., March 5, 1874.
15. Ibid., April 23, May 21, and June 25, 1874.
16. Ibid., May 21 and June 25, 1874.
17. Freeman, *Midnight and Noonday*, 168.
18. *Sumner County Press*, August 6, 1874.
19. Ibid., and Freeman, *Midnight and Noonday*, 168n.
20. Freeman, *Midnight and Noonday*, 158-169.
21. *Sumner County Press*, July 30, 1874.
22. McNeal, *When Kansas Was Young*, 16-17.
23. The raid on Caldwell is described in the *Sumner County Press*, July 30, 1874; Rideout, *Six Years on the Border*, 95-109; and Freeman, *Midnight and Noonday*, 170-173.
24. The lynching is described in the *Sumner County Press*, July 30 and August 6, 1874; Freeman, *Midnight and Noonday*, Freeman, *Midnight and Noonday*, 173-175; and Rideout, *Six Years on the Border*, 101-109.
25. Freeman, *Midnight and Noonday*, 175.
26. *Sumner County Press*, August 6, 1874.
27. The murder and subsequent lynching are described in the *Sumner County Press*, September 3, 1874; Rideout, *Six Years on the Border*, 84-86; and Freeman, *Midnight and Noonday*, 176-178.

Chapter 4: Caldwell Becomes a Community

1. *Sumner County Press*, December 24, 1874, and January 7, 1875.
2. Ibid., May 20, 1875.
3. Ibid., October 28, December 23, and December 30, 1875.
4. Ibid., January 20, February 10, March 2, and April 13, 1876.
5. Rideout, *Six Years on the Border*, 133-135.
6. The Rideout ministry in Caldwell is related with rich, poignant detail by Mrs. Rideout in *Six Years on the Border*.
7. Ibid., 64, 180.
8. Ibid., 127, 154, 183-184. For sample weddings see the *Sumner County Press*, October 7 and December 16, 1875; April 13, August 10, and November 2, 1876; March 22, April 19, July 12, and November 8, 1877; January 3, 1878.
9. *Sumner County Press*, March 1 and November 15, 1877; April 17, 1878.
10. *Sumner County Press*, August 30, 1877; Rideout, *Six Years on the Border*, 197.
11. *Sumner County Press*, October 14, 1875; August 10, 1876.
12. Ibid., February 8 and 13, March 1, April 26, and June 7, 1877.
13. Ibid., June 1, 1876; May 17 and November 8, 1877.
14. Ibid., May 13, 1875.
15. Billington, *America's Frontier Heritage*, 78, 88.
16. *Sumner County Press*, September 16, 1876; February 10, April 13, May 4, 1876; March 14 and May 4, 1878.
17. Ibid., August 24, 1876, and November 24, 1878.
18. Ibid., September 7, 1876, October 11 and December 13, 1877; "Early Day School Record Books...," *Caldwell Messenger*, Centennial Edition, May 8, 1961.
19. Rideout, *Six Years on the Border*, 208-209; *Sumner County Press*, December 14, 1876, and January 3, 1878.
20. *Sumner County Press*, June 17 and 24, and July 6, 1875.
21. Rideout, *Six Years on the Border*, 191-192; *Sumner County Press*, July 13, 1876, and July 22, 1878.
22. *Sumner County Press*, September 25, 1876; September 20, 1877; July 25, 1878.
23. White, *The Border Queen*, 101. *Sumner County Press*, December 17, 1874; April 13, 1876; March 8 and November 15, 1877; February 28 and November 14, 1878.

Chapter Five: Boss Town of the Southwest
1. *Caldwell Post*, July 17, 1879.
2. Dykstra, *Cattle Towns*, 70-72.
3. *Caldwell Post*, January 2, 1879.
4. Ibid., January 9, 1879.
5. Ibid., January 9 and February 6, 1879.
6. Ibid., January 16 and July 24, 1879.
7. Ibid., January 23 and May 15, 1879.
8. Ibid., March 6, April 3 and 10, September 25, 1879.
9. Freeman, *Midnight and Noonday*, 198.
10. Freeman, *Midnight and Noonday*, 130-134; *Caldwell Post*, May 1, 1879.
11. Freeman, *Midnight and Noonday*, 133-134.
12. There are two primary accounts of this fight: *Caldwell Post*, July 10, 1879, and Freeman, *Midnight and Noonday*, 185-191.
13. *Caldwell Post*, April 10, 1879.
14. Ibid., September 25 and October 2, 1879.
15. Freeman, *Midnight and Noonday*, 192.
16. *Caldwell Post*, September 25, 1879.
17. Ibid., January 9 and October 2, 9 and 16, 1879; June 17, 1880.
18. Ibid., October 30, 1879, and October 23, 1884.
19. Miller and Snell, *Great Gunfighters of the Kansas Cowtowns*, 142.
20. *Caldwell Post*, February 20, November 20, and December 4, 1879; February 26, 1880.
21. Ibid., November 27, 1879; January 8 and 29, 1880.
22. Ibid., February 19, and March 4 and 25, 1880.
23. See the *Caldwell Post*, May 15, 1879 and February 26, 1880, and the Caldwell town plat.
24. *Caldwell Post*, January 8 and February 26, 1880.
25. Ibid., April 10, 1879.
26. Ibid., March 11, 1880.
27. Ibid., May 13, 1880.
28. Ibid., May 20 and June 3, 1880.
29. Rod Cook has related the story of Caldwell's Red Light in *George and Maggie and the Red Light Saloon*. For the background of George and Maggie see pp. 2-9.
30. *Caldwell Post*, September 4, 1879.
31. Cook, *Red Light Saloon*, 22-23.
32. *Caldwell Post*, May 13 and 20, 1880; Freeman, *Midnight and Noonday*, 193-194, 202-205.
33. Dykstra, *Cattle Towns*, 69-72.
34. *Caldwell Post*, June 3, 1880.
35. Ibid.

Chapter Six: Last Railhead on the Chisholm Trail
1. *Caldwell Post*, June 3, 17, and 24, 1880.
2. Ibid., June 17, 1880.
3. Dykstra, *Cattle Towns*, 72; *Caldwell Post*, November 25. 1880.
4. *Caldwell Post*, November 11, 1880; June 16, 23 and 30, 1881; August 18, 1881.
5. *Caldwell Post*, August 18 and 25, 1881; Emmett, *Shanghai Pierce: A Fair Likeness*.
6. *Caldwell Post*, September 8, 1881.
7. Ibid., September 8 and 29, and October 13, 1881; January 26, February 9, 16, 23, March 2, 9, 16, 1882.
8. Ibid., February 2, 9, 23 and March 9, 1882.
9. Ibid., January 26, 1882.
10. Ibid., June 16, 1881.
11. Ibid., August 18, 1881.
12. Ibid., November 6 and December 11, 1879; March 29, April 11, May 20, June 3 and 24, 1880; December 1 and 8, 1881.

13. *Caldwell Messenger*, April 7, 1993; *Caldwell Post*, November 17 and December 15, 1881; January 5, March 30, and April 27, 1882.
14. *Caldwell Post*, January 13, 1881.
15. Ibid., September 23, October 21, November 18 and 25, December 9, 1880.
16. Ibid., October 25 and November 8, 1883.
17. Ibid., October 20 and 27, November 10, 17 and 24, December 1 and 15, 1881; January 5, 12 and 19, May 11, 1882.
18. Ibid., September 1, 8 and 29, December 15, 1881; May 18, 1882.
19. Ibid., June 8 and 15, 1882.
20. Ibid., August 12, October 14 and 21, December 9, 1880; August 4, October 6 and 27, November 17 and 24, 1881; February 23 and June 15, 1882.
21. Ibid., November 11, 1880; June 2, 23 and 30, July 7 and 21, August 4, September 29, December 15, 1881; January 12, February 9, June 22, 1882.
22. Ibid., September 1, 1881.
23. Colcord, *Autobiography of Charles Francis Colcord*, 94-95.
24. Ibid., 39.
25. Ibid., 112.
26. Ibid., 56, 94, 96, 97.
27. Ibid., 94.
28. The spree is described in Colcord, *Autobiography*, 95-96.
29. REVISED ORDINANCES OF THE CITY OF CALDWELL, published in the *Caldwell Post*, May 4, 1882. For badges see the *Caldwell Commercial*, August 26, 1880.
30. *Caldwell Post*, April 15, May 6, 13 and 27, and June 10, 1880.
31. The killing is described in detail in the *Post*, June 24, 1880.
32. *Caldwell Post*, July 1 and 8, November 11, 1880; *Caldwell Commercial*, November 11, 1880; April 28, 1881.
33. *Caldwell Post*, September 9, 1880.
34. Ibid., October 14 and 28, 1880.
35. *Caldwell Commercial*, August 25, 1881; *Caldwell Post*, August 25, 1881; Cook, *George and Maggie and the Red Light Saloon*, 38-50.
36. *Wichita Eagle*, December 22, 1881.
37. Ibid., January 4, 1877.
38. The gun battle and subsequent pursuit were related in the *Caldwell Post*, December 22, 1881, and by George Freeman, a witness to the shootout and a participant in the pursuit, in *Midnight and Noonday*, 250-266. Sam P. Ridings, another citizen of Caldwell during this era, also described the Talbot shootout, "a matter of general knowledge," in Ridings, *The Chisholm Trail*, 470-486.
39. Freeman, *Midnight and Noonday*, 254; Ridings, *Chisholm Trail*, 475-476.
40. Colcord, *Autobiography*, 111-112.
41. *Caldwell Post*, December 22, 1881.
42. Miller and Snell, *Great Gunfighters*, 367-368; *Caldwell Post*, February 2, 1882.
43. *Caldwell Commercial*, March 9, 1882.
44. Ibid., June 29, 1882.
45. *Caldwell Post*, October 19 and 26, 1882.
46. Freeman, *Midnight and Noonday*, 209; *Caldwell Commercial*, June 29, 1882.

Chapter Seven: The Town Tamers

1. Freeman, *Midnight and Noonday*, 304-305; *Sumner County Press*, June 29, 1882.
2. *Caldwell Commercial*, June 22, 1882; *Caldwell Post*, July 6, 1882.
3. Dykstra, *The Cattle Towns*, 142-148. In a chart on page 144, Dykstra outlined "Cattle Town Homicides" during the heydays of Abilene, Dodge City, Ellsworth, Wichita, and Caldwell. This compilation reveals that fewer than two violent deaths per year occurred while the railheads were at their wildest.
4. *Caldwell Post*, July 6, 1882; Freeman, *Midnight and Noonday*, 307.

5. *Caldwell Commercial*, July 6, 1882; *Caldwell Post*, July 6, 1882.
6. *Caldwell Post*, July 6 and 13, 1882.
7. *Caldwell Commercial*, July 13 and November 9, 1882; Freeman, *Midnight and Noonday*, 305-307.
8. *Caldwell Post*, July 13, 1882; *Caldwell Commercial*, July 20, 1882.
9. *Caldwell Commercial*, August 24, 1882.
10. Ibid., August 24, 1882.
11. *Caldwell Commercial*, September 7, 1882.
12. Freeman, *Midnight and Noonday*, 308-309.
13. Joe Wiedeman, related to Chester C. Heizer and reprinted in the *Caldwell Messenger*, May 8, 1961. Freeman, *Midnight and Noonday*, 307-309. On page 307 Freeman described Brown as "a man similar in character to Carr, with the exception that he seldom smiled, was sober, candid and determined in expression and mind, therefore was not familiar with the children, or a man with whom the ladies loved to converse. He dressed neatly, was gentlemanly and won friends immediately upon his arrival in Caldwell."
14. *Caldwell Commercial*, October 12, 1882; *Caldwell Post*, December 22, 1881. The rewards were posted by Mayor Cass Burrus of Caldwell ($500), Sheriff Thralls ($200), W. E. Campbell of Caldwell ($200), and J. M. Steele of Wichita ($200).
15. *Caldwell Commercial*, October 12, 1882; *Caldwell Post*, October 12, 1882.
16. *Caldwell Commercial*, September 28 and October 5, 1882; *Caldwell Post*, October 12, 1882.
17. *Caldwell Commercial*, October 12 and November 9, 1882.
18. Ibid., October 19, 1882.
19. *Caldwell Commercial*, November 9 and December 21, 1882; *Caldwell Post*, November 9 and 23, 1882.
20. *Caldwell Commercial*, December 21, 1882; Freeman, *Midnight and Noonday*, 307, 310. D. D. Leahy, at the time a Caldwell merchant, half a century later said that "Batt Carr left Caldwell under a cloud of some sort that I have never heard explained." Leahy, "Random Recollections of Other Days," *Wichita Morning Eagle*, April 13, 1932.
21. Wiedeman, related to Heitzer and reprinted in the *Caldwell Messenger*, May 8, 1961.

Chapter Eight: Caldwell's Outlaw Marshal
1. Siringo, *A Cowboy Detective*, 13.
2. Ibid., 13-14.
3. Ibid., 15-16.
4. Information about the boyhood of Henry Brown was provided to the author by genealogist John M. Usury of Rolla, Missouri. For Brown's 1876 killing in the Texas Panhandle, see Siringo, *A Texas Cowboy*, 110, and Siringo, *History of "Billy the Kid,"* introduction and 69-70.
5. Literature on the Lincoln County War and Billy the Kid is voluminous, beginning with three excellent general histories: Keleher, *Violence in Lincoln County, 1876-1881*; Mullin, ed., Maurice Garland Fulton's *History of the Lincoln County War*; and Nolan, *The Lincoln County War, A Documentary History*.
6. O'Neal, *Henry Brown, Outlaw Marshal*, 23-84. Quotes about Brown's temper are from Rasch, "A Note on Henry Newton Brown," *Warriors of Lincoln County*.
7. Colcord, *Autobiography of Charles Francis Colcord*, 111.
8. Siringo, *A Cowboy Detective*, 14.
9. For quote, see *Caldwell Post*, December 28, 1882. John Phillips had been hired as city marshal at $60 per month, but when the $10 monthly reduction was approved by the Council he resigned. Three years later he accepted an appointment as Caldwell marshal—at $100 per month—six days after Henry Brown's death. *Caldwell Journal* (May 8, 1884); and *Caldwell Commercial* (July 7, 1881).
10. Freeman, *Midnight and Noonday*, 310.
11. *Caldwell Journal*, May 8, 1884.
12. All contemporary references are to "Ben Wheeler."
13. *Caldwell Post*, October 26, 1882.
14. *Caldwell Commercial*, January 4, 1883; and *Caldwell Post*, January 4, 1883. The *Post* reported

that "Henry is as proud of his gun as a boy of a new top." The two newspapers offered different versions—each inaccurate—of the inscription. (*Commercial:* "Presented to City Marshal H. N. Brown for valuable services rendered the citizens of Caldwell, Kansas, A. M. Colson, Mayor, Dec., 1882." *Post:* "Presented to H. N. Brown by his many friends, as a reward for the efficient services rendered the citizens of Caldwell. A. M. Colson, Mayor, Jan. 1, A.D. 1883") The correct inscription was reported to the author by T. L. Rhodes of Richardson, Texas, who was an owner of the rifle. The Kansas State Historical Society has now acquired this rifle.

15. *Caldwell Commercial*, February 1, 1883; *Caldwell Post*, October 26, 1882; *Rolla Weekly Herald*, February 8, 1883, and May 15, 1884.

16. *Caldwell Commercial*, March 8, 1883.

17. Ibid., March 22, 1883.

18. Ibid., March 29, 1883; and *Caldwell Journal*, May 17, 1883.

19. *Caldwell Commercial*, March 29, 1883.

20. Ibid., April 15, 1883.

21. Miller and Snell, *Great Gunfights of the Kansas Cowtowns*, 141-142.

22. *Caldwell Commercial*, April 12, 1883.

23. Rideout, *Six Years on the Border*, 144-145; *Caldwell Post*, September 23 and December 9, 1880, and May 18, 1882.

24. The Spotted Horse incident was described in detail in the *Caldwell Journal*, May 17, 1883. G. D. Freeman also depicted the event in *Midnight and Noonday*, 333-337. "The marshal thinking to frighten him, fired his revolver twice above the Indian's head," stated Freeman on page 335.

25. *Caldwell Journal*, August 2, 1883; Police Docket Records of Caldwell, July 1882—May 1884, cited in Miller and Snell, *Great Gunfights of the Kansas Cowtowns*, 54; Joe Wiedeman, related to Chester C. Heitzer and reprinted in the *Caldwell Messenger*, September 7, 1957.

26. *Caldwell Journal*, May 31, 1883.

27. Ibid., August 9, 1883.

28. The story of the fight between Brown and Joyce is described at length in the *Caldwell Journal*, December 20, 1883.

29. *Caldwell Journal*, May 2, 1884.

30. Leahy, "Random Recollections," *Wichita Morning Eagle*, April 3, 1932.

31. *Caldwell Journal*, January 24, 1884.

Chapter Nine: Tragedy at Medicine Lodge

1. Leahy, "Random Recollections," *Wichita Morning Eagle*, April 3, 1932; and in interview with Dave Leahy (son of D. D.) at his residence in Wichita, January 10, 1971. On May 8, 1884, the *Caldwell Journal* referred to Alice Levagood Brown as "a most estimable young lady." *Caldwell Post*, August 31, 1882, for Maude's adoption and graduation information.

2. Marriage License, Sumner County Records, Wellington, Kansas; *Caldwell Journal*, March 27, 1884.

3. Inventory of Henry N. Brown estate, Sumner County Court Records, Case number 633. The sale was concluded on April 2, 1884, between Brown and Mr. and Mrs. Robert E. Stock. The property in question was located on lots 21 and 23 of block 102, which was just north of the middle of the block on the west side of Main Street.

4. Deed Record, Sumner County, Kansas, April 2, 1884; Administrator's Deed, Sumner County, Kansas, July 7, 1884; Affidavit showing that Henry Brown borrowed $300 from Caldwell Savings Bank with Levi Thrailkill and William Morris as sureties, Sumner County Court Records, Wellington, Ks. The *Caldwell Journal*, May 2, 1884, stated that Brown and Wheeler were being paid "$1,500 and $1,200 a year respectively." This was a $10 per month raise for Wheeler, and an increase for Brown from $100 to $125 per month. The extra $300 per year obviously did not seem enough to the newlywed marshal.

5. The history of Medicine Lodge is depicted in Yost, *Medicine Lodge*.

6. *Caldwell Journal*, May 8, 1884.

7. Ibid., May 8, 1884.

8. Ibid., May 8, 1884; Freeman, *Midnight and Noonday*, 317.

9. *Rolla Weekly Herald*, May 18, 1884.

10. Yost, *Medicine Lodge*, 79; interview with Luke Chapin in Medicine Lodge, January 11, 1871.

11. Yost, *Medicine Lodge*, 83, 95, 99.

12. Interview with Gus Palmer (Medicine Lodge, January 11, 1971). Reference in this paragraph to temporary quarters used by county officials bring up the point that the first permanent courthouse—an imposing brick structure located southeast of the old jail—was built in 1886.

13. Freeman, *Midnight and Noonday*, 316; McNeal, *When Kansas Was Young*, 154; *Caldwell Journal*, May 8, 1884; Yost, *Medicine Lodge*, 16.

14. Freeman, *Midnight and Noonday*, 317; *Caldwell Journal*, May 8, 1884.

15. Yost, *Medicine Lodge*, 95.

16. Freeman, *Midnight and Noonday*, 317.

17. Yost, *Medicine Lodge*, 96-97.

18. The dead end defile was unnamed until tourists began arriving after the bank robbery, whereupon the now noted site was christened "Jackass Canyon."

19. *Medicine Lodge Cressett*, May 1, 1884, quoted in Yost, *Medicine Lodge*, 84.

20. Freeman, *Midnight and Noonday*, 318.

21. *Medicine Lodge Cressett*, May 1, 1884, quoted in Yost, *Medicine Lodge*, 88.

22. "It is stated that when the time arrived for the prisoners to stand, so that the photograph could be taken, our former brave city marshal got down on his knees and implored for mercy." Freeman, *Midnight and Noonday*, 320.

23. This letter no longer exists, presumably disposed of or lost by Maude Brown. It was reproduced in area newspapers, released either by Mrs. Brown or by Medicine Lodge authorities before mailing it. A few sentences were not published: "such parts as are of a purely business character and of no interest to the public. They contained minute directions of how to dispose of his property and as to the payment of some debts." *Caldwell Journal* (May 8, 1884).

24. McNeal, *When Kansas Was Young*, 157.

25. *Medicine Lodge Cressett*, May 1, 1884.

26. Ibid., May 8, 1884.

27. Ibid., May 1, 1884.

28. Blanchard, *Conquest of Southwest Kansas*, 227; McNeal, *When Kansas Was Young*, 158.

29. Freeman, *Midnight and Noonday*, 321-322; McNeal, *When Kansas Was Young*, 159; Charles Colcord was present, and left an eyewitness account of the lynching in the *Autobiography of Charles Francis Colcord*, 112-115.

30. *Medicine Lodge Cressett*, May 1, 1884; McNeal, *When Kansas Was Young*, 159.

31. Yost, *Medicine Lodge*, 99.

32. Ibid.

33. Miller, Langsdorf, and Richmond, *Kansas in Newspapers*, 104; *Medicine Lodge Cressett*, May 8, 1884, quoted in Yost, *Medicine Lodge*, 87-88.

34. Yost, *Medicine Lodge*, 100-101; Miller, Langsdorf, and Richmond, *Kansas in Newspapers*, 104; *Medicine Lodge Cressett*, May 1, 1884; E. W. Payne gravestone, Medicine Lodge.

Chapter Ten: The End of Caldwell's Gunfighter Era

1. *Caldwell Journal*, May 8, 1884.

2. Ibid.; "Marshal Henry Brown's In-Laws," unpublished manuscript by Rod Cook.

3. *Medicine Lodge Cressett*, May 8, 1884, quoted in Yost, *Medicine Lodge*, 87-88.

4. Freeman, *Midnight and Noonday*, 322.

5. *Caldwell Journal*, May 8, 1884.

6. Ibid.

7. Freeman, *Midnight and Noonday*, pp. 323-324. "Mr. Mayor and gentlemen of the council: Your committee to whom was referred the matter of drafting resolutions, expressive of the sentiments of the people of Caldwell in regard to the Medicine Lodge tragedy, have had the matter under consideration and submit the following report:

> WHEREAS, Two men in whom the Government and people of Caldwell have heretofore reposed great trust and confidence, have to the unutterable amazement and mortifi-

cation of our citizens, proved themselves murderers, robbers, cowards and villains of the worst type, by their criminal attack on the Medicine Valley bank, of Medicine Lodge, Kansas; and the wanton murder of Mr. Payne and Mr. Geppert, President and Cashier of said bank, and

WHEREAS, We recognize in the untimely death of Mr. Payne and Mr. Geppert, not only an irreparable loss to the city of Medicine Lodge and Barber county, but by loss to Kansas of two of the best citizens of which our State could boast; and

WHEREAS, We recognize the fact that the two men who were the murderers of Mr. Payne and Mr. Geppert had received a large degree of credit, by reason of their employment by this city as peace officers, we deem it due to the citizens of Medicine Lodge that we should take some official notice of the terrible crime that has so shocked their community in regard to the terrible deed. Therefore be it

Resolved of their Mayor and councilmen of the city of Caldwell that the people of Caldwell are horrified by the awful deed which so tragically ended the lives of Mr. Payne and Mr. Geppert, and that they extend to the friends of the gentlemen, their deepest and best sympathies in their inconsolable loss, that the people of Caldwell keenly feel the disgrace which her former officers, by their desperately criminal conduct, have brought upon our community. That in no manner whatever, do our citizens entertain any semblance of sympathy for the depraved creatures who have proved themselves the worst enemies of civilized society. And while our people deplore the necessity for lynch law in any case, they do most heartily approve of the summary manner in which the sturdy men of Medicine Lodge administered justice to the scoundrels who so rudely brought death and sorrow to their door.

8. Yost, *Medicine Lodge*, 102.

9. See Yost, *Medicine Lodge*, 100; and Blanchard, *Southwest Kansas*, 227. Robert R. Foster, whose grandmother lived in Caldwell for four months in 1884 and became fast friends with Maude Brown, stated that the new widow "went to get his body and brought it back to Caldwell, Kansas." Foster's statement, October 10, 1976. Caldwell native Rod Cook, a superb grass-roots historian, and a team of biological anthropologists from Wichita State University conducted a search of the Caldwell City Cemetery for the final burial site of Henry Brown. On October 31, 2003, two likely gravesites were excavated—and found to be empty.

10. Yost, *Medicine Lodge*, 101-102.

11. *Caldwell Journal*, May 8, 1884.

12. Richards, "Tracing a Bandit's Gun," *Guns* (February 1961), 55.

13. This complete story is related in the *Caldwell Messenger*, October 1976. This edition was mailed to me by the gracious and helpful Grace and Mahlon Reck of Caldwell. Also see the statement by Robert R. Foster, October 10, 1976, a copy of which was forwarded to me by T. L. Rholes of Richardson, Texas.

14. See: Deed Record, Sumner County, Kansas, April 2, 1884; affidavit releasing Alice M. Brown from $300 note to Caldwell Savings Bank, with Levi Thrailkill and William Morris assuming payment; paper showing that Dan W. Jones, E. T. Battin, and J. R. Swartzel were appointed appraisers of estate; and report of sale of real estate (lots 21 and 23, block 102 in New Caldwell addition, July 3, 1884). Henry Brown's widow retained the following items:

One book case	$15	Eight window curtains	20
One bed lounge	12	One bedroom suit	50
Two rockers	12	Kitchen furniture & dishes	20
Two small stands	2	Chamber set	4
Parlor stove and pipe	10	One cow	25
Hanging lamp	7		
58 yards of carpet	19		$181

15. *Caldwell Journal*, May 22, 1884; *Caldwell Post*, November 7, 1882; Letters from Alice M. Brown, Devil's Lake, Dakota Territory, September 5 and December 24, 1887; *Frankfort, Indiana, Times*, May 26, 1935.

16. Colcord, *Autobiography of Charles Francis Colcord*, 112; Freeman, *Midnight and Noonday*, 44; McNeal, *When Kansas Was Young*, 188.

Chapter Eleven: The Cherokee Strip Livestock Association
1. Savage, *Cherokee Strip Livestock Association*, 131.
2. Rainey, *Cherokee Strip*, 39-41.
3. Ibid., 162.
4. Ibid. Cowboying for years on the Strip was a memorable experience for Rainey. Later he wrote *Cherokee Strip*, a volume of vivid reminiscences, and he helped to organize and served as president of The Cherokee Strip Cowpunchers Association.
5. Savage, *Cherokee Strip Livestock Association*, 19-20.
6. Ibid., 23-26.
7. Rainey, *Cherokee Strip*, 163; *Caldwell Post*, September 1, October 6, 13 and 27, 1881.
8. Savage, *Cherokee Strip Livestock Association*, 24, 54; Rainey, *Cherokee Strip*, 163; *Caldwell Post*, October 19, 1882.
9. *Caldwell Post*, March 2 and 9, 1882.
10. Ibid., November 16 and December 14, 1882.
11. Ibid., March 1, 1883.
12. *Daily Journal*, reported in the Post, March 1, 1883.
13. *Caldwell Post*, March 8, 1883.
14. Ibid., March 15, 1883.
15. Ibid., March 15, April 26, and May 31, 1883.
16. Ibid., May 31, 1883; Savage, *Cherokee Strip Livestock Association*, 58-63.
17. *Caldwell Post*, May 10, 1883, and January 17, 1884.
18. Freeman, *Midnight and Noonday*, 283, 285; Rainey, *Cherokee Strip*, 192.
19. Siringo, *Riata and Spurs*, 116; *Caldwell Journal*, September 13, 1883.
20. Siringo, *Riata and Spurs*, 117-118; *Caldwell Journal*, June 4, 1885.
21. *Caldwell Journal*, March 13 and October 30, 1884, and April 16, 1885; Siringo, *Riata and Spurs*, 118-119.
22. *Caldwell Journal*, March 13, 1884, covered the convention in detail.
23. *Caldwell Journal*, March 13 and May 15, 1884.
24. Ibid., March 13 and November 27, 1884.
25. Ibid., September 18, 1884.
26. Ibid., October 16, 1884.
27. The shooting and inquest are described in the *Caldwell Journal*, November 20, 1884.
28. *Caldwell Journal*, February 19 and March 26, 1885.
29. Ibid., June 4 and September 17, 1885.
30. Ibid., March 25, 1886.
31. The event was covered in the *Caldwell Journal*, September 15, 1887.
32. *Davenport, Iowa, Times*, article reproduced in the *Caldwell Journal*, September 22, 1887.
33. *Caldwell Journal*, September 22, 1887.
34. Ibid., November 3, 1887.
35. Ibid., April 12, 1888.
36. Savage, *Cherokee Strip Livestock Association*, 104-109.
37. *Caldwell Journal*, September 20, 1888.
38. *Caldwell Journal*, November 1, 1888; Savage, *Cherokee Strip Livestock Association*, 109-111.
39. *Caldwell Journal*, December 6, 1888.
40. Ibid., December 20, 1888.
41. Ibid., March 21, 1887.
42. Ibid., and Savage, *Cherokee Strip Livestock Association*, 115-116.
43. Savage, *Cherokee Strip Livestock Association*, 116-121.
44. *Caldwell Journal*, September 25, November 20, December 4, 1890.
45. Ibid., July 16, 1891.
46. Savage, *Cherokee Strip Livestock Association*, 112-129.

Chapter 12: Life in the Border Queen

1. The commencement was described in the Journal, May 19 and 26, 1887.
2. *Caldwell Journal*, May 24, 1888.
3. Ibid., April 30 and September 17, 1885.
4. Ibid., October 1 and 8, 1885.
5. Ibid., August 4 and 11, 1887; May 24, 1888; May 18, 1893.
6. Ibid., January 31 and February 7, 1884.
7. Ibid., February 7, 1884; Dykstra, *Cattle Towns*, 210-214.
8. Ibid., July 10, August 21, November 6, 13 and 27, December 11 and 25, 1884; January 15 and 22, 1885.
9. Ibid., December 28, 1886; October 13, 1887; September 3, 1889.
10. Ibid., March 21, 1889; *Caldwell News*, December 31, 1891; November 10, 1892.
11. *Caldwell Journal*, June 3, 1886, and August 18, 1887.
12. Ibid., June 28 and July 5, 1883; July 10, 1884; July 9, 1885; July 8, 1886. For Siringo's stand see the *Journal*, June 18 and August 13, 1885. In *Riata and Spurs*, 118, Siringo correctly relates winning the gold ring for his wife by spearing small rings with a long pole from a galloping horse. But he sets his victory in a "grand cowboy tournament at the fair grounds" on May 1, 1885, instead of the Fourth of July celebration. He beat out two opponents in the ring race on the Fourth, but at his fictional cowboy tournament he vanquished "dozens of competitors." Siringo also awarded himself "a fine silver cup" for winning the steer-roping match—a competition he lost on the Fourth. These windies, of course, fell within the long established frontier tradition of tall tales.
13. *Caldwell Journal*, March 5 September 10. and October 8, 1885.
14. Ibid., July 12, 1888.
15. Ibid., April 17, 1890; *Caldwell News*, March 17, 1892. In 1984 the University of Oklahoma Press published an annotated volume of *Midnight and Noonday*, with an illuminating introduction and notes by Richard L. Lane, whose efforts make the book even more useful.
16. *Caldwell Post*, December 8, 1881; April 27, 1882; *Caldwell Journal*, April 30, November 12, and December 24, 1885; July 16, 1891.
17. *Caldwell Journal*, July 29, 1886; September 22 and November 3, 1887; June 21, July 5 and 12, 1888.
18. Ibid., October 30 and December 25, 1884; January 22 and 29, February 5, 1885.
19. Ibid., September 8, 1887; March 16, 1897.
20. Ibid., July 21 and November 24, 1887; October 17, 1889; September 19, 1890; April 9, 1891.
21. Ibid., May 15, 1884; January 5 and May 10, 1888.
22. *Caldwell Post*, October 21, November 43, December 2, 1880.
23. Ibid., October 28, 1882; *Caldwell Journal*, September 4, 1884.
24. *Caldwell Journal*, May 14, 1885.
25. Ibid., November 14, 1889; September 24, 1891.
26. Ibid., April 7, 1892.
27. *Caldwell News*, March 24, 1892.
28. *Caldwell Journal*, October 23, 1885.
29. Ibid., December 10, 1885.
30. Ibid., December 10, 17 and 24, 1885.
31. Ibid., July 23 and 30, November 12, 1885.
32. Ibid., January 24 and August 14, 1884; December 24, 1885.
33. Ibid., January 7, 1886; September 8, 1887.
34. Ibid., May 25, 1887.
35. Ibid., May 15, 1890; July 30, 1891.
36. Ibid., January 22, 1891.
37. Ibid., December 11, 1890; May 14, 1891.
38. Ibid., August 21, 1890; May 14 and August 27, 1891; Shirley, *West of Hell's Fringes*, 62-67; Rainey, *Cherokee Strip*, 255-260.
39. *Caldwell Journal*, July 9, 1885.
40. Ibid., August 20 and 27, September 3, and October 15, 1885; June 24, 1886.

41. Ibid., February 4, 11 and 18, April 22, May 6, June 24, August 12 and 26, September 2 and 9, 1886.
42. Ibid., August 18, 1887; March 16, 1893.
43. Ibid., October 8 and November 5, 1885; January 14, April 8, June 10 and 24, August 19, September 2, 1886.
44. Ibid., June 10 and September 22, 1886; February 10, June 16, July 7, August 25, September 1, 1887.
45. Ibid., January 1, 1885, April 28, 1887; and Society and Church directories, May 10, 1888.
46. *Caldwell Journal*, June 19, 1890.

Chapter Thirteen: Boomers and Land Rushes
1. Billington, *Westward Expansion*, 705, 708.
2. *Caldwell Journal*, April 21 and 28, September 8, 1987.
3. Ibid., December 16, 1886; January 27, 1887.
4. *Caldwell Post*, July 6, 1882; Caldwell Journal, June 14, 1883.
5. *Caldwell Journal*, June 28, July 19, August 9, 1883.
6. Ibid., August 2, 1883; January 17, July 3, 1884; July 15, 1886; August 1, 8, 29, 1889; June 18, October 1, 1891.
7. Ibid., August 1, 1889; April 23, June 18, 1891.
8. Hoig, *David L. Payne*, 1-56.
9. Ibid., xi-xii, 57-206.
10. *Caldwell Post*, November 4, December 9, 1880.
11. Ibid., December 16, 1880; Hoig, *David L. Payne*, 99-104.
12. *Caldwell Journal*, December 4, 1884.
13. *Caldwell Post*, January 6 and November 10, 1881.
14. *Caldwell Journal*, October 16, 1884.
15. Ibid., June 18, July 16, 1885.
16. Ibid., January 29, February 5, 1885; May 1, 1890.
17. Ibid., January 15, February 26, March 5, May 5, 1885.
18. Ibid., May 14 and 28, 1885.
19. Ibid., May 21 and July 16, 1885.
20. Ibid., April 23, September 3, 1885; April 10, 1890.
21. Billington, *Westward Expansion*, 720-721.
22. *Caldwell Journal*, December 17, 1888; January 10 and February 7, 1889.
23. Ibid., March 7, 1889.
24. See ads in the *Journal* on April 11 and 18, 1887.
25. *Caldwell Journal*, April 11 and 18, 1889.
26. Ibid., April 25, 1889.
27. Ibid., May 2, 1889; May 1, 1870.
28. Turner, *The Frontier in American History*, 1; *Caldwell Journal*, November 20, 1890.
29. *Caldwell Journal*, August 27, 1891.
30. Ibid., December 4, 18, 25, 1890.
31. Ibid., January 15, August 20, 1891.
32. *Caldwell News*, March 9, 1893.
33. Ibid., March 9, 1893. The text of the bill in its entirety is printed in this issue.
34. *Caldwell News*, March 16 and 23, 1893.
35. Ibid., May 25, July 20, August 10, 31, 1893; *Caldwell Journal*, August 24, 1893; Rainey, *Cherokee Strip*, 262-269.
36. *Caldwell News*, August 31, 1893.
37. Ibid., September 7 and 14, 1893.
38. Ibid., September 14 and 21, 1893.
39. Ibid., September 14, 1893; Rainey, *Cherokee Strip*, 268-271.
40. Rainey, *Cherokee Strip*, 276-279; *Caldwell News*, September 21, 1893.
41. Rainey, *Cherokee Strip*, 277.
42. *Caldwell News*, September 21, 1893.

43. "John F. Ryland…," *Caldwell Messenger*, Centennial Edition, May 8, 1961.
44. Rainey, *Cherokee Strip*, 276; *Caldwell News*, September 21, 1893.
45. *Caldwell News*, September 21, 1893.
46. Ibid.
47. Ibid., September 21, October 5, 1893.
48. Ibid., September 21, 1893.
49. Ibid., September 21, 1893; "John F. Ryland...," *Caldwell Messenger*, Centennial Edition, May 8, 1961.

Chapter Fourteen: Celebration of the Border Queen

1. Detailed accounts of the shooting are in both Caldwell newspapers of September 28, 1893, the *News* and the *Journal*.
2. *Caldwell News*, September 30, 1893.
3. The Western movies *Dodge City*, *Abilene Town*, *Wichita*, and *Tumbleweeds* are available on DVD.

Bibliography

Books

Appleman, Roy E. *Charles Siringo, Cowboy Detective.* Falls Creek, Virginia: The Pioneer America Society Press, 1968.

Billington, Ray Allen. *America's Frontier Heritage.* New York: Holt, Rinehart and Winston, 1966.

Billington, Ray Allen. *Westward Expansion: A History of the American Frontier.* Fourth Edition. New York: The Macmillan Company, 1963.

Boucher, Troy. *Prince of the Plains.* College Station, TX: Virtualbookworm.com Publishing Inc., 2002.

Brown, Richard Maxwell. *Strain of Violence: Historical Studies of American Violence and Vigilantism.* New York: Oxford University Press, 1975.

Colcord, Charles Francis. *The Autobiography of Charles Francis Colcord, 1859–1934.* N.p.: C.C. Helmerich, 1970.

Cook, Rod. *George and Maggie and the Red Light Saloon.* New York: Universe, Inc., 2003.

Cook, Rod. *The Legend Accounts, Narratives of Personal Experiences in Caldwell's Legendary Tunnels.* Privately published, 2006.

Dale, Edward Everett. *The Cherokee Strip Live Stock Association and Charter and By-Laws of the Cherokee Strip Live Stock Association.* Wichita, Kansas: First National Bank in Wichita, 1951.

Dobie, J. Frank. *The Longhorns.* Boston: Little, Brown and Company, 1941.

Drago, Harry Sinclair. *Wild, Woolly & Wicked.* New York: Clarkson N. Potter, Inc., 1960.

Dykstra, Robert R. *The Cattle Towns.* New York: Alfred A. Knopf, 1968.

Emmett, Chris. *Shanghai Pierce: A Fair Likeness.* Norman: University of Oklahoma Press, 1953.

Fehrenbach, T. R. *Lone Star, A History of Texas and the Texans.* New York: The Macmillan Company, 1968.

Fitzgerald, Daniel. *Ghost Towns of Kansas.* Lawrence: University Press of Kansas, 1988.

Flanagan, Sue. *Trailing the Longhorns, A Century Later.* Austin: Madrona Press, Inc., 1974.

Frantz, Joe B. *Texas, A Bicentennial History.* New York: W. W. Norton & Company, Inc., 1976.

Freeman, G. D. *Midnight and Noonday.* Caldwell, Kansas: G. D. Freeman, 1892.

Fulbright, Jim. *Trails to Old Pond Creek, The Early Days of Trade & Travel in Northwestern Oklahoma.* Goodlettsville, Tennessee: Mid-South Publications, 2005.

Gard, Wayne. *The Chisholm Trail.* Norman: University of Oklahoma Press, 1954.

———. *Frontier Violence.* Norman: University of Oklahoma Press, 1949.

Haley, J. Evetts. *Charles Goodnight, Cowman & Plainsman.* Norman: University of Oklahoma Press, 1936.

Halsell, H. H. *Cowboys and Cattleland, Memories of a Frontier Cowboy.* Fort Worth: Texas Christian University Press, 1983.

Haywood, C. Robert. *Victorian West, Class & Culture in Kansas Cattle Towns*. Lawrence: University Press of Kansas, 1991.

Hollon, W. Eugene. *Frontier Violence: Another Look*. New York: Oxford University Press, 1974.

Hunter, J. Marvin. *The Trail Drivers of Texas*. Austin: University of Texas Press, 1992.

Johnson, Mary E. *From a 'whirlpool of death ... to victory', Civil War Remembrances of Jesse Tyler Sturm, 14th West Virginia Infantry*. Charleston, W.V.: West Virginia History, 2002.

Keleher, William A. *Violence in Lincoln County, 1869-1881*. Albuquerque: University of New Mexico Press, 1957.

Lake, Stuart N. *Wyatt Earp, Frontier Marshal*. Boston: Houghton Mifflin Company, 1931.

Lefebure, Irene Sturm. *Cherokee Strip in Transition, Circumstances, Conflicts and Challenges*. Enid, OK: Cherokee Strip Centennial Foundation, Inc., 1991.

Massey, Sara R., ed. *Texas Women on the Cattle Trails*. College Station: Texas A&M University Press, 2006.

McNeal, T. A. *When Kansas Was Young*. New York: The Macmillan Co., 1922.

Metz, Leon C. *Dallas Stoudenmire*, El Paso Marshal. Norman: University of Oklahoma Press, 1969.

Miller, Benjamin S. *Ranch Life in Southern Kansas and the Indian Territory*. New York: Fless & Ridge Printing Company, 1896.

Miller, Nyle H., Edgar Langsdorff, and Robert W. Richmond. *Kansas in Newspapers*. Topeka: Kansas State Historical Society, 1963.

Miller, Nyle H., and Joseph W. Snell. *Great Gunfighters of the Kansas Cowtowns, 1867-1967*. Lincoln: University of Nebraska Press, 1967.

Miller, Nyle H., and Joseph W. Snell. *Why the West Was Wild*. Topeka: Kansas State Historical Society, 1963.

Miner, Craig. *Kansas, The History of the Sunflower State, 1854-2000*. Lawrence: University Press of Kansas, 2002.

Miner, Craig. *West of Wichita, Settling the High Plains of Kansas, 1865-1890*. Lawrence: University Press of Kansas, 1986.

Miner, Craig. *Wichita, The Early Years, 1865-1880*. Lincoln: University of Nebraska Press, 1982.

Morris, John W., Charles R. Goins, and Edwin C. McReynolds. *Historical Atlas of Oklahoma*, Third Edition. Norman: University of Oklahoma Press, 1986.

Mullin, Robert N., ed. *Maurice Garland Fulton's History of the Lincoln County War*. Tucson: University of Arizona Press, 1968.

Nolan, Frederick. *The Lincoln County War, A Documentary History*. Norman: University of Oklahoma Press, 1992.

Official State Atlas of Kansas. Philadelphia: L. H. Evarts & Co., 1987.

O'Neal, Bill. *Henry Brown, The Outlaw Marshal*. College Station, Texas. Creative Publishing Company, 1980.

Onley, Glen. *Sunset*. Santa Fe: Sunstone Press, 2003.

Peavy, Charles D. *Charles A. Siringo, A Texas Picaro*. Austin, Texas: Steck-Vaughn Company, 1967.

Pingenot, Ben E. *Siringo*. College Station: Texas A&M University Press, 1989.

Postlewait, Dilmond D. and Evelyn L. *Caldwell, Kansas, City Cemetery*. N.p., 2000.

Prassel, Frank Richard. *The Great American Outlaw: A Legacy of Fact and Fiction*. Norman: University of Oklahoma Press, 1993.

Rainey, George. *The Cherokee Strip*. Guthrie, OK: Co-Operative Publishing Co., 1933.

Rasch, Philip J. *Warriors of Lincoln County*. Edited by Robert K. DeArment. The National Association for Outlaw and Lawman History, 1998.

Records, Laban Samuel, and Ellen Jayne Maris Wheeler, ed. *Cherokee Outlet Cowboy, Recollections of Laban S. Records*. Norman: University of Oklahoma Press, 1995.

Rideout, Mrs. J. B. *Six Years on the Border; or, Sketches of Frontier Life*. Philadelphia: Presbyterian Board of Publication, 1883.

Ridings, Sam P. *The Chisholm Trail, A History of the World's Greatest Cattle Trail*. Guthrie, OK: Co-Operative Publishing Company, 1936.

Savage, William W., Jr. *The Cherokee Strip Live Stock Association*. Norman: University of Oklahoma Press, 1990.

Shirley, Glenn. *West of Hell's Fringes*. Norman: University of Oklahoma Press, 1978.

Silva, Lee A. *Wyatt Earp, A Biography of the Legend*. Vol. I: The Cowtown Years. Santa Ana, CA: Graphic Publishers, 2002.
Siringo, Charles. *History of "Billy the Kid."* Santa Fe: Charles A. Siringo, 1920.
——. *Riata and Spurs*. Boston: Houghton Mifflin Company, 1912.
——. *A Texas Cowboy*. Lincoln: University of Nebraska Press, 1950 (originally published in 1912).
Smith, Thomas T., ed. *A Dose of Frontier Soldiering, The Memoirs of Corporal E. A. Bode, Frontier Regular Infantry, 1877-1882*. Lincoln: University of Nebraska Press, 1994.
Socolofsky, Homer E., and Huber Self. *Historical Atlas of Kansas*, Second Edition. Norman: University of Oklahoma Press, 1988.
Streeter, Floyd Benjamin. *Prairie Trails & Cow Towns*. Boston: Chapman & Grimes, 1936.
Turner, Frederick Jackson. *The Frontier in American History*. New York: Holt, Rinehart and Winston, 1962.
Tyler, Ron, editor-in-chief. *The New Handbook of Texas*. 6 vols. Austin: Texas State Historical Association, 1996.
Webb, Walter P. *The Great Plains*. New York: Grosset & Dunlap, 1931.
White, Donald. *The Border Queen, A History of Early Day Caldwell, Kansas*. Wyandotte, OK: The Gregath Publishing Company, 1998.
Worcester, Don. *The Chisholm Trail, High Road of the Cattle Kingdom*. Lincoln: University of Nebraska Press, 1980.
Yost, Nellie Snyder. *Medicine Lodge: The Story of a Kansas Frontier Town*. Chicago: The Swallow Press, Inc., 1970.

Articles
Dewey, Ernest. "Henry Packed a Powerful Punch." *Hutchinson News-Herald*, January 20, 1952.
Heizer, Chester C. "Henry Brown: Marshal and Murderer." *Sumner County Herald*. Vol. IV, January 1954–April 1957.
Leahy, D. D. "Random Recollections of Other Days." *Wichita Morning Eagle*, April 13, 1932.
Rasch, Philip J. "A Note on Henry Newton Brown." *Los Angeles Westerners Brand Book*, Vol. V, 1953.
White, Owen P. "Bullet-Proof Brown." *Collier's*, Vol. LXXXIX, No. 9, February 27, 1932.

Newspapers
Caldwell Commercial
Caldwell Journal
Caldwell Messenger
Caldwell News
Caldwell Post
Frankfort, Indiana Times
Medicine Lodge Cressett
Rolla, Missouri Weekly Herald
Sumner County Press, Wellington

Miscellaneous
Cook, Rod. "Border Queen Police Dockets: 1879-1885." Unpublished manuscript, n.d.
——. "Caldwell's Boot Hill." Unpublished manuscript, 2006.
——. "Marshal Henry Brown's In-laws." Unpublished manuscript, 2004.
——. "Soiled Doves of the Border Queen." Unpublished manuscript, n.d.
Tucker, George R. Autobiographical manuscript. John Alley Collection, Western History Collection, University of Oklahoma, Norman.

Index

Abilene, Kansas, 1, 5, 8, 9, 32, 73, 78, 94, 102, 146, 171, 216, 217
Abilene Town (movie), 217
Achenbach, Jacob, 133, 137
Adams, Andy, 180, 217
Adams, Jake, 64, 65, 68, RIP
Adkins, John, 45
Akin, Rev. Dudley E., 124
American Revolution, 22
Anderson, Doc, 21-22, 24, 147
Arizona Rangers, 218
Arkansas City, Kansas, 68, 199, 201, 204, 207
Atchison, Topeka & Santa Fe RR, 32, 33, 56, 61, 73, 75-76, 77
Austin, Texas, 82, 112

Badger, A. B., 34
Baker, Frank, 110
Baker, Josh, 37
Banks, Becky, 74
Bates, Clara, 172
Bates, W. H., 80
Battin, E. T. 145
Baufman, Ted, 109
Beals, David T., 80
Beals, E. H., 117
Bell, Alexander Graham, 58
Bell, L. B., 150
Bennett, M. H., 154, 155, 160, 165
Bigtree, Bob, 96, 98
Billington, Ray Allen, 13, 50, 203
Billy the Kid, 109, 110, 179
Blair, John A., 37, 49, 53-54, 57, 140, 153, 155, 160, 165, 175, 190
Border Line Railroad, 191, 192
Boyce, Newt, 118, 120-123, 146, 147, 215

Boyce, Mrs. Newt, 122
Boyd, Ella, 214
Boyd, G. F., 214
Bradley, Lee, 132
Brady, Sheriff William, 110
Brooks, W. O., 188
Brooks, Mrs. W. O., 188, 189
Brooks, William L. "Bully," 37-39, 41-43, 147
Brooks, Mrs. William L., 42,43
Brown, Ellen, 110, 114
Brown, Fannie, 99, 100
Brown, George, 99-100, 101, 102, 147
Brown, Henry N., 102-108, 109-123, 124-136, 138, 140-141, 142, 144, 145, 146, 147, 161, 215
Brown, Maude, 124, 127, 134-135, 140-145
Bryant, Black-Faced Charley, 189
Burkett, Dr. P. J. M., 39, 43
Burrus, Cass, 98
Burton, Ben F. (*see* Ben Wheeler)
Burton, Alice M., 112, 126, 144
Bushyhead, Daniel W., 151, 152, 155, 166, 170, 205
Byron, Oklahoma, 144

Caldwell, Alexander, 2, 9
Caldwell Electric Light Company, 191
Caldwell High School, 172, 173, 174, 177
Caldwell *Journal*, 119, 120, 123, 124, 140, 142, 144, 156, 157, 160, 163, 165, 170, 172, 173, 177, 178, 179, 182, 187, 188, 189, 191, 193, 194, 197, 198, 200, 201, 202, 204, 205, 206
Caldwell *Post*, 61, 62, 63, 65, 68, 69, 70, 71, 72, 73, 74, 75, 76, 77, 78, 79, 81, 82, 83, 86, 87, 88, 91, 92, 93, 96, 101, 102, 116, 152, 154, 155, 156, 197, 199

Caldwell public schools, 34, 46, 49, 50-51, 69, 72, 87-88, 173, 174
Calhoun, John, 62-63
Calkins, Jud, 40-42, 43
Cameron Junction, Missouri, 182
Camp Caldwell, 49, 200
Campbell, B. H., 80
Campbell, W. E., 98, 153, 160
Carr, B. P. "Bat," 102-108, 112, 113, 114, 146
Cassidy, Butch, 218
Catholic Church, 3, 194
Caypless, John, 119-120, 141
cemetery, 27, 65, 92, 94, 138, 139, 141, 143, 163, 186, 214, 219
Cherokee Nation, 105, 149, 150, 151, 154, 155, 160, 166, 168, 169, 170, 171, 205, 207
Cherokee Strip/Outlet, 61, 81, 89, 90, 105, 111, 125, 127, 149, 150, 151, 152, 154, 155, 157, 160, 161, 163, 168, 169, 170, 171, 181, 198, 202, 205, 206, 207, 215, 217, 218, 219
Cherokee Strip Live Stock Association, 105, 148-171, 174, 180, 181, 194, 197, 198, 219
Cheyenne Wyoming, 45, 112
Chicago, Illinois, 83, 88, 159, 163, 164, 165, 179, 180
Chicago and Rock Island Railroad, 192
Chicago Comedy Company, 177
Chisholm, Jesse, 5
Chisholm Trail, 1-2, 5, 6, 8, 9, 10, 11, 28, 32, 35, 36, 56, 60, 69, 73, 74, 75, 77, 78, 82, 83, 89, 100, 150, 156, 159, 160, 162, 163, 171, 194, 197, 198, 200, 215, 216, 219
Christian Church, 87, 194
Cincinnati Red Stockings, 49
Circle Bar ranch, 181
Civil War, 4, 12, 18, 29, 34, 49, 51, 94, 196, 198, 200, 202
Clark, J. F., 186
Clark, Jennie, 186
Clark, Johnnie, 186
Clark, Mary, 51
Clark, Roll, 132
Clark, S. S., 51
Clay, John, 1-2
Cleveland, Grover, 206, 208
Colbert, Henry, 57
Colcord, Charles, 89-91, 92, 98, 111, 146
Colcord, William, 111
Colorado City, Texas, 103, 106-107
Colson, A. M., 11, 12, 17, 39, 43, 83, 68, 81, 102, 107, 114, 127, 157, 160, 164, 165, 177, 178, 183, 190, 200, 205, 213
Colson, Fawnie, 157, 184
Colson, Mary A., 68
Colson, Mary Goldy, 157

Cook, Rod, 8
Cooper, I. N., 30, 31, 55-56
Coronado, Francisco Vasquez de, 3
Córtes, Hernán, 3
Couch, W. L., 201, 202, 203, 204, 205
Covington, ——, 117
Cowley, Sumner & Fort Smith Railroad, 61, 62
Crabtree, Lotta, 165
Crats, Fred, 12
Crist, T. L., 122

Dagner, James H., 9
Dalton, ——, 29-30
Danford, J. S., 83-84, 86
Davidson, Elmer, 188
Davidson, H. H., 19
Davis, Charlie, 94
Davis, Sheriff John G., 39-41, 43
Day, A. J., 154
Dean, John, 91-92
Decatur, Texas, 189
Denn, Sam, 129-130, 135
Denver, Colorado, 45
Devil's Lake, D. T., 145
Devore, Lou, 47
Dillard, James A., 40, 41
Dixon, Ballard, 29
Dixon, Carrie, 50
Dixon, Julia, 68
Dixon, N. J., 19, 58, 59, 68
Dobson, John, 175, 189
Dodge City (movie), 217
Dodge City, Kansas, 1, 3, 8, 38, 56, 61, 73, 77, 78, 107, 146, 150, 217
Donaldson, Jessie, 50
Donaldson, Walter, 172
Doran, Tom, 132
Drumm, Andrew, 111, 152, 154, 155, 168, 185
Dykstra, Robert, 175

Earp, Wyatt, 13-14, 95, 217
Eddleman, Dick, 96, 98, 99
El Camino Real, 3
El Paso, Texas, 146
El Rancho Grande, Texas, 79
Eldred, Charles, 140, 155
Ellis, Dr. A. N., 50
Ellsworth, Kansas, 36, 56
Elsfelder, Lucy, 172
Enid, Oklahoma, 189, 213
Epps, George, 17, 18-19, 21, 147
Everhart, Charles, 114-115

Fay, Charles H., 89

Index

Fehrenbach, T. R., 6
Fielder, Dan, 25
Fielder, Eugene, 21, 147
First Chance-Last Chance, 8, 9, 10, 23-24, 26, 28, 35, 36, 39, 40, 59, 220
First Methodist Church, 87, 124, 194
Fitzgerald, Milam, 10, 11
Flatt, Fannie Lamb, 68, 92, 93
Flatt, George, 63, 64-65, 68, 69, 91-92, 93, 101, 102, 118, 147, 215
Flatt, Georgie, 93
Fleming, John, 132
Flynn, Errol, 217
Folks, J. H., 65
Ford, Thomas, 29
Ford, Thomas G. (*see* Tom Smith)
Fort Griffin, Texas, 9, 83
Fort Larned, Kansas, 29
Fort Reno, I.T., 200
Fort Richardson, Texas, 9
Fort Riley, Kansas, 10
Fort Sill, I.T., 9, 35, 37, 39
Fort Worth, Texas, 36, 74
Fossett, Bill, 96-97, 98
Foster, Mollie, 144
Foster, P. J., 144
Fourth of July celebrations, 49, 52, 53, 56, 178
Fox, Dr. B. W., 19, 30, 34, 36, 39, 57
Frankfort, Indiana, 145
Frantz, Joe B., 1
Freeman, George D., 1, 8, 9, 11, 12, 15, 16, 17, 18, 19-20, 22, 23, 24, 25, 26, 27, 28, 29, 30, 33, 33, 54, 63-64, 65, 75, 96, 97, 101, 107, 112, 146, 157, 161, 180, 181
Friedley, Rev. George, 129, 132, 133

Gall, Franz Joseph, 109
Gambril, Charles, 171
Garrett, Pat, 125
Geppert, George, 127, 128-129, 132, 133, 135, 138-139, 140, 141
Giddings, Texas, 20
Gilbert, C. F., 9
Gilliman, Robert, 107
Gillon, Margaret Ann (see Mag Wood)
Given, Dr. O. G., 35
Godfrey, G. G., 59
Goodnight, Charles, 7
Goodnight-Loving Trail, 5
Grand Canyon, 3
Grand Central Hotel, 72, 73, 84-85
Grand Opera House, 164, 169, 172, 174, 175, 176, 177, 178, 182, 183, 191, 195, 209, 215, 220
Grant, Fred, 52

Grant, Ulysses, 36, 52
Graul, George, 34
Great Western Band, 184
Green, Jess, 100
Green, Steve, 100
Groh, A. S., 88
Gunsmoke (TV series), 217
Guthrie, Oklahoma, 170
Gyp Hills, Kansas, 128, 131-132, 133

Haines, G. W., 33, 36, 47, 50, 57, 58, 59
Hall, Henry, 39
Halsell, H. H., 5, 8
Hamilton, J. W., 155
Hansen, Rev. J. P., 34
Harbaugh, Ben, 128, 138
Harper, Kansas, 127, 128
Harris, Grant, 117
Harris, James, 26-27, 147
Harrison, Benjamin, 169, 170, 204, 205, 206, 207
Hart, William S., 214, 217, 218, 219
Harvest Fair and Festival, 197
Hasbrouck, L. B., 39, 41, 42-43, 147
Hatch, Edward, 200, 201, 202
Hawley, Ed, 214, 215
Hays City, Kansas, 94
Hennessey, Oklahoma, 189
Hennessey, Pat, 40
Herron, J. H., 115, 116
Hewins, Ed, 83, 84, 155, 165, 166, 169
Hickok, Wild Bill, 94, 102, 125, 217
Higgins, Pink, 7
Hill, Doug, 98, 99
Hill, Harry (*see* John Wesley)
Hindman, George, 110
Hollister, Cassius M., 68-69, 115-116, 119-121, 147, 186, 187
Hollister, Sarah Rhodes, 68-69, 71, 205
Hood, Frank, 185
Hopkins, Henry, 57, 147
Horner, S. H. "Harve," 82, 87, 88, 140, 141, 145, 182, 183, 195, 214
Horseman, William, 89, 92, 93
House, Mr. and Mrs. E. W., 177
Houston, Samuel Dunn, 90-93
Hubbell, W. N., 68, 89, 98, 147, 205
Huff, J. M., 65
Hugo, Colorado, 91, 93
Hulbert, C. F., 89, 121, 156
Hume, Dr., 204
Hunnewell, Kansas, 75, 77-78, 83, 84, 90, 93, 94, 115, 116, 147, 150, 152, 156, 161, 165, 186, 187, 195
Hunt, Frank, 69, 92, 93-94, 101, 147

Hunter, Lem, 83
Hussen, F. G., 59
Hutchison, W. H., 152

Iago, 125
Indianola, Nebraska, 112, 126
Izee Sheep Shooters, 148

Jackson, —— (city marshal), 116
Jackson, Lou, 212
Jennison, Colonel, 103
Johnson, "I-Bar", 127
Johnson, James, 92, 94
Jones, —— (saloon operator), 36
Jones, Dan, 92, 94, 145
Jones, Frank, 113
Jones, Hiram, 58, 147
Jones, Lengthy, 98
Jones, Red Bill, 91

Kansas City, Missouri, 10, 13, 77, 83, 152, 161, 165, 168
Kansas City, Burlington & Southwestern Railway, 61
Kansas City, Lawrence and Southern Railroad, 75, 77, 84
Kansas Pacific Railroad, 5, 32
Kelley, Billy, 136
Kelly, J. D., 51, 59, 61, 62, 68, 96, 102, 104, 105, 106
Kelly, J. D., Jr., 61, 68, 78
Kelly, W. C., 64
Kelly's cornet band, 70, 72
Kelpatrick, Lizzie, 172
Killibrew, Mack, 162
King, W. B. "Buffalo," 11, 12
Kingsley, C. M., 172, 174
Kiser, W. H., 64
Kuhlman, Fred, 94

Lamb, Fannie (*see* Fannie Flatt)
Leah, Harry, 144
Leahy, D. D., 122, 123, 124
Leland Hotel, 70-71, 84, 85, 86, 94, 104, 109, 110, 121, 154, 156, 169, 209, 210, 212, 215, 220
Levagood, Alice Maude (*see* Maude Brown)
Lillie, Gordon W. "Pawnee Bill", 203, 204, 206
Lincoln County War, New Mexico, 110
Lipe, D. W., 151, 152
Little Missouri Stockmen's Association, 148
Littlefield, George, 110
Lloyd, Mamie (*see* Mamie Siringo)
Love, Tom, 96, 98, 99
Lovell, Belle, 172

LX Ranch, 80, 81, 82, 83, 110
Lyeth, J. C., 87
Lynch, Charles, 22
Lynch, John D., 25, 147
Lyons, Charles, 58, 147
Lytle, Vernon, 132

Mack, George, 17
Mackenzie, Ranald S., 51
Maggard, Dr. Felix, 58, 59
Malaley, W. E., 175
Manning, Frank, 18-20
Manning, George "Doc," 19-20
Manning, Jim, 18-20
Manning, John, 18-20
Manning, Lem, 184-185
Manning, William, 18, 21, 147
Mardis, David, 55
Marion, Jasper, 39
Marshall, John E. "Curly," 8, 9, 23, 24, 26, 36
Marshall, Pony, 37
Martin, Howard, 132
Martin, Hurricane Bill, 37
Martin, Jim, 96, 98
May, Frank, 177
Mayes, Joel B., 166, 167, 168, 169, 170, 171
McAtee, J. L., 164, 165, 171
McCamnant, Doc, 63
McCarty, Michael, 20-22, 23, 24-25, 26, 147
McCloskey, William, 110
McCoy, Joseph G., 5, 32, 78, 80, 83, 152
McCrea, Joel, 217
McCullough, —— (constable), 120
McKinney, Alec, 132
McKinney, Wayne, 132
McLean, A. C., 36, 39, 40, 41
McNeal, T. A., 143, 146, 157
Meagher, Jenny, 71, 94
Meagher, John, 92, 94, 95, 98, 99
Meagher, Mike, 92, 94-98, 101, 115, 118, 147, 199
Medicine Lodge, Kansas, 58, 125-126, 127, 128, 130, 133, 134, 135, 140, 141, 142, 143, 144, 147, 152, 156, 157
Medicine Valley Bank, 125, 126, 128, 129, 130, 131, , 156, 157
Meloy, Bertha, 172
Mendoza, Antonio, 3
Merchants & Drovers Bank, 83-84, 86
Merritt, Wesley, 202
Metcalf, Willis, 100
Miller, Ben S., 81, 82, 83, 84, 140, 141, 148, 152, 153, 154, 155, 160, 163, 165, 175, 178, 180, 181
Miller, J. N., 124

Miller, Josephine Bowen, 181
Mitchell, ———, 185
Mitchell, Alonzo T., 7
Montana Stock Growers Association, 148
Moore, Della, 129
Moore, Frank, 26-27, 147
Moore, L. W., 129
Moore, Thomas G. (*see* Tom Smith)
Moore, Dr. W. F., 58, 141
Moreland, Jim, 63, 64, 89, 117
Morris, William, 125, 145
Morse, Sheriff, 171
Morton, William, 110
Mosier, Burr, 39
Munson, Bob, 96, 98
Murray, Joe, 83

Neal, Rev. W. N., 48
New Caldwell, 71-72, 73, 75, 84
New Orleans, Louisiana, 4
New York Ideal Concert Co., 209
New York Opera Co., 177
Newton, Kansas, 32, 36, 38, 73, 78, 171, 175, 216
Nicholson, ———, 24
Noble, John W., 82, 170
Noble, Dr. W. A., 59, 68, 82, 87, 92, 93, 94, 105, 114-115, 122, 160, 163, 215
Noble, Mrs. W. A., 68, 71
Norton, Dr. B. D., 52, 54
Noyes, Frank, 147, 186-188, 218
Nyce, John W., 135, 171, 182, 187

Oakes, James, 10
O'Bannon, ———, 15-16, 17, 147
O'Connor, Barney, 111, 125, 128, 130-131, 132, 133, 134, 142, 144
Odum, D. M., 69
O'Folliard, Tom, 110
Oklahoma City, 89, 181, 199, 204, 205
Oklahoma War Chief (newspaper), 199, 202
Old Chisholm Trail, The (ballad), 216
Olive, Print, 27-28, 80
Oliver, L. L., 44, 147
Overall, Asa, 29, 53, 82, 181-182
Overall, Monroe, 182

Palo Duro Canyon, 3
Paris, Texas, 127, 137
Payne, David L., 198, 199-200, 201
Payne, Edward Wylie, 126, 127, 128, 129, 132, 133, 135, 138-139, 140, 141, 155, 156, 157, 161
Peay, George, 15-16, 147
Phillips, John, 162
Pierce, Chris, 9

Pierce, Shanghai, 79, 80, 81, 158, 169, 179
Pizarro, Francisco, 3
Plummer, Henry, 22-23
Polk, Dan, 37
Post, Orville, 144
Powell, Sylvester, 95
Pratt, Frank, 103
Presbyterian Church, 34, 47, 48, 52, 87, 139, 187, 194
Priest, Nate, 132

Rachal, Nate, 11
Rainey, George, 150, 151, 152, 157, 210, 211
Rathbun, Ed, 97
Ratliff, J. V., 51
Red Light Dance Hall and Saloon, 73-75, 89, 93-94, 95, 96, 98, 99, 100, 101, 147, 220
Reid, Christena, 34
Reid, John, 21
Rhodes, James, 172
Rhodes, Sarah (*see* Sarah Rhodes Hollister)
Ricer, Frederick, 43-44, 147
Rideout, Rev. J. B., 34-35, 36-38, 41, 43, 45, 46, 47-48, 52, 53, 186
Rideout, Mrs. J. B., 25, 34-35, 36-38, 40, 41-44, 45, 46, 47, 48, 52, 54-55, 116, 186
Ridings, Sam P., 97, 98, 174
Rigg, C. F., 134, 135, 138, 140, 141-142, 144
Riggs, Douglas, 147
Rio Grande, 3
Roberts, Buckshot, 110
Robertson, Ben (*see* Ben Wheeler)
Rock Island Railroad, 163, 165, 188, 189, 192, 193
Rockdale, Texas, 112
Rogers, Samuel H., 92
Rolla, Missouri, 110, 114
Roosevelt, Theodore, 148
Ross, H. A., 88, 212
Ross, T.H.B., 16, 34, 45, 56, 57, 61, 62, 102, 119, 120, 121, 122, 163, 182
Ross, Mrs. T.H.B., 71
Ross family, 115-116, 119
Rowen, Ada, 172
Rue, Robert, 124
Ryan, Rev. A., 48
Ryland, J. A., 11, 12, 17
Ryland, John F., 196, 211, 213

Sain, J. H., 45, 46, 50, 51, 52, 53, 54, 56, 57, 58, 59
Salmon, Emma, 51
Savage, William. W., Jr., 148, 171
Schaeffer, John, 189
Scott, Randolph, 217

Scribner, Dr. N. A., 88, 212
Segerman, Louis, 92
Sewell, Eli, 34
Shank, Rev. O. E., 169
Sharp, Dave, 188
Sharp, Robert, 147
Shawnee Trail (Sedalia Trail), 4-5
Sheridan, Gen. Phil, 200, 201
Sherman, James (*see* Jim Talbot)
Short, Ed, 189
Showalter, John B., 53
Sidney, Willie, 182
Sieber, Alice, 50
Sieber, Charley, 36
Simons, Robert T., 211, 213
Singer, J. W., 138
Siringo, Charles, 81-85, 109-110, 111, 142, 157, 158, 159, 178, 179, 180
Siringo, Mamie Lloyd, 83-84, 109-110, 157, 158, 178
Siringo, Viola, 178
Sister, J. C., 34
Slaughter, William B., 10
Smith, G. W., 9
Smith, Hoke, 207, 210
Smith, "One-armed Charley," 29, 39, 41, 43, 147
Smith, Tom, 29-31, 41, 43-44, 55, 56, 147
Smith, W. F., 93
Smith, William, 126-137, 138, 140, 144
Snelling, George, 172
Snyder, Dudley, 80
Snyder, John, 80
Southwestern Hotel, 85-86, 104, 114, 120, 125, 154, 169, 175, 183, 185, 190, 210, 215
South Western Grazers Association, 168
Spear, C. L., 92
Spear, Dave, 64
Spears, George, 96, 98, 147
Spears, Steve, 94
Spiker, Jefferson, 185
Spiker, Susan, 185
Spiker, Walter, 185
Spotted Horse (Pawnee), 116-119, 146, 147
St. John, Mrs. John P., 84
St. John, Lutie, 84
St. John, William, 105
St. Louis, Kansas and Western Railroad, 72
Standard, Jess, 7
Steele, J. M., 98
Stevenson (coroner), 119
Stock Exchange Bank, 84, 85, 148, 162, 168, 171, 216
Stone, Charles H., 9, 10, 11, 12,13, 14, 15,19, 29, 32, 36, 54, 58, 80

Stoudenmire, Dallas, 20
Sturm, W. A., 179
Sullivan, Charles, 16
Swartzel, J. R., 145
Swayer, Samuel, 100
Sweet, Professor, 114

Tahlequah, I.T., 151, 155, 165, 169, 170, 205
Talbot, Jim, 95-99, 101, 105, 147, 215, 218
Talliaferro, Charlie, 132, 133
Tascosa, Texas, 102, 110, 111, 124, 146
Taylor, Texas, 144
Taylor, E. C., 86
Templeton Opera Co., 175
Terrill, Dave, 26, 36, 41-42, 43
Terwilliger, W. R., 83
Texas and Southwestern Cattle Raisers Association, 148
"Texas Bill," 57
Thomas, Heck, 125
Thomas, James M., 10, 12, 21, 23, 30, 36, 53, 56, 57, 58, 59, 65
Thomas, Mrs. J. M., 50, 53
Thomas, Oscar, 147, 162
Thrailkill, Levi, 63, 89, 125, 145
Thralls, J. M., 40, 98, 99, 105, 106
Thralls, Wes, 116
Tilghman, Bill, 125
Tombstone, Arizona, 146
Topeka, Kansas, 62, 84, 145
Tracey, J. L., 147, 188
Tumbleweeds (movie), 214, 217, 219
Tunstall, John, 110
Tuttle, Sol, 154, 164, 165, 175

Union Pacific Railroad, 5
Union Stock Yards, Chicago, 165
Unsell, H. C., 122, 175, 213

Vantilberg, George, 9
Van Meter, Chet, 119-121
Vasey, May, 173, 174
Vernon, Texas, 127, 137
Vilas, William, 168

Waco, Texas, 145
Walton, Tell, 79, 82, 87, 96, 152, 156, 160
Wamsley, Clementine (*see* Sain, Clementine Wamsley)
Ward, Carson, 80
Warrington, Fannie, 51
Watkins, Alex, 37
Webb, ——, 21-22
Weller, Lee, 140-141
Wellington, Kansas, 19, 25, 30, 35, 38, 40, 41,

43, 49, 52, 56, 58, 59, 62, 65, 70, 75, 77, 86, 92, 98, 99, 101, 116, 119, 120, 122, 124, 147, 171, 178, 186, 195, 200, 214
Wells, O. G., 47
Wendels, J. G., 102-103
Wendels, Lizzie, 50
Wesley, John, 126-127, 128, 132, 133, 134, 136, 137, 138, 140, 142, 144
Western Trail, 1, 5, 56, 61, 150
Wheeler, Ben, 107, 112-113, 114,115,116,119-122, 126-138, 140, 141, 142, 144, 147
Wheeler, Gen. Joe, 19
Wichita, Kansas, 5, 9, 10, 11, 23, 26, 32, 35, 36, 37, 38, 50, 54, 56, 59, 61, 63, 69, 73, 74, 78, 84, 90, 94, 95, 96, 98, 101, 116, 163, 171, 175, 189, 199, 201, 204, 216, 217

Wichita (movie), 217
Wichita Town, 217
Wichita Trail, 5
Wiedeman, Joe, 105, 107
Wiley, Joe 131
Williams, Jerry, 39
Williams, Newt, 25, 26
Williamson, L. T., 43
Wilson, John, 64-65, 68, 95-98, 147
Witzelben, ——, 135, 162
Women's Christian Temperance Union, 187
Wood, Geo., 74, 147
Wood, Mary, 74, 75
Wyoming Stock Growers Association, 148

Zuber, Hank, 56, 57, 59

BILL O'NEAL is the author of more than thirty books and 300 articles and book reviews. He was selected as *True West Magazine*'s "Best Living Non-fiction Writer, 2007." Bill's book, *The Johnson County War*, was voted 2005 Book of the Year by the National Association for Outlaw and Lawman History (NOLA) and in 2007 he was inducted into NOLA's Hall of Fame. Bill has appeared on TV documentaries about the Old West on TBS, The History Channel, A&E, The Discovery Channel, and TNN. He is regularly featured on the nationally syndicated radio show *Chronicles of the Old West*.

Bill is a member of the Western Writers of America and of numerous historical organizations. He taught history for thirty-three years at Panola College in Carthage, Texas, where his teaching awards included a Piper Professorship in 2000. Bill's wife, Karon, teaches in Panola's math department and assists with research and manuscript preparation for each of his books.

www.ingramcontent.com/pod-product-compliance
Lightning Source LLC
Chambersburg PA
CBHW081847170426
43199CB00018B/2836